**WILLIAM BLAKE**

# SONGS OF INNOCENCE AND OF EXPERIENCE

# OUR BOOKS ON LITERATURE

1. An Evaluation of His Poetry
**JOHN KEATS**
2. The Rape of the Lock
**ALEXANDER POPE**
3. An Evaluation of His Poetry
**P.B. SHELLEY**
4. An Evaluation of His Poetry
**W.B. YEATS**
5. The Prologue
**GEOFFREY CHAUCER**
6. The Pardoner's Tale
**GEOFFREY CHAUCER**
7. Songs of Innocence and of Experience
**WILLIAM BLAKE**
8. Select Poems, Vol. I
**ROBERT BROWNING**
9. Select Poems, Vol. II
**ROBERT BROWNING**
10. Select Poems
**ALFRED TENNYSON**
11. Select Poems
**JOHN DONNE**
12. Select Poems
**W.H. AUDEN**
13. An Evaluation of His Poetry
**WILLIAM WORDSWORTH**
14. Preface to the Lyrical Ballads
**WILLIAM WORDSWORTH**
15. Essays of Elia
**CHARLES LAMB**
16. Bacon's Essays
**FRANCIS BACON**
17. Doctor Faustus
**CHRISTOPHER MARLOWE**
18. The Duchess of Malfi
**JOHN WEBSTER**
19. Essays in Criticism
**MATTHEW ARNOLD**
20. An Essay of Dramatic Poesy
**JOHN DRYDEN**
21. An Apology for Poetry
**PHILIP SIDNEY**
22. The Poetics
**ARISTOTLE**
23. Biographia Literaria
**S.T. COLERIDGE**
24. The Rime of Ancient Mariner
**S.T. COLERIDGE**
25. An Evaluation of His Poetry
**S.T. COLERIDGE**
26. Preface to Shakespeare
**DR. JOHNSON**
27. Sons and Lovers
**D.H. LAWRENCE**
28. The Rainbow
**D.H. LAWRENCE**
29. Women in Love
**D.H. LAWRENCE**
30. A Passage to India
**E.M. FORSTER**
31. Oliver Twist
**CHARLES DICKENS**
32. David Copperfield
**CHARLES DICKENS**
33. Great Expectations
**CHARLES DICKENS**
34. Hard Times
**CHARLES DICKENS**
35. The Tale of Two Cities
**CHARLES DICKENS**
36. Tess of the D'Urbervilles
**THOMAS HARDY**
37. The Return of the Native
**THOMAS HARDY**
38. Lord Jim
**JOSEPH CONARD**
39. Heart of Darkness
**JOSEPH CONRAD**
40. The Secret Agent
**JOSEPH CONRAD**
41. Vanity Fair
**W.M. THACKERAY**
42. Arms and the Man
**BERNARD SHAW**
43. To the Lighthouse
**VIRGINIA WOOLF**
44. The Mill on the Floss
**GEORGE ELIOT**
45. Middlemarch
**GEORGE ELIOT**
46. Sceptical Essays
**BERTRAND RUSSELL**
47. Unpopular Essays
**BERTRAND RUSSELL**
48. Waiting for Godot
**SAMUEL BECKETT**
49. The Waste Land & Other Poems
**T.S. ELIOT**
50. The Critic
**T.S. ELIOT**
51. Murder in the Cathedral
**T.S. ELIOT**
52. The Cocktail Party
**T.S. ELIOT**
53. History and Principles of Literary Criticism
*Edited by* **LISA ROY**
54. The Old Man & the Sea
**ERNEST HEMINGWAY**
55. A Farewell to Arms
**ERNEST HEMINGWAY**
56. The Scarlet Letter
**NATHANIELHAWTHORNE**
57. The Portrait of a Lady
**HENRY JAMES**
58. The Adventures of Huckleberry Finn
**MARK TWAIN**
59. Death of a Salesman
**ARTHUR MILLER**
60. Select Poems
**ROBERT FROST**
61. Select Poems
**WALT WHITMAN**
62. Gitanjali
**RAVINDRANATH TAGORE**
63. The Guide
**R.K. NARAYAN**
64. The Serpent and the Rope
**RAJA RAO**
65. Kanthapura
**RAJA RAO**
66. Coolie
**MULK RAJ ANAND**
67. Untouchable
**MULK RAJ ANAND**
68. Nineteen Eighty Four
**GEORGE ORWELL**
69. The Power & the Glory
**GRAHAM GREENE**
70. Wuthering Heights
**EMILY BRONTE**
71. Look Back in Anger
**JOHN OSBORNE**
72. Gulliver's Travels
**JONATHAN SWIFT**
73. Mansfield Park
**JANE AUSTEN**
74. Pride and Prejudice
**JANE AUSTEN**
75. Advanced Literary Essays
*Edited by* **LISA ROY**
76. In Memoriam
**ALFRED TENNYSON**
77. Paradise Lost, Book II
**JOHN MILTON**
78. Paradise Lost, Book I
**JOHN MILTON**
79. Paradise Lost, Book IV
**JOHN MILTON**
80. Minor Poems
**JOHN MILTON**
81. Paradise Lost, Book IX
**JOHN MILTON**
82. Silver Poets of the Sixteenth Century
*Edited by* **LISA ROY**
83. All for Love
**JOHN DRYDEN**
84. Life of Pope
**SAMUEL JOHNSON**
85. Life of Milton
**SAMUEL JOHNSON**
86. The Pilgrim's Progress
**JOHN BUNYAN**
87. The Man-Eater of Malgudi
**R.K. NARAYAN**
88. Much Ado About Nothing
**WILLIAM SHAKESPEARE**
89. The Winter's Tale
**WILLIAM SHAKESPEARE**
90. King Lear (Text with Notes)
**WILLIAM SHAKESPEARE**
91. Macbeth
**WILLIAM SHAKESPEARE**
92. Othello
**WILLIAM SHAKESPEARE**
93. Henry V
**WILLIAM SHAKESPEARE**
94. Antony & Cleopatra
**WILLIAM SHAKESPEARE**
95. A Midsummer Night's Dream
**WILLIAM SHAKESPEARE**
96. As You Like It
**WILLIAM SHAKESPEARE**
97. Richard II
**WILLIAM SHAKESPEARE**
98. Hamlet (A Critical Study)
**WILLIAM SHAKESPEARE**
99. Henry IV, Part I
**WILLIAM SHAKESPEARE**
100. The Tempest
**WILLIAM SHAKESPEARE**
101. Julius Caeser
**WILLIAM SHAKESPEARE**
102. Twelfth Night
**WILLIAM SHAKESPEARE**
103. The Merchant of Venice
**WILLIAM SHAKESPEARE**
104. Jane Eyre
**CHARLOTTE BRONTE**
105. The Way of the World
**WILLIAM CONGREVE**
106. Lord of the Flies
**WILLIAM GOLDING**
107. Crime and Punishment
**FYODOR DOSTOYEVSKY**
108. Tom Jones
**HENRY FIELDING**

William Blake

# SONGS OF INNOCENCE AND OF EXPERIENCE

[Inclusive of Text of All Poems, Analysis and Criticism]

**Aditya Nandwani**
B.A. English (Hons) , Delhi University;
M.A. (English), IGNOU; Print Journalism (English) YMCA

**ANMOL PUBLICATIONS PVT. LTD.**
**NEW DELHI - 110 002 (INDIA)**

**ANMOL PUBLICATIONS PVT. LTD.**

*H.O.:* 4374/4B, Ansari Road, Darya Ganj,
New Delhi-110 002 (India)
Ph.: 23278000, 23261597

*B.O.:* No. 1015, Ist Main Road, BSK IIIrd Stage
IIIrd Phase, IIIrd Block
Bangalore - 560 085 (India)
*Visit us at:* www.anmolpublications.com

*Songs of Innocence and of Experience*

First Published, 2009



PRINTED IN INDIA

Printed at Mehra Offset Press, Delhi.

# Contents

# Preface

If one follow Blake's mind through the several stages of his poetic development it is impossible to regard him as a naïf, a wild man, a wild pet for the supercultivated. The strangeness is evaporated, the peculiarity is seen to be the peculiarity of all great poetry: something which is found in Homer and Æschylus and Dante and Villon, and profound and concealed in the work of Shakespeare—and also in another form in Montaigne and in Spinoza. It is merely a peculiar honesty, which, in a world too frightened to be honest, is peculiarly terrifying. It is an honesty against which the whole world conspires, because it is unpleasant.

Blake's poetry has the unpleasantness of great poetry. Nothing that can be called morbid or abnormal or perverse, none of the things which exemplify the sickness of an epoch or a fashion, have this quality; only those things which, by some extraordinary labour of simplification, exhibit the essential sickness or strength of the human soul. And this honesty never exists without great technical accomplishment. The question about Blake the man is the question of the circumstances that concurred to permit this honesty in his work, and what circumstances define its limitations.

The Book is a crtical study of Blake's Poetry.The following book encorporates the similar notion and disscusses Blake's poetry in greater detail.

*Author*

# Preface

If one follows Blake's mind through the several stages of his poetic development it is impossible to regard him as a naïf, a wild man, a wild pet for the supercultivated. The strangeness is evaporated, the peculiarity is seen to be the peculiarity of all great poetry: something which is found in Homer and Aeschylus and Dante and Villon, and profound and concealed in the work of Shakespeare—and also in another form in Montaigne and in Spinoza. It is merely a peculiar honesty, which, in a world too frightened to be honest, is peculiarly terrifying. It is an honesty against which the whole world conspires, because it is unpleasant.

Blake's poetry has the unpleasantness of great poetry. Nothing that can be called morbid or abnormal or perverse, none of the things which exemplify the sickness of an epoch or a fashion, have this quality; only those things which, by some extraordinary labour of simplification, exhibit the essential sickness or strength of the human soul. And this honesty never exists without great technical accomplishment. The question about Blake the man is the question of the circumstances that concurred to permit this honesty in his work, and what circumstances define its limitations.

The Book is a critical study of Blake's Poetry. The following book encorporates the similar notion and discusses Blake's poetry in greater detail.

Author

# Chapter 1

# Introduction

Blake is one of the major Romantic poets, whose verse and artwork became part of the wider movement of Romanticism in late Eighteenth and early Nineteenth century European Culture. His writing combines a variety of styles: he is at once an artist, a lyric poet, a mystic and a visionary, and his work has fascinated, intrigued and sometimes bewildered readers ever since. For the nineteenth century reader Blake's work posed a single question: was he sane or mad? The poet Wordsworth, for example, commented that there "is no doubt that this poor man was mad, but there is something in his madness which interests me more than the sanity of Lord Byron and Walter Scott" and John Ruskin similarly felt that Blake's work was "diseased and wild", even if his mind was "great and wise".. In the Twentieth century, however, following W.B. Yeats's three volume edition of his works, Blake has been recognized as a highly original and important poet, artist and writer, and as a member of an enduring tradition of visionary artists and philosophers, an individualist, a libertarian, and an uncompromising critic of orthodoxy and authoritarianism...

Blake's work can be difficult at times, mainly because the reader is offered Blake's visions in Blake's own terms. Blake draws on a highly powerful, but essentially personal, mythological system of his own devising, but one that also draws on a variety of mythological, poetic and philosophical sources. On this, Blake himself remarked that he had to "create a System, or be enslaved by another Man's." In part also, what Blake seeks to express can only be presented in terms of vague abstractions and allusions, with a cosmic perspective on issues of faith, religion, philosophy and belief, and this must also mean that the reader has to work hard. Yet the effort is worth it. Blake is a revolutionary and visionary artist and poet, and his work represented a decisively new direction in the course of English Poetry and the Visual Arts.

Blake's works range from the deceptively simple and lyrical style of the Songs of Innocence and Experience, through speculative works such as The Marriage of Heaven and Hell, to the highly elaborate visionary and apocalyptic style of America, The Four Zoas, Milton and The Book of Urizen.

Chapter 2

# William Blake: List of Works

1. All Religions are One
2. There is No Natural Religion [a]
3. There is No Natural Religion [b]
4. The Book of Thel
5. Songs of Innocence and of Experience
6. For Children: The Gates of Paradise
7. The Marriage of Heaven and Hell
8. Visions of the Daughters of Albion
9. America a Prophecy
10. Europe a Prophecy
11. The Song of Los
12. The [First] Book of Urizen
13. The Book of Ahania
14. The Book of Los
15. Milton: a Poem in 2 Books
16. Jerusalem: The Emanation of The Giant Albion frontispiece

To the Public

Chap: 1 [plates4-27]

To the Jews

"The fields from Islington to Marybone

Chap: 2 [plates 28-50]

To the Deists

"I saw a Monk of Charlemaine"

Chap 3 [plates 53-75]

To the Christians

"I stood among my valleys of the south"

"England! Awake!..."

C[hap] 4 [plates 78-99]

17. For the Sexes: The Gates of Paradise
18. On Homers Poetry
19. On Virgil
20. The Ghost of Abel
21. [Laocoön]
22. Tiriel
23. The French Revolution
24. The Four Zoas
    - Vala Night the First
    - Vala Night the [Second]
    - Vala Night the Third
    - Vala Night the Fourth
    - Vala Night the Fifth
    - Vala Night the Sixth
    - Vala Night the Seventh
    - Vala Night the Eighth
    - Vala Night the Ninth Being The Last Judgment

1. Poetical Sketches
2. [An Island in the Moon]
3. [Songs and Ballads] (Index)
4. [The Pickering Manuscript] (Index)
5. [Satiric Verses and Epigrams]

6. The Everlasting Gospel
7. [Blake's Exhibition and Catalogue of 1809]
8. [Descriptions of the Last Judgment]
9. [Blake's Chaucer: Prospectuses]
10. [Public Address]

Annotations to:

- Lavater's Aphorisms on Man
- Swedenborg's Heaven and Hell
- Swedenborg's Divine Love and Divine Wisdom
- Swedenborg's Divine Providence
- An Apology for the Bible by R. Watson
- Bacon's Essays Moral, Economical and Political
- Boyd's Historical Notes on Dante
- The Works of Sir Joshua Reynolds
- Spurzheim's Observations on Insanity
- Berkeley's Siris
- Wordsworth's Poems
- Wordsworth's Preface to The Excursion
- Thorton's The Lord's Prayer, Newly Translated
- Cellini
- Young's Night Thoughts.
  - [Inscriptions and Notes On or For Pictures]
  - [Miscellaneous Prose]
  - [The Letters]

# Chapter 3

# Biography of William Blake

William Blake was born in London in 1757. His father, a hosier, soon recognized his son's artistic talents and sent him to study at a drawing school when he was ten years old. At 14, William asked to be apprenticed to the engraver James Basire, under whose direction he further developed his innate skills. As a young man Blake worked as an engraver, illustrator, and drawing teacher, and met such artists as Henry Fuseli and John Flaxman, as well as Sir Joshua Reynolds, whose classicizing style he would later come to reject. Blake wrote poems during this time as well, and his first printed collection, an immature and rather derivative volume called *Poetical Sketches,* appeared in 1783. *Songs of Innocence* was published in 1789, followed by *Songs of Experience* in 1793 and a combined edition the next year bearing the title *Songs of Innocence and Experience showing the Two Contrary States of the Human Soul.*

A rebel all of his life, Blake was once arrested on a trumped up charge of sedition. Of course, he was a complete sympathizer with the forces of revolution, both in America and France. He was a personal friend of Thomas Paine and made the American War of Independence and French Revolution parts of his grand mythology in his America: A Prophecy and Europe: A Prophecy.

Blake is frequently referred to as a mystic, but this is not really accurate. He deliberately wrote in the style of the Hebrew prophets and apocalyptic writers. He envisioned his works as expressions of prophecy, following in the footsteps (or, more precisely strapping on the sandals) of Elijah and Milton. In fact, he clearly believed himself to be the living embodiment of the spirit of Milton.

Most of Blake's paintings (such as "The Ancient of Days" above, the frontispiece to *Europe: a Prophecy*) are actually prints made from copper plates, which he etched in a method he claimed was revealed to him in a dream. He and his wife coloured these prints with water colours. Thus each print is itself a unique work of art.

As an artist Blake broke the ground that would later be cultivated by the Pre-Raphaelites. His work is for the most part done on a very small scale. His illuminated works and engravings are all only inches in size, yet they are meticulous in detail. And each of them is, in a sense, merely a part of a titanic whole.

Blake's political radicalism intensified during the years leading up to the French Revolution He began a seven-book poem about the Revolution, in fact, but it was either destroyed or never completed, and only the first book survives. He disapproved of Enlightment, rationalism, of institutionalized religion, and of the tradition of marriage in its conventional legal and social form (though he was married himself). His unorthodox religious thinking owes a debt to the Swedish philosopher Emmanuel Swedenborg (1688-1772), whose influence is particularly evident in Blake's *The Marriage of Heaven and Hell*. In the 1790s and after, he shifted his poetic voice from the lyric to the prophetic mode, and wrote a series of long prophetic books, including *Milton* and *Jerusalem*. Linked together by an intricate mythology and symbolism of Blake's own creation, these books propound a revolutionary new social, intellectual, and ethical order.

Blake published almost all of his works himself, by an original process in which the poems were etched by hand, along with illustrations and decorative images, onto copper plates. These plates were inked to make prints, and the prints were then coloured in with paint. This expensive and labour-intensive production method resulted in a quite limited circulation of Blake's poetry during his life. It has also posed a special set of challenges to scholars of Blake's work, which has interested both literary critics and art historians. Most students of Blake find it necessary to consider his graphic art and his writing together; certainly he himself thought of them as inseparable. During his own lifetime, Blake was a pronounced failure, and he harbored a good deal of resentment and anxiety about the public's apathy toward his work and about the financial straits in which he so regularly found himself. When his self-crated exhibition of his works met with financial failure in 1809, Blake sank into depression and withdrew into obscurity; he remained alienated for the rest of his life. His contemporaries saw him as something of an eccentric—as indeed he was. Suspended between the neoclassicism of the 18th century and the early phases of Romanticism, Blake belongs to no single poetic school or age. Only in the 20th century did wide audiences begin to acknowledge his profound originality and genius.

British poet, painter, visionary mystic, and engraver, who illustrated and printed his own books, Blake proclaimed the supremacy of the imagination over the rationalism and materialism of the 18th- century. He joined for a time the Swedenborgian Church of the New Jerusalem in London and considered Newtonian science to be superstitious nonsense. Misunderstanding shadowed his career as a writer and artist and it was left to later generations to recognize his importance.

Blake was born in London, where he spent most of his life. His father was a successful London hosier and attracted by the doctrines of Emmanuel Swedenborg. Blake was first educated at home, chiefly by his mother. His parents encouraged him to collect prints of the Italian masters, and in 1767 sent him to Henry Pars' drawing school. From his early years, he experienced visions of angels and ghostly monks; he saw and conversed with the angel Gabriel, the Virgin Mary, and various historical figures.

At the age of 14 Blake was apprenticed for seven years to the engraver James Basire. Gothic art and architecture influenced him deeply. After studies at the Royal Academy School, Blake started to produce watercolours and engrave illustrations for magazines. In 1783 he married Catherine Boucher, the daughter of a market gardener. Blake taught her to draw and paint and she assisted him devoutly. In 1774 Blake opened with his wife and younger brother Robert a print shop at 27 Broad Street, but the venture failed after the death of Robert in 1787. Blake's important cultural and social contacts included Henry Fuseli, Reverend A.S. Mathew and his wife, John Flaxman (1755-1826), a sculptor and draughtsman, Tom Paine, William Godwin, and Mrs. Elizabeth Montague (1720-1800), married to the wealthy grandson of the earl of Sandwich.

His early poems Blake wrote at the age of 12. His first book of poems, Poetical Sketches, appeared in 1783 and was followed by Songs of Innocence (1789), and Songs of Experience (1794). His most famous poem, 'The Tyger', was part of his Songs of Experience. Typical for Blake's poems were long, flowing lines and violent energy, combined with aphoristic clarity and moments of lyric tenderness. He approved of free love, and sympathized with the actions of the French revolutionaries until the events of 1794 sickened him. In 1790 Blake engraved The Marriage of Heaven and Hell, a book of paradoxical aphorisms and his principal prose work. It expressed Blake's revolt against the established values of his time. "Prisons are built with stones of Law, brothels with bricks of Religion." Radically he sided with the Satan in Milton's Paradise Lost and attacked the conventional religious views in a series of aphorisms. But the poet's life in the realms of images did not please his wife who once remarked: "I have very little of Mr. Blake's company. He is always in Paradise." Some of Blake's contemporaries called him a harmless lunatic.

The Blakes moved south of the Thames to Lambeth in 1790. During this time Blake began to work on his 'prophetic books', where he expressed his lifelong concern with the struggle of the soul to free its natural energies from reason and organized religion. He wrote The Visions of the Daughters of Albion (1793), America: A Prophesy (1793), The Book of

Urizen (1794), and The Song of Los (1795). Blake hated the effects of the Industrial Revolution in England and looked forward to the establishment of a New Jerusalem "in England's green and pleasant land." Between 1804 and 1818 he produced an edition of his own poem Jerusalem with 100 engravings.

In 1800 Blake was taken up by the wealthy William Hayley, poet and patron of poets. The Blakes lived in Hayley's house at Felpham in Sussex, staying there for three years. At Felpham Blake worked on Milton: A Poem in Two Books, to Justify the Ways of God to Men. It was finished and engraved between 1803 and 1808. In 1803 Blake was charged at Chichester with high treason for having 'uttered seditious and treasonable expressions, such as "D-n the King, d-n all his sibjects..."' but was acquitted. In 1809 Blake had a commercially unsuccessful exhibition at the shop once owned by his brother. However, economic problems did not depress him, but he continued to produce energetically poems, aphorisms, and engravings. "The tigers of wrath are wiser than the horses of instruction," he wrote.

From 1818 Blake started to enjoy the admiration of a group of young disciples. Blake's last years were passed in obscurity, quarreling even with some of the circle of friends who supported him. Among Blake's later artistic works are drawings and engravings for Dante's Divine Comedy and the 21 illustrations to the book of Job, which was completed when he was almost 70 years old. Blake never shook off the poverty, in large part due to his inability to compete in the highly competitive field of engraving and his expensive invention that enabled him to design illustrations and print words at the same time.

Independent through his life, Blake left no debts at his death on August 12, 1827. He was buried in an unmarked grave at the public cemetery of Bun hill Fields. Wordsworth's verdict after Blake's death reflected many opinions of the time: "There was no doubt that this poor man was mad, but there is something in the madness of this man which interests me more than the sanity of Lord Byron and Walter Scott." Blake's influence grew through Pre-Raphaelites and W.B. Yeats especially in Britain. His interest in legend was revived with the Romantics' rediscovery of the past, especially the Gothic and medieval. In the 1960s Blake's work was acclaimed by the Underground movement.

## Chapter 4

# Blake: As a Poet

IF one follow Blake's mind through the several stages of his poetic development it is impossible to regard him as a naïf, a wild man, a wild pet for the super cultivated. The strangeness is evaporated, the peculiarity is seen to be the peculiarity of all great poetry: something which is found (not everywhere) in Homer and Æschylus and Dante and Villon, and profound and concealed in the work of Shakespeare—and also in another form in Montaigne and in Spinoza. It is merely a peculiar honesty, which, in a world too frightened to be honest, is peculiarly terrifying. It is an honesty against which the whole world conspires, because it is unpleasant. Blake's poetry has the unpleasantness of great poetry.

Nothing that can be called morbid or abnormal or perverse, none of the things which exemplify the sickness of an epoch or a fashion, have this quality; only those things which, by some extraordinary labour of simplification, exhibit the essential sickness or strength of the human soul. And this honesty never exists without great technical accomplishment. The question about Blake the man is the question of the circumstances that concurred to permit this honesty in his work, and what circumstances define its limitations. The favouring conditions probably include these two: that, being early apprenticed to a manual occupation, he was not compelled to acquire any other education in literature than he wanted, or to acquire it for any other reason than that he wanted it; and that, being a humble engraver, he had no journalistic-social career open to him.

There was, that is to say, nothing to distract him from his interests or to corrupt these interests: neither the ambitions of parents or wife, nor the standards of society, nor the temptations of success; nor was he exposed to imitation of himself or of anyone else. These circumstances—not his supposed inspired and untaught spontaneity—are what make him innocent. His early poems show what the poems of a boy of genius ought to show, immense power of assimilation. Such early poems are not, as usually supposed, crude attempts to do something beyond the boy's capacity; they are, in the case of a boy of real promise, more likely to be quite mature and successful attempts to do something small. So with Blake, his early poems are technically admirable, and their originality is in an occasional rhythm. The verse of Edward III deserves study. But his affection for certain Elizabethans is not as surprising as his affinity with the very best work of his own century. He is very like Collins, he is very eighteenth century. The poem Whether on Ida's shady brow is eighteenth-century work; the movement, the weight of it, the syntax, the choice of words—

The languid strings do scarcely move!
The sound is forced, the notes are few!

this is contemporary with Gray and Collins; it is the poetry of a language which has undergone the discipline of prose. Blake up to twenty is decidedly a traditional.

Blake's beginnings as a poet, then, is as normal as the beginnings of Shakespeare. His method of composition, in his mature work, is exactly like that of other poets. He has an idea (a feeling, an image), he develops it by accretion or expansion, alters his verse often, and hesitates often over the final choice. 1 The idea, of course, simply comes, but upon arrival it is subjected to prolonged manipulation. In the first phase Blake is concerned with verbal beauty; in the second he becomes the apparent naïf, really the mature intelligence. It is only when the ideas become more automatic, come more freely and are less manipulated, that we begin to suspect their origin, to suspect that they spring from a shallower source.

The Songs of Innocence and of Experience, and the poems from the Rossetti manuscript, are the poems of a man with a profound interest in human emotions, and a profound knowledge of them. The emotions are presented in an extremely simplified, abstract form. This form is one illustration of the eternal struggle of art against education, of the literary artist against the continuous deterioration of language.

It is important that the artist should be highly educated in his own art; but his education is one that is hindered rather than helped by the ordinary processes of society which constitute education for the ordinary man. For these processes consist largely in the acquisition of impersonal ideas which obscure what we really are and feel, what we really want, and what really excites our interest. It is of course not the actual information acquired, but the conformity which the accumulation of knowledge is apt to impose, that is harmful. Tennyson is a very fair example of a poet almost wholly encrusted with parasitic opinion, almost wholly merged into his environment. Blake, on the other hand, knew what interested him, and he therefore presents only the essential, only, in fact, what can be presented, and need not be explained. And because he was not distracted, or frightened, or occupied in anything but exact statement, he understood. He was naked, and saw man naked, and from the centre of his own crystal. To him there was no more reason why Swedenborg should be absurd than Locke. He accepted Swedenborg, and eventually rejected him, for reasons of his own. He approached everything with a mind unclouded by current opinions. There was nothing of the superior person about him. This makes him terrifying.

But if there was nothing to distract him from sincerity there were, on the other hand, the dangers to which the naked man is exposed. His philosophy, like his visions, like his insight, like his technique, was his own. And accordingly he was inclined to attach more importance to it than an artist should; this is what makes him eccentric, and makes him inclined to formlessness.

But most through midnight streets I hear
How the youthful harlot's curse
Blasts the new-born infant's tear,
And blights with plagues the marriage hearse,

is the naked vision?

Love seeketh only self to please,
To bind another to its delight,
Joys in another's loss of ease,
And builds a Hell in Heaven's despite,

is the naked observation; and The Marriage of Heaven and Hell is naked philosophy, presented. But Blake's occasional marriages of poetry and philosophy are not so felicitous.

He who would do well to another must do it in Minute Particulars.

General Good is the plea of the scoundrel, hypocrite, and flatterer;

For Art and Science cannot exist but in minutely organized particulars....

One feels that the form is not well chosen. The borrowed philosophy of Dante and Lucretius is perhaps not so interesting, but it injures their form less. Blake did not have that more Mediterranean gift of form which knows how to borrow as Dante borrowed his theory of the soul; he must need create a philosophy as well as poetry. A similar formlessness attacks his draughtsman ship. The fault is most evident, of course, in the longer poems—or rather, the poems in which structure is important. You cannot create a very large poem without introducing a more impersonal point of view, or splitting it up into various personalities. But the weakness of the long poems is certainly not that they are too visionary, too remote from the world. It is that Blake did not see enough, became too much occupied with ideas.

We have the same respect for Blake's philosophy (and perhaps for that of Samuel Butler) that we have for an ingenious piece of home-made furniture: we admire the man who has put it together out of the odds and ends about the house. England has produced a fair number of these resourceful Robinson Crusoes; but we are not really so remote from the Continent, or from our own past, as to be deprived of the advantages of culture if we wish them.

We may speculate, for amusement, whether it would not have been beneficial to the north of Europe generally, and to Britain in particular, to have had a more continuous religious history. The local divinities of Italy were not wholly exterminated by Christianity, and they were not reduced to the dwarfish fate which fell upon our trolls and pixies.

The latter, with the major Saxon deities, were perhaps no great loss in themselves, but they left an empty place; and perhaps our mythology was further impoverished by the divorce from Rome. Milton's celestial and infernal regions are large but insufficiently furnished apartments filled by heavy conversation; and one remarks about the Puritan mythology an historical thinness.

And about Blake's supernatural territories, as about the supposed ideas that dwell there, we cannot help commenting on a certain meanness of culture. They illustrate the crankiness, the eccentricity, which frequently affects writers outside of the Latin traditions, and which such a critic as Arnold should certainly have rebuked. And they are not essential to Blake's inspiration. 8

Blake was endowed with a capacity for considerable understanding of human nature, with a remarkable and original sense of language and the music of language, and a gift of hallucinated vision. Had these been controlled by a respect for impersonal reason, for common sense, for the objectivity of science, it would have been better for him.

What his genius required, and what it sadly lacked, was a framework of accepted and traditional ideas which would have prevented him from indulging in a philosophy of his own, and concentrated his attention upon the problems of the poet. Confusion of thought, emotion, and vision is what we find in such a work as Also Sprach Zarathustra; it is eminently not a Latin virtue. The concentration resulting from a framework of mythology and theology and philosophy is one of the reasons why Dante is a classic, and Blake only a poet of genius.

The fault is perhaps not with Blake himself, but with the environment which failed to provide what such a poet needed; perhaps the circumstances compelled him to fabricate, perhaps the poet required the philosopher and mythologist; although the conscious Blake may have been quite unconscious of the motives

## Blake – As an Anarchist

In the popular imagination William Blake is known as an opium muncher and poet. Peter Marshall embarks on a journey to dispel the myths that surround this radical thinker who lived over two centuries ago. In Marshall's words "he (William Blake) demands bread for all and a fair return for a fairs day work. He would like to see an end to capital, tax and empire. He calls for complete sexual and racial equality and celebrates universal toleration".

Peter Marshall examines the influences on Blake's life, he looks at the events that shaped his visionary ideas and dissects the society he lived in.

Reading this little pamphlet just 65 pages long gives you an insight into how the historical process washes out everything that doesn't fit into the dominant ideology of the period. Just two centuries after Blake's death the radical egalitarian aspects of his thoughts and works have been banished to the dustbin of history. The exoskeleton survives providing a framework on which every historian and their dog hangs out their prejudices about Blake.

Marshall has ignored the historical interpretations of Blake's work and has gone back to the original sources to try to establish what Blake was trying to say. He has placed Blake in his historical context (No man is an island) and has tried to discover the formative influences on his work. Marshall believes that Blake like his contemporary, William Godwin, was a forerunner of the anarchist movement. Extrapolating from Marshall's analysis, it's possible to see Blake's ideas as a logical extension of the Levellers ideas.

All in all William Blake a visionary Anarchist is a well thought out exercise that places Blake among anarchism's significant thinkers.

# Chapter 5

# Blake as A Romantic Poet

Blake's peculiar method of reproducing his writings, and the comparative seclusion in which he lived, prevented his works from exercising any influence on their age, though Wordsworth, Coleridge, Southey and Lamb knew and admired portions of them. Yet, few responded so directly and in so many ways to the quickening impulse of the romantic revival.

It is true that his early years coincided with an awakened interest in our older literature, which was already exercising a limited influence on contemporary work; and, moreover, as has been seen, his juvenile reading was in this field. But the root of the matter seems to have lain deeper. The whole temper of his genius was essentially opposed to the classical tradition, with its close regard to intellectual appeal and its distrust of enthusiasm.

In the Laocoon sentences and in the engraved notes On Homer's Poetry and On Virgil, he identifies it with the devastating errors of materialism and morality, and, in the Public Address, he is vehement in denouncing Dryden's presumption in "improving" Milton, and Pope's "niggling" formalism: as he puts it, the practitioners of this school "knew enough of artifice, but little of art." Such a judgment, though not wholly just to classicism at its best, was the fighting creed of the romantics, and Blake maintained it more uncompromisingly than most. His mystical faith freed him from the barren materialism of his age, and opened to him in vision the world lying beyond the range of the physical senses. Hence, the greater warmth of his ethical creed; and his preoccupation with the supernatural, which he never consciously shaped to literary ends, is yet the source of the peculiar imaginative quality of his work. It also looks forward to the use of the supernatural in such works as The Ancient Mariner and Christabel.

Though he probably intended it otherwise, the effective and complete revelation of the new spirit within him is made, not in his definitely dogmatic writing, but in his verse, which he seems to have rated below his other work; he scarcely ever speaks of it as he does of his art or his mystical writings. Yet, his lyric poetry, at its best, displays the characteristics of the new spirit some years before it appeared elsewhere.

His first volume of poems contained songs such as had not been sung for more than a century; the nearest parallel in time is Burns. While Wordsworth was still a schoolboy, Blake had found, and was using with consummate art, diction almost perfect in its simplicity, aptness and beauty. His earlier attitude to nature, as has already been noticed, has none of the complacency that distinguishes his age: to him, it was the revelation of a universal spirit of love and delight, the Divine Image, less austere than Wordsworth's "overseeing power."

It has also been seen that he had the romantic sympathy with quaint or terrible imaginings, such as appeared later in Keats and Shelley. His passion for freedom was, also, akin to that which moved Wordsworth, Coleridge and Southey in their earlier years, though, in its later form, it came nearer to Shelley's revolt against convention. There is, indeed, an unusual degree of fellowship between these two: the imagery and symbolism, as well as the underlying spirit, of The Revolt of Islam, Alastor and Prometheus Unbound find their nearest parallel in Blake's prophetic books. Both had visions of a world regenerated by a gospel of universal brotherhood, transcending law; though, perhaps, the firmer spirit of Blake brought his faith in imagination nearer to life than Shelley's philosophic dream of intellectual beauty. For the final note of Blake's career is not one of tragedy: his own works and the record of others show that he had subdued the world to his own spirit; he died singing.

Much like William Wordsworth, Blake wrote from the heart, letting natural expression take over. Many of the writers of the Romantic period felt they had entered an imaginative climate, which some of them called "the Spirit Age." During this "Spirit Age," many authors felt that freedom and spontaneity were the key elements in poetry.

Before this creative revolution, a poem was considered a classical work of art, assimilated to please an audience. In Romanticism, the "rules" hanging over poetry were dropped and a piece of work could become, as Blake described, "an embodiment of the poet's imagine vision." Blake used these free-formed ideas and concepts in his later works. These essays, All Religions Are One, There is No Natural Religion (a), and There is No Natural Religion (b), all show Blake's views against Christian Orthodox, religion based on ancient scripture and against "Natural Religion," the belief that God is as an

Mary Wollstonecraft wrote "A Vindication of the Rights of Women. All Religions Are One, There is No Natural Religion and there is No Natural Religion were composed in hopes of bringing change to the public's spiritual life. In the end, Blake reminds us that are all things in this world were accepted as "natural," then "the Philosophic and Experimental would soon be at the ratio of all things, and stand still unable to do other than repeat the same dull round over again. He wrote three works around 1788, to illustrate his views on religion, All Religions Are One, There is No Natural Religion (a), and There is No Natural Religion (b). He wrote All Religions Are One directed against Deism or "Natural Religion" and against Christian Orthodoxy. " People of this era felt his works tested the boundaries of good art. He states that the desires and perceptions of man are not natural or organic, but are things taught to us. Many of the other writers of this time also challenged previously accepted ideas. During the war, Blake was faced with charges of "speaking against his King and country. Blake soon rebelled, calling Haley the enemy of his spiritual life.

Many of the writers of the Romantic period were highly influenced by the war between England and France and the French Revolution. " We as humans, are too dependent upon acceptance and not enough on independence. Haley attempted to change Blake's free art into conventional and breadwinning art. " He states that "The Jewish and Christian Testaments are an original derivation from the Poetic Genius," supporting his theory that man has imagined God.

# Chapter 6

# A Note on Romanticism

## Characteristics

In a general sense, the term "Romanticism" has been used to refer to certain artists, poets, writers, musicians, as well as political, philosophical and social thinkers of the late eighteenth and early nineteenth centuries. It has equally been used to refer to various artistic, intellectual, and social trends of that era. Despite this general usage of the term, a precise characterization and specific definition of Romanticism has been the subject of debate in the fields of intellectual history and literary history throughout the twentieth century, without any great measure of consensus emerging.

Arthur Lovejoy attempted to demonstrate the difficulty of this problem in his seminal article "On The Discrimination of Romanticisms" in his Essays in the History of Ideas (1948); some scholars see romanticism as completely continuous with the present, some see it as the inaugural moment of modernity, some see it as the beginning of a tradition of resistance to the Enlightenment, and still others date it firmly in the direct aftermath of the French Revolution. Another definition comes from Charles Baudelaire: "Romanticism is precisely situated neither in choice of neither subject nor exact truth, but in a way of feeling."

Many intellectual historians have seen Romanticism as a key movement in the Counter-Enlightenment, a reaction against the Age of Enlightenment. Whereas the thinkers of the Enlightenment emphasized the primacy of deductive reason, Romanticism emphasized intuition, imagination, and feeling, to a point that has led to some Romantic thinkers being accused of irrationalism.

## Romanticism and Music

In general, the term "Romanticism" when applied to music has come to mean the period roughly from the 1820s until around 1900. The contemporary application of 'romantic' to music did not coincide with modern categories: in 1810 E.T.A. Hoffmann called Mozart, Haydn and Beethoven the three "Romantic Composers", and Ludwig Spohr used the term "good Romantic style" to apply to parts of Beethoven's Fifth Symphony. Technically, Mozart is considered classical and by most standards Beethoven is the start of the musical Romantic period. By the early twentieth century, the sense that there had been a decisive break with the musical past led to the establishment of the nineteenth century as "The Romantic Era," and as such it is referred to in the standard encyclopedias of music.

The traditional modern discussion of the music of Romanticism includes elements, such as the growing use of folk music, which are also directly related to the broader current of Romantic nationalism in the arts

## Frédéric Chopin

Some aspects of Romanticism are already present in eighteenth-century music. The heightened contrasts and emotions of Sturm und Drang (German for "Storm and Stress") seem a precursor of the Gothic novel in literature, or the sanguinary elements of some of the operas of the period of the French Revolution the concept of the Romantic musician begins to reveal itself— the man who ]. The libretti of Lorenzo da Ponte for Mozart, and the eloquent music the latter wrote for them, convey a new sense of individuality and freedom. The romantic generation viewed Beethoven as their ideal of a heroic artist—a man who first dedicated a symphony to Consul Bonaparte as a champion of freedom and then challenged Emperor Napoleon by striking him out from the dedication of the Eroica Symphony. In Beethoven's Fidelio he creates the apotheosis of the 'rescue operas' which were another feature of French musical culture during the revolutionary period, in order to hymn the freedom which underlay the thinking of all radical artists in the years of hope after the Congress of Vienna.

**Felix Mendelssohn**

In the contemporary music culture, the romantic musician followed a public career, depending on sensitive middle-class audiences rather than on a courtly patron, as had been the case with earlier musicians and composers. Public persona characterized a new generation of virtuosi who made their way as soloists, epitomized in the careers of Paganini and Liszt.

Beethoven's use of tonal architecture in such a way as to allow significant expansion of musical forms and structures was immediately recognized as bringing a new dimension to music. The later piano music and string quartets, especially, showed the way to a completely unexplored musical universe.

The writer, critic (and composer) Hoffmann was able to write of the supremacy of instrumental music over vocal music in expressiveness, a concept which would previously have been regarded as absurd. Hoffmann himself, as a practitioner both of music and literature, encouraged the notion of music as 'programmatic' or telling a story, an idea which new audiences found attractive, however irritating it was to some composers (e.g. Felix Mendelssohn).

New developments in instrumental technology in the early nineteenth century—iron frames for pianos, wound metal strings for string instruments—enabled louder dynamics, more varied tone colours, and the potential for sensational virtuosity. Such developments swelled the length of pieces, introduced programmatic titles, and created new genres such as the free standing overture or tone-poem, the piano fantasy, nocturne and rhapsody, and the virtuoso concerto, which became central to musical romanticism.

## Richard Wagner

In opera, a new Romantic atmosphere combining supernatural terror and melodramatic plot in a folkloric context was most successfully achieved by Weber's Der Freischütz (1817, 1821). Enriched timbre and colour marked the early orchestration of Hector Berlioz in France, and the grand operas of Meyerbeer. Amongst the radical fringe of what became mockingly characterized (adopting Wagner's own words) as 'artists of the future', Liszt and Wagner each embodied the Romantic cult of the free, inspired, charismatic, perhaps ruthlessly unconventional individual artistic personality.

It is the period of 1815 to 1848 which must be regarded as the true age of Romanticism in music - the age of the last compositions of Beethoven (d. 1827) and Schubert (d. 1828), of the works of Schumann (d. 1856) and Chopin (d.1849), of the early struggles of Berlioz and Richard Wagner, of the great virtuosi such as Paganini (d. 1840), and the young Liszt and Thalberg. Now that we are able to listen to the work of Mendelssohn (d. 1847) stripped of the Biedermeier reputation unfairly attached to it, he can also be placed in this more appropriate context.

After this period, with Chopin and Paganini dead, Liszt retired from the concert platform at a minor German court, Wagner effectively in exile until he obtained royal patronage in Bavaria, and Berlioz still struggling with the bourgeois liberalism which all but smothered radical artistic Endeavour in Europe, Romanticism in music was surely past its prime—giving way, rather, to the period of musical romantics.

## Visual Art and Literature

In visual art and literature, "Romanticism" typically refers to the late 18th century through the mid 19th century.

Recurring themes found in Romantic literature are the criticism of the past, emphasis on women and children, and respect for nature. Furthermore, several romantic authors, such as Nathaniel Hawthorne, based their writings on the supernatural/occult and human psychology, which they were fascinated with.

The Scottish poet James McPherson influenced the early development of Romanticism with the international success of his Ossian cycle of poems published in 1762, inspiring both Goethe and the young Walter Scott.

An early German influence came from Johann Wolfgang Goethe whose 1774 novel The Sorrows of Young Werther had young men throughout Europe emulating its protagonist, a young artist with a very sensitive and passionate temperament. At that time Germany was a multitude of small separate states, and Goethe's works would have a seminal influence in developing a unifying sense of nationalism. Important writers of early German romanticism were Ludwig Tieck, Novalis (Heinrich von Ofterdingen, 1799) and Friedrich Hoelderlin.

Heidelberg later became a centre of German romanticism, where writers and poets such as Clemens Brentano, Achim von Arnim and Joseph von Eichendorff met regularly in literary circles. Romanticists often focused on emotions and dreams in their works. Other important motifs in German Romanticism are travelling, nature and ancient myths. The late German Romanticism (of, for example, E.T.A. Hoffmann's Der Sandmann - The Sandman, 1817, and Eichendorff's Das Marmorbild - The Marble Statue, 1819) was somewhat darker in its motifs and has some gothic elements.

The Fighting Téméraire tugged to her last Berth to be broken, J.M.W. Turner

Romanticism in British literature developed in a different form slightly later, mostly associated with the poets William Wordsworth and Samuel Taylor Coleridge, whose co-authored book "Lyrical Ballads" (1798) sought to reject Augustan poetry in favour of more direct speech derived from folk traditions.

Both poets were also involved in Utopian social thought in the wake of the French Revolution. The poet and painter William Blake is the most extreme example of the Romantic sensibility in Britain, epitomized by his claim "I must create a system or be enslaved by another man's." Blake's artistic work is also strongly influenced by Medieval illuminated books. The painters J.M.W. Turner and John Constable are also generally associated with Romanticism. Lord Byron, Percy Bysshe Shelley, Mary Shelley and John Keats constitute another phase of Romanticism in Britain. The historian Thomas Carlyle and the Pre-Raphaelite Brotherhood represent the last phase of transformation into Victorian culture. William Butler Yeats, born in 1865, referred to his generation as "the last romantics."

**Liberty Leading the People by Eugène Delacroix**

In predominantly Roman Catholic countries Romanticism was less pronounced than in Germany and Britain, and tended to develop later, after the rise of Napoleon. François-René de Chateaubriand is often called the "Father of French Romanticism". In France, the movement is associated with the nineteenth century, particularly in the paintings of Théodore Géricault and Eugène Delacroix, the plays, poems and novels of Victor Hugo (such as Les Misérables and Ninety-Three), and the novels of Stendhal. The composer Hector Berlioz is also important.

Inside Russia, the principal exponent of Romanticism is Alexander Pushkin. Mikhail Lermontov attempted to analyse and bring to light the deepest reasons for the Romantic idea of metaphysical discontent with society and self, and was much influenced by Lord Byron. The poet Fyodor Tyutchev was also an important figure of the movement in Russia, and was heavily influenced by the German Romantics.

Romanticism played an essential role in the national awakening of many Central European peoples lacking their own national states, not least in Poland, which had recently lost its independence when Russia's army crushed the Polish Rebellion under the reactionary Nicholas I. Revival and reinterpretation of ancient myths, customs and traditions by Romantic poets and painters helped to distinguish their indigenous cultures from those of the dominant nations and crystallize the mythography of Romantic nationalism. Patriotism, nationalism, revolution and armed struggle for independence also became popular themes in the arts of this period. Arguably, the most distinguished Romanticist poet of this part of Europe was Adam Mickiewicz, who developed an idea that Poland was the Messiah of Nations, predestined to suffer just as Jesus had suffered to save all the people.

A Romantic heroine: in The Lady of Shalott (1888) John William Waterhouse's realistic technique depicts a neo-medieval subject drawn from Arthurian Romance

In the United States, the romantic gothic made an early appearance with Washington Irving's Legend of Sleepy Hollow (1820) and Rip Van Winkle (1819), followed from 1823 onwards by the fresh Leatherstocking tales of James Fenimore Cooper, with their emphasis on heroic simplicity and their fervent landscape descriptions of an already-exotic mythicized frontier peopled by "noble savages", similar to the philosophical theory of Rousseau, like Uncas, "The Last of the Mohicans". There are picturesque "local colour" elements in Washington Irving's essays and especially his travel books. Edgar Allan Poe's tales of the macabre and his balladic poetry were more influential in France than at home, but the romantic American novel developed fully in Nathaniel Hawthorne's atmosphere and melodrama. Later Transcendentalist writers such as Henry David Thoreau and Ralph Waldo Emerson still show elements of its influence, as does the romantic realism of Walt Whitman.

But by the 1880s, psychological and social realism was competing with romanticism in the novel. The poetry which Americans wrote and read was all romantic until the 1920s: Poe and Hawthorne, as well as Henry Wadsworth Longfellow. The poetry of Emily Dickinson – nearly unread in her own time – and Herman Melville's novel Moby-Dick can be taken as epitomes of American Romantic literature, or, by interpreting their sometimes subversive subtexts, as successors to it. As elsewhere (England, Germany, France), literary Romanticism had its counterpart in American visual arts, most especially in the exaltation of untamed America found in the paintings of the Hudson River School. Painters like Thomas Cole, Albert Bierstadt and Frederic Edwin Church and others often combined a sense of the sublime with underlying religious and philosophical themes. Thomas Cole's paintings feature strong narratives as in The Voyage of Life series painted in the early 1840s that depict man trying to survive amidst an awesome and immense nature, from the cradle to the grave.

Romanticism is an artistic, literary, and intellectual movement that originated around the middle of the 18th century in Western Europe, and gained strength during the Industrial Revolution. It was partly a revolt against aristocratic, social, and political norms of the Enlightenment period and a reaction against the scientific rationalization of nature in art and literature.

The movement stressed strong emotion as a source of aesthetic experience, placing new emphasis on such emotions as trepidation, horror, and the awe experienced in confronting the sublimity of untamed nature. It elevated folk art, nature and custom, as well as arguing for an epistemology based on nature, which included human activity conditioned by nature in the form of language, custom and usage. It was influenced by ideas of the Enlightenment and elevated medievalism and elements of art and narrative perceived to be from the medieval period.

The name "romantic" itself comes from the term "romance" which is a prose or poetic heroic narrative originating in medieval literature and romantic literature. The ideologies and events of the French Revolution and Industrial Revolution are thought to have influenced the movement. Romanticism elevated the achievements of what it perceived as misunderstood heroic individuals and artists that altered society. It also legitimized the individual imagination as a critical authority which permitted freedom from classical notions of form in art. There was a strong recourse to historical and natural inevitability in the representation of its ideas.

In its intense focus on the individual consciousness, it was both a continuation of and a reaction against the Enlightenment. Romanticism emphasized the individual, the subjective, the irrational, the imaginative, the personal, the spontaneous, the emotional, the visionary, and the transcendental. Among its attitudes were a deepened appreciation of the beauties of nature; a general exaltation of emotion over reason and of the senses over intellect; a turning in upon the self and a heightened examination of human personality; a preoccupation with the genius, the hero, and the exceptional figure; a new view of the artist as a supremely individual creator; an emphasis on imagination as a gateway to transcendent experience and spiritual truth; a consuming interest in folk culture, national and ethnic cultural origins, and the medieval era; and a predilection for the exotic, the remote, the mysterious, the weird, the occult, the monstrous, the diseased, and even the satanic.

Chapter 7

# A Note on Romantic Poetry

## Historical Considerations

It is one of the curiosities of literary history that the strongholds of the Romantic Movement were England and Germany, not the countries of the romance languages themselves. Thus it is from the historians of English and German literature that we inherit the convenient set of terminal dates for the Romantic period, beginning in 1798, the year of the first edition of Lyrical Ballads by Wordsworth and Coleridge and of the composition of Hymns to the Night by Novalis, and ending in 1832, the year which marked the deaths of both Sir Walter Scott and Goethe. However, as an international movement affecting all the arts, Romanticism begins at least in the 1770's and continues into the second half of the nineteenth century, later for American literature than for European, and later in some of the arts, like music and painting, than in literature. This extended chronological spectrum (1770-1870) also permits recognition as Romantic the poetry of Robert Burns and William Blake in England, the early writings of Goethe and Schiller in Germany, and the great period of influence for Rousseau's writings throughout Europe.

The early Romantic period thus coincides with what is often called the "age of revolutions"—including, of course, the American (1776) and the French (1789) revolutions—an age of upheavals in political, economic, and social traditions, the age which witnessed the initial transformations of the Industrial Revolution. A revolutionary energy was also at the core of Romanticism, which quite consciously set out to transform not only the theory and practice of poetry (and all art), but the very way we perceive the world. Some of its major precepts have survived into the twentieth century and still affect our contemporary period.

## Imagination

The imagination was elevated to a position as the supreme faculty of the mind. This contrasted distinctly with the traditional arguments for the supremacy of reason. The Romantics tended to define and to present the imagination as our ultimate "shaping" or creative power, the approximate human equivalent of the creative powers of nature or even deity. It is dynamic, an active, rather than passive power, with many functions. Imagination is the primary faculty for creating all art. On a broader scale, it is also the faculty that helps humans to constitute reality, for (as Wordsworth suggested), we not only perceive the world around us, but also in part create it. Uniting both reason and feeling (Coleridge described it with the paradoxical phrase, "intellectual intuition"), imagination is extolled as the ultimate synthesizing faculty, enabling humans to reconcile differences and opposites in the world of appearance. The reconciliation of opposites is a central ideal for the Romantics. Finally, imagination is inextricably bound up with the other two major concepts, for it is presumed to be the faculty which enables us to "read" nature as a system of symbols.

## Nature

"Nature" meant many things to the Romantics. As suggested above, it was often presented as itself a work of art, constructed by a divine imagination, in emblematic language. For example, throughout "Song of Myself," Whitman makes a practice of presenting commonplace items in nature—"ants," "heap'd stones," and "poke-weed"—as containing divine elements, and he refers to the "grass" as a natural "hieroglyphic," "the handkerchief of the Lord." While particular perspectives with regard to nature varied considerably—nature as a healing power, nature as a source of subject and image, nature as a refuge from the artificial constructs of civilization, including artificial language—the prevailing views accorded nature the status of an organically unified whole.

It was viewed as "organic," rather than, as in the scientific or rationalist view, as a system of "mechanical" laws, for Romanticism displaced the rationalist view of the universe as a machine (e.g., the deistic image of a clock) with the analogue of an "organic" image, a living tree or mankind itself. At the same time, Romantics gave greater attention both to describing natural phenomena accurately and to capturing "sensuous nuance"—and this is as true of Romantic landscape painting as of Romantic nature poetry. Accuracy of observation, however, was not sought for its own sake. Romantic nature poetry is essentially a poetry of meditation.

## Symbolism and Myth

Symbolism and myth were given great prominence in the Romantic conception of art. In the Romantic view, symbols were the human aesthetic correlatives of nature's emblematic language. They were valued too because they could simultaneously suggest many things, and were thus thought superior to the one-to-one communications of allegory. Partly, it may have been the desire to express the "inexpressible"—the infinite—through the available resources of language that led to symbol at one level and myth (as symbolic narrative) at another.

## Other Concepts: Emotion, Lyric Poetry, and the Self

Other aspects of Romanticism were intertwined with the above three concepts. Emphasis on the activity of the imagination was accompanied by greater emphasis on the importance of intuition, instincts, and feelings, and Romantics generally called for greater attention to the emotions as a necessary supplement to purely logical reason. When this emphasis was applied to the creation of poetry, a very important shift of focus occurred. Wordsworth's definition of all good poetry as "the spontaneous overflow of powerful feelings" marks a turning point in literary history. By locating the ultimate source of poetry in the individual artist, the tradition, stretching back to the ancients, of valuing art primarily for its ability to imitate human life (that is, for its mimetic qualities) was reversed.

In Romantic theory, art was valuable not so much as a mirror of the external world, but as a source of illumination of the world within. Among other things, this led to a prominence for first-person lyric poetry never accorded it in any previous period. The "poetic speaker" became less a persona and more the direct person of the poet. Wordsworth's Prelude and Whitman's "Song of Myself" are both paradigms of successful experiments to take the growth of the poet's mind (the development of self) as subject for an "epic" enterprise made up of lyric components.

Confessional prose narratives such as Goethe's Sorrows of Young Werther (1774) and Chateaubriand's Rene (1801), as well as disguised autobiographical verse narratives such as Byron's Childe Harold (1818), are related phenomena. The interior journey and the development of the self recurred everywhere as subject material for the Romantic artist. The artist-as-hero is a specifically Romantic type.

**Contrasts With Neoclassicism**

Consequently, the Romantics sought to define their goals through systematic contrast with the norms of "Versailles neoclassicism." In their critical manifestoes—the 1800 "Preface" to Lyrical Ballads, the critical studies of the Schlegel brothers in Germany, the later statements of Victor Hugo in France, and of Hawthorne, Poe, and Whitman in the United States—they self-consciously asserted their differences from the previous age (the literary "ancien regime"), and declared their freedom from the mechanical "rules." Certain special features of Romanticism may still be highlighted by this contrast. We have already noted two major differences: the replacement of reason by the imagination for primary place among the human faculties and the shift from a mimetic to an expressive orientation for poetry, and indeed all literature. In addition, neoclassicism had prescribed for art the idea that the general or universal characteristics of human behaviour were more suitable subject matter than the peculiarly individual manifestations of human activity. From at least the opening statement of Rousseau's Confessions, first published in 1781—"I am not made like anyone I have seen; I dare believe that I am not made like anyone in existence. If I am not superior, at least I am different."—this view was challenged.

### Individualism: The Romantic Hero

The Romantics asserted the importance of the individual, the unique, even the eccentric. Consequently they opposed the character typology of neoclassical drama. In another way, of course, Romanticism created its own literary types. The hero-artist has already been mentioned; there were also heaven-storming types from Prometheus to Captain Ahab, outcasts from Cain to the Ancient Mariner and even Hester Prynne, and there was Faust, who wins salvation in Goethe's great drama for the very reasons—his characteristic striving for the unattainable beyond the morally permitted and his insatiable thirst for activity—that earlier had been viewed as the components of his tragic sin. (It was in fact Shelley's opinion that Satan, in his noble defiance, was the real hero of Milton's Paradise Lost.)

In style, the Romantics preferred boldness over the preceding age's desire for restraint, maximum suggestiveness over the neoclassical ideal of clarity, free experimentation over the "rules" of composition, genre, and decorum, and they promoted the conception of the artist as "inspired" creator over that of the artist as "maker" or technical master. Although in both Germany and England there was continued interest in the ancient classics, for the most part the Romantics allied themselves with the very periods of literature that the neoclassicists had dismissed, the Middle Ages and the

Baroque, and they embraced the writer whom Voltaire had called a barbarian, Shakespeare. Although interest in religion and in the powers of faith were prominent during the Romantic period, the Romantics generally rejected absolute systems, whether of philosophy or religion, in favour of the idea that each person (and humankind collectively) must create the system by which to live.

### The Everyday and the Exotic

The attitude of many of the Romantics to the everyday, social world around them was complex. It is true that they advanced certain realistic techniques, such as the use of "local colour" (through down-to-earth characters, like Wordsworth's rustics, or through everyday language, as in Emily Bronte's northern dialects or Whitman's colloquialisms, or through popular literary forms, such as folk narratives). Yet social realism was usually subordinate to imaginative suggestion, and what was most important were the ideals suggested by the above examples, simplicity perhaps, or innocence. Earlier, the 18th-century cult of the noble savage had promoted similar ideals, but now artists often turned for their symbols to domestic rather than exotic sources—to folk legends and older, "unsophisticated" art forms, such as the ballad, to contemporary country folk who used "the language of commen men," not an artificial "poetic diction," and to children (for the first time presented as individuals, and often idealized as sources of greater wisdom than adults).

Simultaneously, as opposed to everyday subjects, various forms of the exotic in time and/or place also gained favour, for the Romantics were also fascinated with realms of existence that were, by definition, prior to or opposed to the ordered conceptions of "objective" reason. Often, both the everyday and the exotic appeared together in paradoxical combinations. In the Lyrical Ballads, for example, Wordsworth and Coleridge agreed to divide their labors according to two subject areas, the natural and the supernatural: Wordsworth would try to exhibit the novelty in what was all too familiar, while Coleridge would try to show in the supernatural what was psychologically real, both aiming to dislodge vision from the "lethargy of custom." The concept of the beautiful soul in an ugly body, as characterized in Victor Hugo's Hunchback of Notre Dame and Mary Shelley's Frankenstein, is another variant of the paradoxical combination.

## The Romantic Artist in Society

In another way too, the Romantics were ambivalent toward the "real" social world around them. They were often politically and socially involved, but at the same time they began to distance themselves from the public. As noted earlier, high Romantic artists interpreted things through their own emotions, and these emotions included social and political consciousness—as one would expect in a period of revolution, one that reacted so strongly to oppression and injustice in the world. So artists sometimes took public stands, or wrote works with socially or politically oriented subject matter. Yet at the same time, another trend began to emerge, as they withdrew more and more from what they saw as the confining boundaries of bourgeois life.

In their private lives, they often asserted their individuality and differences in ways that were to the middle class a subject of intense interest, but also sometimes of horror. ("Nothing succeeds like excess," wrote Oscar Wilde, who, as a partial inheritor of Romantic tendencies, seemed to enjoy shocking the bourgeois, both in his literary and life styles.) Thus the gulf between "odd" artists and their sometimes shocked, often uncomprehending audience began to widen. Some artists may have experienced ambivalence about this situation—it was earlier pointed out how Emily Dickinson seemed to regret that her "letters" to the world would go unanswered. Yet a significant Romantic theme became the contrast between artist and middle-class "Philistine." Unfortunately, in many ways, this distance between artist and public remains with us today.

## Spread of the Romantic Spirit

Finally, it should be noted that the revolutionary energy underlying the Romantic Movement affected not just literature, but all of the arts—from music (consider the rise of Romantic opera) to painting, from sculpture to architecture. Its reach was also geographically significant, spreading as it did eastward to Russia, and westward to America. For example, in America, the great landscape painters, particularly those of the "Hudson River School," and the Utopian social colonies that thrived in the 19th century, are manifestations of the Romantic spirit on this side of the Atlantic.

**Recent Developments**

Some critics have believed that the two identifiable movements that followed Romanticism—Symbolism and Realism—were separate developments of the opposites which Romanticism itself had managed, at its best, to unify and to reconcile. Whether or not this is so, it is clear that Romanticism transformed Western culture in many ways that survive into our own times. It is only very recently that any really significant turning away from Romantic paradigms has begun to take place, and even that turning away has taken place in a dramatic, typically Romantic way.

Today a number of literary theorists have called into question two major Romantic perceptions: that the literary text is a separate, individuated, living "organism"; and that the artist is a fiercely independent genius who creates original works of art. In current theory, the separate, "living" work has been dissolved into a sea of "intertextuality," derived from and part of a network or "archive" of other texts—the many different kinds of discourse that are part of any culture. In this view, too, the independently sovereign artist has been demoted from a heroic, consciously creative agent, to a collective "voice," more controlled than controlling, the intersection of other voices, other texts, ultimately dependent upon possibilities dictated by language systems, conventions, and institutionalized power structures. It is an irony of history, however, that the explosive appearance on the scene of these subversive ideas, delivered in what seemed to the establishment to be radical manifestoes, and written by linguistically powerful individuals, has recapitulated the revolutionary spirit and events of Romanticism itself.

## Chapter 8

# Major Romantic Poets

The Romantic poets wrote during a period of the late 18th to early 19th century. Most commonly known among English speakers are the British Romantic poets. While there were many poets that would fit the Romantic poets "framework," generally the ones considered most relevant are William Blake, William Wordsworth, Samuel Taylor Coleridge, Percy Bysshe Shelley, John Keats and Lord Byron.

Though each of the Romantic poets had their own special qualities, they all had things in common. They triumphed the belief that nature and emotion were the places in which one found spiritual truth, a response to the "Age of Enlightenment," poets preceding them. Most attributed to children special innate gifts, as Wordsworth stated, they come from heaven "trailing clouds of glory." As well, they wrote poetry as a "spontaneous overflow of feelings," again a Wordsworthian concept.

The Romantic poets particularly changed the way in which poetry was written. Many wrote in a style of free verse at times, moving away from the elaborate rhyming patterns of poets preceding them. The Romantic poets were also much more interested in triumphing the rights of women. Shelley was married to Mary Wollstonecraft, whose mother wrote one of the earliest and most celebrated feminist tracts, A Vindication of the Rights of Women. Mary Shelley can be considered an important Romantic novelist of the period with her masterpiece Frankenstein.

Nature was of supreme importance to the Romantic poets. The idea of immersing oneself in the natural or beautiful, or in some cases the natural and frightening as in Blake's The Tiger is distinctly Romantic. Blake contrasts the concept of the fierce burning tiger to his poem The Lamb which seems like a child's nursery poem in its innocence and sweetness. When Blake inquires in The Tiger "Did he who made the lamb make thee?" he is essentially questioning the great mysteries of nature in its contrast of beautiful and fearsome.

It is difficult to pick just a few of the pieces that most resemble the Romantic poets as examples. However, a few examples can give one the sense of the variety of the Romantic poets as well as their sentiments.

Samuel Taylor Coleridge is especially known for The Rhyme of the Ancient Mariner. William Blake is known for poems like The Tiger and especially for his collected works in Songs of Innocence and Songs of Experience. William Wordsworth's Ode: Intimations of Immortality from Recollections of Early Childhood is a fundamental work. However, many of his other poems are quite frequently quoted. Lord Byron's narrative poems are greatly celebrated, including Childe Harold and Don Juan.

John Keats' Ode on a Grecian Urn and Ode to a Nightingale are among his most well known works. Keats had a very short life, dying when he was 25. Literary critics often see this as a tremendous tragedy given his early potential.

Percy Bysshe Shelley also died quite young, at the age of 30. His most celebrated works include Ozymandias, Ode to the West Wind and To a Skylark.

Taken in sum, the Romantic poets may be seen as reactionary and humanist. They forever changed poetry, inventing new forms and influencing later poets. Nowhere is their influence felt more than in the American poets and writers of the mid 19th century. Many suspect the poetry of Walt Whitman, or the theories of Ralph Waldo Emerson could not exist without the influence of the Romantic poets.

## Chapter 9

# Songs of Innocence: Introduction

In Songs of Innocence, this faculty of "spiritual sensation" transfigures rather than transforms. Thus, in The Lamb, pleasure in the natural image persists, but is carried further and exalted by the implication of a higher significance. It is the manifest spontaneity of this mystical insight that carries Blake safely over dangerous places. A little faltering in the vision or straining after effect would have sunk him, by reason of the simplicity of theme, diction and meter, now the sources of peculiar pleasure, into unthinkable depths of feebleness. Contrast with the strength of these seemingly fragile lines the more consciously didactic pieces like The Chimney Sweeper and The Little Black Boy. These, indeed, have the pleasant qualities of an unpretentious and sincere spirit; but their burden of instruction brings them too near to the well-meant but somewhat pedagogic verse that writers like Nathaniel Cotton and Isaac Watts thought most suitable for the young. Blake regarded children more humanly as the charming "Introduction" to these Songs bears witness, or the poem Infant Joy, a perfect expression of the appeal of infancy. And, in The Cradle Song, almost certainly suggested by Watt's lines beginning "Hush! my dear, lie still and slumber," Blake's deeper humanity lifts him far above the common-place moralizing of his model.

The first critic to read the "Introduction" as a Blakean commentary upon the process of artistic creation, Joseph Wick steed claims that Blake's "main interest" in the poem is putting into exact and expressive imagery his own experience as the singer of the songs which follow. Thus the piper's experience mirrors the experience Blake has undergone in composing the Songs of Innocence. The piper begins upon the "wild" earth, is lifted momentarily into direct intercourse with a heavenly vision (the "child" on the "cloud"), and finally returns to earth to sing a note of "joy." This movement symbolizes Blake's—or any other poet's—own creative process: first the poet amuses himself with his craft, then becomes inspired by artistic vision, and finally transforms this vision into material art. Thus the "Introduction" expresses "the theme of all Blake's greatest work": however one explores the realms of vision, one cannot remain there, and must return to earth.

Howard Justin also reads the "Introduction" as Blake's recognition of the increasing materialization and humanization of art, or "the descent of Innocence into the world with the contingent loss of ideality". For Justin, the poem is an elucidation of a single, necessarily ambiguous line, "And I stained the water clear," which should be glossed as both "by dipping my pen in the water, I stained it," and "I stained the water into clarity." Justin interprets the "pen" as art, and the "water" as nature; thus Blake is claiming that art leaves a blemish upon nature, and that art (though itself a blemish) stains nature into clarity. Material art, then, is both a corruption of "Ideal art"—which is symbolized by the "child" on the "cloud" who is himself "piping down the valleys"—and a transformative medium with the power to clarify existence.

In a direct response to Justin's reading, William Bowden asserts that the "Introduction" describes not the descent of ideal art into corrupted, material poetry, but the ascent inherent in the creative process: "it is not the disparagement of art, but a proud poetic credo". Bowden insists that it is Blake, not the "child," who opens the poem by "Piping down the valleys wild". Thus the evolution of the piper's song from pleasurable tune, to a song infused with specific meaning, to written verse addressed to "every child" symbolizes the creative process in which Blake (and every artist) participates.

Blake recognizes that each artist bears a responsibility to compose not only work which is pleasurable, but work which is fraught with meaning. Moreover, this art must be disseminated and preserved for posterity, so that all "may joy to hear."

The first critic to read the "Introduction" as not primarily an exploration of the artist's creative process, but as an elucidation of the state of innocence, Margaret Giovannini claims that Blake consciously employs the style of ballad verse as well suited to his purpose: to introduce the songs which follow. Giovannini reads the "child" as a symbol of happy innocence who understands the "Lamb" only as the infant Christ, and not as the tragic figure of the crucifixion. For the child's state is one of innocence untainted by the tragic knowledge of experience; he, like all the children present in the Songs of Innocence, reflects a joy which issues from a perfectly innocent faith.

Robert Gleckner's reading of the poem both disputes the claim that the state illuminated exists free from the looming presence of experience, and affirms that Blake is graphically representing the process of artistic creation. Concluding that in the "Introduction" the "shadow of experience constantly impinges upon innocence," Gleckner finds in the child's thoughts of the "Lamb"—which symbolizes the Lamb of God, Christ—a vision of loveliness which is tinged with sorrow by knowledge of the crucifixion. This provides a hint that innocence is a temporary state, knowledge of which demands either a retreat to infantilism, or an advance to higher innocence through experience. In the final two stanzas—the "introduction proper to the Songs of Innocence"—the piper faces just such a choice when the child who inspires his song disappears: he may return to the state of selfish glee in which he opened the poem, or he may crystallize his vague feelings of change into a creative act. By composing the songs, the piper chooses creation: "the most divine act a human can perform".

Donald Dike also perceives in the state of innocence illuminated in the "Introduction" an intimation of the state of experience which must inevitably come to pass. The celebrations of innocence are never complete; they are always disturbed by a sense of vulnerability which anticipates the coming of the state of experience. Even in the "Introduction" there exists a "faint elegiac strain": a clue that the freedoms present in the state of innocence cannot long be imagined.

Unlike Dike, John Holloway does not perceive the world of innocence described in the "Introduction" as being threatened by the coming of experience, but as a "world of harmonious oneness". And unlike Justin, Holloway reads the line "And I stained the water clear" not as ambiguous, but as the line from which the poem's harmonious oneness springs. The phrase "the water" refers back to the child's tears; thus, since these tears issue from a cloud, they are also to be read as "joyous showers of rain". The poem's harmonious oneness, then, exists in the dual image Blake inscribes: the spiritual image of a poet singing to the presence of the divine (the child), and, "different but not different," the natural image of a springtime landscape containing lambs in meadows and rain-bearing clouds above.

Like Wick steed, Justin, Bowden, and Gleckner before him, E.D. Hirsch reads the "Introduction" as a Blakean commentary upon the process of artistic creation. More specifically, Hirsch reads the poem as a symbolic account of the way Blake was inspired to compose the Songs of Innocence. In the poem Blake examines both the moment of religious and artistic expression, and the process of making poetry out of this inspiration. And, although C.M. Bowra had earlier claimed that Blake makes a distinction between the lyric poetry of the Songs, which the poet feels compelled to sing, and the visionary prophecies, which are the words of a prophet summoning his generation to new life, Hirsch views the "Introduction" as both lyric and prophecy. The poem's form is simple and lyrical, but its purpose is prophetic: to directly reveal the "joy" of artistic creation that is divinely inspired to all who "may joy to hear."

Heather Glen reads Blake's attitude toward artistic creation as more problematic: rather than simply being infused with a sensation of "joy" in the moment of creation, the poet experiences a dual sensation of loss and empowerment. In the "Introduction," Blake reveals that shaping a book involves abandoning a form of communication which is constantly changing and directly heard for one which is fixed and visible. The work becomes abstracted from real life, and spontaneity and face-to-face communication are lost. However, such abstraction allows the poet to address a wider audience—allows for a potentially joyful relationship with not one, but "every child." Thus art is not a reified object, but an agent which possesses the potential to stimulate the faculties of other children. This dual moment of artistic creation is neither a paradox nor a contradiction: both attitudes are part of a "coherent poetic vision" whose implications are worked out in the following Songs of Innocence.

Stanley Gardner discovers evidence for reading the "Introduction" as a Blakean commentary on the artistic process in the poems design. The figures within the looping tendrils of the vines which frame the plate's text illuminate "the care, the instruction, the elation, thee good seed, the inspiration, and the mechanics of publishing".

Throughout the Songs of Innocence and of Experience, the illustrations often refer back to a condition which gave rise to the poem, or provides an alternative depiction of the proposition introduced in the poem. In the "Introduction" the design accomplishes the latter function. The text describes the ways in which a divine vision (the child) motivates communication and transforms the piper's "songs of pleasant glee" into something more profound; the design reveals, by its references to publishing, that the text can be read as a commentary on the process of poetic creation.

Claiming that the piper's unhesitating response to the cloud- borne child implies that adults have something to learn from children, Zachary Leader admonishes critics who would ignore the example of the sympathetic piper and approach the

"Introduction" with the "adult's instinctive desire to anatomize or abstract or categorize" (a group which would certainly include those who read the poem as a Blakean commentary on artistic creation).

Leader emphasizes the poem's dramatic context, and claims that a proper reading of the poem should begin on the literal level, and not with an examination of the symbolic meaning of the poem (for which he admonishes Gleckner). Read in this way, the child can be seen as divinely human, not a divine agent inspiring the human piper.

Harvey Birenbaum also takes issue with critics who would approach the "Introduction" with an eye toward analyzing its symbolic meaning. Birenbaum claims that the Songs of Innocence define innocence through the song process; that is, innocence is not just the subject of the verses, but each poem is itself an innocent song which is not to be read ironically.

Read properly, the "Introduction" allows the reader to experience what it is like to adopt the persona of one in the state of innocence. Thus the reader becomes the voice of the song, and can ignore the ironic implications of certain clusters of words.

In his claim that the "Introduction" encourages its reader to abandon analysis and realise the perspective of one in the state of innocence, Birenbaum is anticipated by B.H. Fairchild. Although earlier Alice Ostriker had claimed that the meter of the "Introduction" provides enough slight variation to prevent sing- song monotony, Fairchild argues that the Songs of Innocence all contain "time meter" which is characteristic of many nursery rhymes. This submerged, insistent tempo pulls the reader closer to a "child-like, 'innocent' sensitivity which appeals to the child's ear within the adult ear". The last stanza especially evinces the pull of this temporal regularity.

Unlike Leader and Birenbaum, Edward Larrissy claims that with the vine-like designs which often frame the text of the Songs of Innocence, Blake is depicting the personas of the poems as limited, and thus they require an extra-textual level of interpretation to explain them. In the "Introduction," the staining of the water, the disappearance of the child (the source of the piper's vision), and the contrast between voice and writing all suggest that in writing down the songs the piper has corrupted the original inspiration of the idea. This could indicate that the state of innocence which this poem evinces— as well as introduces— has already fallen.

# Chapter 10

# Songs of Innocence: Complete Text

### Introduction

Piping down the valleys wild,
Piping songs of pleasant glee,
On a cloud I saw a child,
And he laughing said to me:
"Pipe a song about a Lamb!"
So I piped with a merry chear.

"Piper, pipe that song again;"
So I piped: he wept to hear.

"Drop thy pipe, thy happy pipe;
Sing thy songs of happy chear:"

So I sung the same again,
While he wept with joy to hear.

"Piper, sit thee down and write
In a book, that all may read."

So he vanish'd from my sight,
And I pluck'd a hollow reed,
And I made a rural pen,
And I stain'd the water clear,
And I wrote my happy songs,
Every child may joy to hear.

**The Shepherd**

How sweet is the Shepherd's sweet lot!
From the morn to the evening he strays;
He shall follow his sheep all the day,
And his tongue shall be filled with praise.

For he hears the lamb's innocent call,
And he hears the ewe's tender reply;
He is watchful while they are in peace,
For they know when their Shepherd is nigh.

**The Echoing Green**

The Sun does arise,
And make happy the skies;
The merry bells ring
To welcome the Spring;
The skylark and thrush,
The birds of the bush,
Sing lounder around
To the bells' chearful sound,
While our sports shall be seen
On the Echoing Green.

Old John, with white hair,
Does laugh away care,
Sitting under the oak,
Among the old folk.
They laugh at our play,
And soon they all say:

"Such, such were the joys
When we all, girls & boys,
In our youth time were seen
On the Echoing Green."

Till the little ones, weary,
No more can be merry;
The sun does descend,
And our sports have on end.

Round the laps of their mothers
Many sisters and brothers,

Like birds in their nest,
Are ready for rest,
And sports no more seen
On the darkening Green.

**The Lamb**

Little Lamb, who made thee?

Dost thou know who made thee?

Gave thee life, & bid thee feed
By the stream & o'er the mead;
Gave thee clothing of delight,
Softest clothing, wooly, bright;
Gave thee such a tender voice,
Making all the vales rejoice?
Little Lamb, who made thee?
Dost thou know who made thee?
Little Lamb, I'll tell thee,
Little Lamb, I'll tell thee,
He is called by thy name,
For he calls himself a Lamb.

He is meek, & he is mild;
He became a little child.

I a child, & thou a lamb,
We are called by his name.
Little Lamb, God bless thee!
Little Lamb, God bless thee!

**The Little Black Boy**

My mother bore me in the southern wild,
And I am black, but O! my soul is white;
White as an angel is the English child,
But I am black, as if bereav'd of light.

My mother taught me underneath a tree,
And sitting down before the heat of day,
She took me on her lap and kissed me,
And pointing to the east, began to say:

"Look on the rising sun: there God does live,
And gives his light, and gives his heat away;
And flowers and trees and beasts and men receive
Comfort in morning, joy in the noonday.

"And we are put on earth a little space,
That we may learn to bear the beams of love;
And these black bodies and this sunburnt face
Is but a cloud, and like a shady grove.

"For when our souls have learn'd the heat to bear,
The cloud will vanish; we shall hear his voice,
Saying: 'Come out from the grove, my love & care,
And round my golden tent like lambs rejoice.'"

Thus did my mother say, and kissed me;
And thus I say to little English boy:
When I from black and he from white cloud free,
And round the tent of God like lambs we joy,
I'll shade him from the heat, till he can bear
To lean in joy upon our father's knee;
And then I'll stand and stroke his silver hair,
And be like him,and he will then love me.

## The Blossom

Merry, Merry Sparrow!
Under leaves so green
A happy Blossom
Sees you swift as arrow
Seek your cradle narrow
Near my Bosom.

Pretty, Pretty Robin!
Under leaves so green
A happy Blossom
Hears you sobbing, sobbing,
Pretty, Pretty Robin,
Near my Bosom.

## The Chimney Sweeper

When my mother died I was very young,
And my father sold me while yet my tongue

Could scarcely cry "'weep! 'weep! 'weep! 'weep!"
So your chimneys I sweep, & in soot I sleep.

There's little Tom Dacre, who cried when his head,
That curl'd like a lamb's back, was shav'd: so I said
"Hush, Tom! never mind it, for when you head's bare
You know that the soot cannot spoil your white hair."

And so he was quiet, & that very night,
As Tom was a-sleeping, he had such a sight!
That thousands of sweepers, Dick, Joe, Ned, & Jack,
Were all of them lock'd up in coffins of black.
And by came an Angel who had a bright key,
And he open'd the coffins & set them free;
Then down a green plain leaping, laughing, they run,
And wash in a river, and shine in the Sun.

Then naked & white, all their bags left behind,
They rise upon clouds and sport in the wind;
And the Angel told Tom, if he'd be a good boy,
He'd have God for his father, & never want joy.

And so Tom awoke; and we rose in the dark,
And got with our bags & our brushes to work,
Tho the morning was cold, Tom was happy & warm,
So if all do their duty they need not fear harm.

### The Little Boy Lost

"Father! father! where are you going?
O do not walk so fast.

Speak, father, speak to your little boy,
Or else I shall be lost."

The night was dark, no father was there;
The child was wet with dew;
The mire was deep, & the child did weep,
And away the vapour flew.

### The Little Boy Found

The little boy lost in the lonely fen,
Led by the wand'ring light,

Began to cry; but God, ever nigh,
Appear'd like his father in white.

He kissed the child & by the hand led
And to his mother brought,
Who in sorrow pale, thro' the lonely dale,
Her little boy weeping sought.

## Laughing Song

When the green woods laugh with the voice of joy,
And the dimpling stream runs laughing by;

When the air does laugh with our merry wit,
And the green hill laughs with the noise of it;

When the meadows laugh with lively green,
And the grasshopper laughs in the merry scene,
When Mary and Susan and Emily
With their sweet round mouths sing "Ha, Ha, He!"
When the painted birds laugh in the shade,
Where our table with cherries and nuts is spread,
Come live & be merry, and join with me,
To sing the sweet chorus of "Ha, Ha, He!"

## A Cradle Song

Sweet dreams, form a shade
O'er my lovely infant's head;

Sweet dreams of pleasant streams
By happy, silent, moony beams.

Sweet sleep, with soft down
Weave thy brows an infant crown.

Sweep sleep, Angel mild,
Hover o'er my happy child.

Sweet smiles, in the night
Hover over my delight;
Sweet smiles, Mother's smiles,
All the livelong night beguiles.

Sweet moans, dovelike sighs,
Chase not slumber from thy eyes.

Sweet moans, sweeter smiles,
All the dovelike moans beguiles.

Sleep, sleep, happy child,
All creation slept and smil'd;
Sleep, sleep, happy sleep,
While o'er thee thy mother weep.

Sweet babe, in thy face
Holy image I can trace.

Sweet babe, once like thee,
Thy maker lay and wept for me,
Wept for me, for thee, for all,
When he was an infant small
Thou his image ever see,
Heavenly face that smiles on thee,
Smiles on thee, on me, on all;
Who became an infant small.

Infant smiles are his own smiles;
Heaven & earth to peace beguiles.

## The Divine Image

To Mercy, Pity, Peace, and Love
All pray in their distress;
And to these virtues of delight
Return their thankfulness.

For Mercy, Pity, Peace, and Love
Is God, our father dear,
And Mercy, Pity, Peace, and Love
Is Man, his child and care.

For Mercy has a human heart,
Pity a human face,
And Love, the human form divine,
And Peace, the human dress.

Then every man, of every clime,
That prays in his distress,
Prays to the human form divine,
Love, Mercy, Pity, Peace.

And all must love the human form,
In heathen, turk, or jew;
Where Mercy, Love, & Pity dwell
There God is dwelling too.

## Holy Thursday

'T was on a Holy Thursday, their innocent faces clean,
The children walking two & two, in red & blue & green,
Grey-headed beadles walk'd before, with wands as white as snow,
Till into the high dome of Paul's they like Thames' waters flow.

O what a multitude they seem'd, these flowers of London town!
Seated in companies they sit with radiance all their own.

The hum of multitudes was there, but multitudes of lambs,
Thousands of little boys & girls raising their innocent hands.

Now like a mighty wind they raise to heaven the voice of song,
Or like harmonious thunderings the seats of Heaven among.

Beneath them sit the aged men, wise guardians of the poor;
Then cherish pity, lest you drive an angel from your door.

## Night

The sun descending in the west,
The evening star does shine;
The birds are silent in their nest,
And I must seek for mine.

The moon like a flower
In heaven's high bower,
With silent delight
Sits and smiles on the night.

Farewell, green fields and happy groves,
Where flocks have took delight.

Where lambs have nibbled, silent moves
The feet of angels bright;
Unseen they pour blessing
And joy without ceasing,
On each bud and blossom,
And each sleeping bosom.

They look in every thoughtless nest,
Where birds are cover'd warm;
They visit caves of every beast,
To keep them all from harm.

If they see any weeping
That should have been sleeping,
They pour sleep on their head,
And sit down by their bed.

When wolves and tygers howl for prey,
They pitying stand and weep;
Seeking to drive their thirst away,
And keep them from the sheep;
But if they rush dreadful,
The angels, most heedful,
Receive each mild spirit,
New worlds to inherit.

And there the lion's ruddy eyes
Shall flow with tears of gold,
And pitying the tender cries,
And walking round the fold,
Saying "Wrath, by his meekness,
And by his health, sickness
Is driven away
From our immortal day.

"And now beside thee, bleating lamb,
I can lie down and sleep;
Or think on him who bore thy name,
Graze after thee and weep.

For, wash'd in life's river,
My bright mane for ever

Shall shine like the gold
As I guard o'er the fold."

## Spring

Sound the Flute!
Now it's mute.

Birds delight
Day and Night;
Nightingale

In the dale,

Lark in Sky,
Merrily,
Merrily, Merrily, to welcome in the Year.
Little Boy,
Full of joy;
Little Girl,
Sweet and small;
Cock does crow,
So do you;
Merry voice,
Infant noise,
Merrily, Merrily, to welcome in the Year.

Little Lamb,
Here I am;
Come and lick
My white neck;
Let me pull

Your soft Wool;
Let me kiss
Your soft face:
Merrily, Merrily, we welcome in the Year.

## Nurse's Song

When the voices of children are heard on the green
And laughing is heard on the hill,
My heart is at rest within my breast
And everything else is still.

"Then come home, my children, the sun is gone down
And the dews of night arise;
Come, come, leave off play, and let us away
Till the morning appears in the skies."

"No, no, let us play, for it is yet day
And we cannot go to sleep;
Besides, in the sky the little birds fly
And the hills are all cover'd with sheep."

"Well, well, go & play till the light fades away
And then go home to bed."

The little ones leaped & shouted & laugh'd
And all the hills echoed.

## Infant Joy

"I have no name:
I am but two days old."

What shall I call thee?
"I happy am,
Joy is my name."

Sweet joy befall thee!
Pretty joy!
Sweet joy but two days old,
Sweet joy I call thee:
Thou dost smile,
I sing the while,
Sweet joy befall thee!

## A Dream

Once a dream did weave a shade
O'er my Angel-guarded bed,
That an Emmet lost its way
Where on grass methought I lay.

Troubled, 'wilder'd, and forlorn,
Dark, benighted, travel-worn,
Over many a tangled spray,
All heart-broken I heard her say:

"O, my children! do they cry?
Do they hear their father sigh?

Now they look abroad to see:
Now return and weep for me."
Pitying, I drop'd a tear;
But I saw a glow-worm near,
Who replied: "What wailing wight
Calls the watchman of the night?

"I am set to light the ground,
While the beetle goes his round:
Follow now the beetle's hum;
Little wanderer, hie thee home."

**On Another's Sorrow**

Can I see another's woe,
And not be in sorrow too?

Can I see another's grief,
And not seek for kind relief?

Can I see a falling tear,
And not feel my sorrow's share?

Can a father see his child
Weep, nor be with sorrow fill'd?

Can a mother sit and hear
An infant groan an infant fear?

No, no! never can it be!
Never, never can it be!
And can he who smiles on all
Hear the wren with sorrows small,
Hear the small bird's grief & care,
Hear the woes that infants bear,
And not sit beside the nest,
Pouring pity in their breast;
And not sit the cradle near,
Weeping tear on infant's tear;
And not sit both night & day,
Wiping all our tears away?

O, no! never can it be!
Never, never can it be!

He doth give his joy to all;
He becomes an infant small;
He becomes a man of woe;
He doth feel the sorrow too.

Think not thou canst sigh a sigh
And thy maker is not by;
Think not thou canst weep a tear
And thy maker is not near.

O! he gives to us his joy
That our grief he may destroy;
Till our grief is fled & gone
He doth sit by us and moan.

## Chapter 11

# Songs of Experience: Introduction

Up to this point, Blake's writings preserve the spontaneity and confident strength that mark The Marriage: his faith in the immediate efficacy of passion to free itself by revolt gives energy and freshness to the measure and language. But, from this time, his outlook becomes increasingly overcast. He comes to see that the will to freedom is not all-powerful, but must endure, for a time, the limitations of temporal experience.

Salvation is still to come through passionate revolt, and, in an indefinite way, this is associated with the French revolution; but Blake now emphasizes the strength of the moral heresy, and the impetuous enthusiasm of America and Visions is, to a considerable degree, checked. The simplest indications of this change occur in Songs of Experience (1794) and those poems in the Rossetti MS. belonging to the same period.

The contrast between these and Songs of Innocence is not merely formal, but is the direct expression of the change already referred to. In the early collection, there are no shadows: to Blake's unaccustomed eyes, the first glimpse of the world of vision was pure light. But, in the intervening years, experience had brought a fuller sense of the power of evil, and of the difficulty and loneliness of his lot who would set himself against the current of this world. So he writes of himself

The Angel that presided o'er my birth
Said, "Little creature, formed of Joy and Mirth,
Go, love without the help of anything on Earth."

The title-page for the combined Songs of Innocence and of Experience describes them as "Shewing the Contrary States of the Human Soul' while, in the motto, he writes, in a spirit of disenchantment, The Good are attracted by Men's perceptions

And think not for themselves;
Till Experience teaches them to catch
And to cage the Fairies and Elves,

the catching of the fairies and elves, apparently, signifying the deliberate searching after the hidden mystical meaning of things, in place of a docile acceptance of other men's faith.

Signs of the change lie on every hand. If the introduction in Songs of Experience be compared with its earlier counterpart, the piper is seen to have become the more portentous bard, the laughing child upon a cloud gives place to "the lapsed Soul weeping in the evening dew." And there is, also, apparent, at times, the vague consciousness of "some blind hand" crushing the life of man, as man crushes the fly. This, however, is not quite constant, though something of the same mystery lies behind the question in

The Tyger,
Did he who made the Lamb make thee?

More commonly, Blake lays stress upon the fallacy of law, and this, chiefly, in its relation to love. Thus, in The Clod and the Pebble, his own ethic of the love that "seeketh not itself to please," is set against the concept of love governed by moral duty, and, therefore, cold and interested. Similarly, in Holy Thursday, there is white passion beneath the simplicity and restraint of his picture of the little victims of a niggard charity; perhaps, nothing gives so complete an impression of the change in Blake as the comparison of the earlier and later poems under this title. Moreover, he always opposed any interference with the natural development of the individual genius. "There is no use in education," he told Crab Robinson, "I hold it wrong. It is the great Sin." This text he develops in The Schoolboy and in the two versions, manuscript and engraved, of Infant Sorrow. Something of the kind appears in A Little Boy Lost, though there is also a return to the baiting of the Philistine with paradox, as in The Marriage. For here, as before, churches and priests represent the extreme forms of obscurantism and repression, and the exaltation of the letter of a rigid law above the spirit of love that transcends mere obligation. But by far the greater bulk of the engraved and manuscript verse of this period repeats the theme of Visions, the infallibility of the human instinct towards gratification of appetite, and the iniquity of all that interferes with it. Hence, modesty, continence and asceticism become glossing terms, hiding the deformity and corruption that arise from the covert satisfaction of desire; they are the fair-seeming fruit of the poison-tree, the tree of moral virtue.

Chapter 12

# Songs of Experience: Complete Text

### Introduction

Hear the voice of the Bard!
Who Present, Past, & Future sees;

Whose ears have heard
The Holy Word
That walk'd among the ancient trees,

Calling the lapsed Soul,
And weeping in the evening dew;

That might control

The starry pole,
And fallen, fallen light renew!
"O Earth, O Earth, return!
Arise from out the dewy grass;

Night is worn,
And the morn
Rises from the slumberous mass.
"Turn away no more;

Why wilt thou turn away?
The starry floor,
The wat'ry shore,
Is giv'n thee till the break of day."

### Earth's Answer

Earth raised up her head
From the darkness dread & drear.

Her light fled,
Stony dread!
And her locks cover'd with grey despair.

"Prison'd on wat'ry shore,
Starry Jealousy does keep my den:
Cold and hoar,
Weeping o'er,
I hear the father of the ancient men.

"Selfish father of men!
Cruel, jealous, selfish fear!
Can delight,
Chain'd in night,
The virgins of youth and morning bear?

"Does spring hide its joy
When buds and blossoms grow?
Does the sower
Sow by night,
Or the plowman in darkness plow?

"Break this heavy chain
That does freeze my bones around.

Selfish! vain!
Eternal bane!

That free Love with bondage bound."

### The Clod and the Pebble

"Love seeketh not Itself to please,
Nor for itself hath any care,
But for another gives its ease,
And builds a Heaven in Hell's despair."

So sung a little Clod of Clay
Trodden with the cattle's feet,

But a Pebble of the brook
Warbled out these metres meet:
"Love seeketh only Self to please,
To bind another to Its delight,
Joys in another's loss of ease,
And builds a Hell in Heaven's despite."

## Holy Thursday

Is this a holy thing to see
In a rich and fruitful land,
Babes reduc'd to misery,
Fed with cold and usurous hand?
Is that trembling cry a song?
Can it be song of joy?
And so many children poor?
It is a land of poverty!

And their sun does never shine,
And their fields are bleak & bare,
And their ways are fill'd with thorns:
It is eternal winter there.

For where-e'er the sun does shine,
And were-e'er the rain does fall,
Babe can never hunger there,
Nor poverty the mind appall.

## The Little Girl Lost

In futurity
I prophetic see
That the earth from sleep
(Grave the sentence deep)
Shall arise and seek
For her maker meek;
And in the desart wild
Become a garden mild.

In the southern clime,
Where the summer's prime
Never fades away,
Lovely Lyca lay.

Seven summers old
Lovely Lyca told;
She had wander'd long
Hearing wild birds' song.
"Sweet sleep, come to me
Underneath this tree.

Do father, mother weep,
Where can Lyca sleep?
"Lost in desart wild
Is your little child.

How can Lyca sleep
If her mother weep?
"If her heart does ake
Then let Lyca wake;
If my mother sleep,
Lyca shall not weep.

"Frowning, frowning night,
O'er this desart bright
Let thy moon arise
While I close my eyes."

Sleeping Lyca lay
While the beasts of prey,
Come from caverns deep,
View'd the maid asleep.

The kingly lion stood
And the virgin view'd,
Then he gamboll'd round
O'er the hollow'd ground.

Leopards, tygers, play
Round her as she lay,
While the lion old
Bow'd his mane of gold.

And her bosom lick,
And upon her neck
From his eyes of flame

Ruby tears there came;
While the lioness
Loos'd her slender dress,
And naked they convey'd
To caves the sleeping maid.

### The Little Girl Found

All the night in woe
Lyca's parents go
Over vallies deep,
While the desarts weep.

Tired and woe-begone,
Hoarse with making moan,
Arm in arm seven days
They trac'd the desart ways.

Seven nights they sleep
Among the shadows deep,
And dream they see their child
Starv'd in desart wild.

Pale, thro' pathless ways
The fancied image strays
Famish'd, weeping, weak,
With hollow piteous shriek.

Rising from unrest,
The trembling woman prest
With feet of weary woe:
She could no further go.

In his arms he bore
Her, arm's with sorrow sore;
Till before their way
A couching lion lay.

Turning back was vain:
Soon his heavy mane
Bore them to the ground.

Then he stalk'd around,
Smelling to his prey;

But their fears allay
When he licks their hands,
And silent by them stands.

They look upon his eyes
Fill'd with deep surprise,
And wondering behold
A spirit arm'd in gold.

On his head a crown,
On his shoulders down
Flow'd his golden hair.

Gone was all their care.

"Follow me," he said;
"Weep not for the maid;
In my palace deep
Lyca lies asleep."

Then they followed
Where the vision led,
And saw their sleeping child
Among the tygers wild.

To this day they dwell
In a lonely dell;
Nor fear the wolvish howl
Nor the lion's growl.

## The Chimney Sweep

A little black thing among the snow,
Crying "'weep! 'weep!" in notes of woe!
"Where are thy father & mother? say?"
"They are both gone up to the church to pray.

"Because I was happy upon the heath,
And smil'd among the winter's snow,
They clothed me in the clothes of death,
And taught me to sing the notes of woe.

"And because I am happy & dance & sing,
They think they have done me no injury,

And are gone to praise God & his Priest & King,
Who make up a heaven of our misery."

## Nurse's Song

When the voices of children are heard on the green
And whisp'rings are in the dale,
The days of my youth rise fresh in my mind,
My face turns green and pale.

Then come home, my children, the sun is gone down,
And the dews of night arise;
Your spring & your day are wasted in play,
And your winter and night in disguise.

## The Sick Rose

O Rose, thou art sick!
The invisible worm
That flies in the night,
In the howling storm,
Has found out thy bed
Of crimson joy,
And his dark secret love
Does thy life destroy.

## The Fly

Little Fly,
Thy summer's play
My thoughtless hand
Has brush'd away.

Am not I
A fly like thee?
Or art not thou
A man like me?

For I dance,
And drink, & sing,
Till some blind hand
Shall brush my wing.

If thought is life,
And strength & breath,
And the want
Of thought is death;
Then am I
A happy fly,
If I live
or if I die.

## The Angel

I dreamt a Dream! what can it mean!
And that I was a maiden Queen,
Guarded by an Angel mild:
Witless woe was ne'er beguil'd!
And I wept both night and day,
And he wip'd my tears away,
And I wept both day and night,
And hid from him my heart's delight.

So he took his wings and fled;
Then the morn blush'd rosy red;
I dried my tears, & arm'd my fears
With ten thousand shields and spears.
Soon my Angel came again:
I was arm'd, he came in vain;
For the time of youth was fled,
And grey hairs were on my head.

## The Tyger

Tyger! Tyger! burning bright,
In the forests of the night,
What immortal hand or eye
Could frame thy fearful symmetry?

In what distant deeps or skies
Burnt the fire of thine eyes?

On what wings dare he aspire?
What the hand dare sieze the fire?
And what shoulder, & what art,
Could twist the sinews of thy heart?

And when thy heart began to beat,
What dread hand? & what dread feet?

What the hammer? what the chain?
In what furnace was thy brain?
What the anvil? what dread grasp
Dare its deadly terrors clasp?

When the stars threw down their spears,
And water'd heaven with their tears,
Did he smile his work to see?

Did he who made the Lamb make thee?
Tyger! Tyger! burning bright
In the forests of the night,
What immortal hand or eye
Dare frame thy fearful symmetry?

## My Pretty Rose-Tree

A flower was offer'd to me,
Such a flower as May never bore;
But I said "I've a Pretty Rose-tree,"
And I passed the sweet flower o'er.

Then I went to my Pretty Rose-tree,
To tend her by day and by night;
But my Rose turn'd away with jealousy,
And her thorns were my only delight.

## Ah! Sun-Flower

Ah, Sun-flower! weary of time,
Who countest the steps of the Sun,
Seeking after that sweet golden clime
Where the traveller's journey is done:
Where the Youth pined away with desire
And the pale Virgin shrouded in snow
Arise from their graves, and aspire
Where my Sun-flower wishes to go.

## The Lilly

The modest Rose puts forth a thorn,
The humble Sheep a threat'ning horn;

While the Lilly white shall in Love delight,
Nor a thorn, nor a threat, stain her beauty bright.

## The Garden of Love

I went to the Garden of Love,
And saw what I never had seen:
A Chapel was built in the midst,
Where I used to play on the green.

And the gates of this Chapel were shut,
And "Thou shalt not" writ over the door;
So I turn'd to the Garden of Love
That so many sweet flowers bore;
And I saw it was filled with graves,
And tomb-stones where flowers should be;
And Priests in black gowns were walking their rounds,
And binding with briars my joys & desires.

## The Little Vagabond

Dear Mother, dear Mother, the Church is cold,
But the Ale-house is healthy & pleasant & warm;
Besides I can tell where I am used well,
Such usage in Heaven will never do well.

But if at the Church they would give us some Ale,
And a pleasant fire our souls to regale,
We'd sing and we'd pray all the live-long day,
Nor ever once wish from the Church to stray.

Then the Parson might preach, & drink, & sing,
And we'd be as happy as birds in the spring;
And modest Dame Lurch, who is always at Church,
Would not have bandy children, nor fasting, nor birch.

And God, like a father rejoicing to see
His children as pleasant and happy as he,

Would have no more quarrel with the Devil or the Barrel,
But kiss him, & give him both drink and apparel.

### London

I wander thro' each charter'd street,
Near where the charter'd Thames does flow,
And mark in every face I meet
Marks of weakness, marks of woe.

In every cry of every Man,
In every Infant's cry of fear,
In every voice, in every ban,
The mind-forg'd manacles I hear.

How the Chimney-sweepers cry
Every black'ning Church appalls;
And the hapless Soldier's sigh
Runs in blood down Palace walls.

But most thro' midnight streets I hear
How the youthful Harlot's curse
Blasts the new born Infant's tear,
And blights with plagues the Marriage hearse.

### The Human Abstract

Pity would be no more
If we did not make somebody Poor;
And Mercy no more could be
If all were as happy as we.

And mutual fear brings peace,
Till the selfish loves increase:
Then Cruelty knits a snare,
And spreads his baits with care.

He sits down with holy fears,
And waters the grounds with tears;
Then Humility takes its root
Underneath his foot.

Soon spreads the dismal shade
Of Mystery over his head;

And the Catterpiller and Fly
Feed on the Mystery.

And it bears the fruit of Deceit,
Ruddy and sweet to eat;
And the Raven his nest has made
In its thickest shade.

The Gods of the earth and sea
Sought thro' Nature to find this Tree;
But their search was all in vain:
There grows one in the Human Brain.

**Infant Sorrow**

My mother groan'd! my father wept.
Into the dangerous world I leapt:
Helpless, naked, piping loud:
Like a fiend hid in a cloud.

Struggling in my father's hands,
Striving against my swadling bands,
Bound and weary I thought best
To sulk upon my mother's breast.

**A Poison Tree**

I was angry with my friend:
I told my wrath, my wrath did end.
I was angry with my foe:
I told it not, my wrath did grow.

And I water'd it in fears,
Night & morning with my tears;
And I sunned it with smiles,
And with soft deceitful wiles.

And it grew both day and night,
Till it bore an apple bright;
And my foe beheld it shine,
And he knew that it was mine,
And into my garden stole
When the night had veil'd the pole:

In the morning glad I see
My foe outstretch'd beneath the tree.

## A Little Boy Lost

"Nought loves another as itself,
Nor venerates another so,
Nor is it possible to Thought
A greater than itself to know:
"And Father, how can I love you
Or any of my brothers more?

I love you like the little bird
That picks up crumbs around the door."
The Priest sat by and heard the child,
In trembling zeal he siez'd his hair:
He led him by his little coat,
And all admir'd the Priestly care.

And standing on the altar high,
"Lo! what a fiend is here!" said he,
"One who sets reason up for judge
Of our most holy Mystery."

The weeping child could not be heard,
The weeping parents wept in vain;
They strip'd him to his little shirt,
And bound him in an iron chain;
And burn'd him in a holy place,
Where many had been burn'd before:
The weeping parents wept in vain.

Are such things done on Albion's shore?

## A Little Girl Lost

Children of the future Age
Reading this indignant page,
Know that in a former time
Love! sweet Love! was thought a crime.

In the Age of Gold,
Free from winter's cold,

Youth and maiden bright
To the holy light,
Naked in the sunny beams delight.
Once a youthful pair,
Fill'd with softest care,
Met in garden bright
Where the holy light
Had just remov'd the curtains of night.

There, in rising day,
On the grass they play;
Parents were afar,
Strangers came not near,
And the maiden soon forgot her fear.

Tired with kisses sweet,
They agree to meet
When the silent sleep
Waves o'er heaven's deep,
And the weary tired wanderers weep.

To her father white
Came the maiden bright;
But his loving look,
Like the holy book,
All her tender limbs with terror shook.

"Ona! pale and weak!
To thy father speak:
O, the trembling fear!
O, the dismal care!
That shakes the blossoms of my hoary hair."

## To Tirzah

Whate'er is Born of Mortal Birth
Must be consumed with the Earth
To rise from Generation free:
Then what have I to do with thee?
The Sexes sprung from Shame & Pride,
Blow'd in the morn, in evening died;

But Mercy chang'd Death into Sleep;
The Sexes rose to work & weep.

Thou, Mother of my Mortal part,
With cruelty didst mould my Heart,
And with false self-deceiving tears
Didst bind my Nostrils, Eyes, & Ears:
Didst close my Tongue in senseless clay,
And me to Mortal Life betray.

The Death of Jesus set me free:
Then what have I to do with thee?

**The Schoolboy**

I love to rise in a summer morn
When the birds sing on every tree;
The distant huntsman winds his horn,
And the sky-lark sings with me.

O! what sweet company.
But to go to school in a summer morn,
O! it drives all joy away;
Under a cruel eye outworn,
The little ones spend the day
In sighing and dismay.

Ah! then at times I drooping sit,
And spend many an anxious hour,
Nor in my book can I take delight,
Nor sit in learning's bower,
Worn thro' with the dreary shower.

How can the bird that is born for joy
Sit in a cage and sing?
How can a child, when fears annoy,
But droop his tender wing,
And forget his youthful spring?
O! father & mother, if buds are nip'd
And blossoms blown away,
And if the tender plants are strip'd
Of their joy in the springing day,

By sorrow and care's dismay,
How shall the summer arise in joy,
Or the summer fruits appear?

Or how shall we gather what griefs destroy,
Or bless the mellowing year,
When the blasts of winter appear?

## The Voice of the Ancient Bard

Youth of delight, come hither,
And see the opening morn,
Image of truth new born.

Doubt is fled, & clouds of reason,
Dark disputes & artful teazing.

Folly is an endless maze,
Tangled roots perplex her ways.

How many have fallen there!
They stumble all night over bones of the dead,
And feel they know not what but care,
And wish to lead others, when they should be led.

## The Divine Image

Cruelty has a Human Heart,
And Jealousy a Human Face;
Terror the Human Form Divine,
And Secrecy the Human Dress.

The Human Dress is forged Iron,
The Human Form a fiery Forge,
The Human Face a Furnace seal'd,
The Human Heart is hungry Gorge.

## Chapter 13

# Songs of Innocence and Experience: Summary and Analysis

---

**"The Lamb"**

Little Lamb who made thee
Dost thou know who made thee
Gave thee life & bid thee feed.

By the stream & o'er the mead;
Gave thee clothing of delight,
Softest clothing wooly bright;
Gave thee such a tender voice,
Making all the vales rejoice!
Little Lamb who made thee
Dost thou know who made thee

Little Lamb I'll tell thee,
Little Lamb I'll tell thee!
He is called by thy name,
For he calls himself a Lamb:
He is meek & he is mild,
He became a little child:
I a child & thou a lamb,
We are called by his name.
Little Lamb God bless thee.
Little Lamb God bless thee..

## Summary

The poem begins with the question, "Little Lamb, who made thee?" The speaker, a child, asks the lamb about its origins: how it came into being, how it acquired its particular manner of feeding, its "clothing" of wool, its "tender voice." In the next stanza, the speaker attempts a riddling answer to his own question: the lamb was made by one who "calls himself a Lamb," one who resembles in his gentleness both the child and the lamb. The poem ends with the child bestowing a blessing on the lamb.

## Form

"The Lamb" has two stanzas, each containing five rhymed couplets. Repetition in the first and last couplet of each stanza makes these lines into a refrain, and helps to give the poem its song-like quality. The flowing l's and soft vowel sounds contribute to this effect, and also suggest the bleating of a lamb or the lisping character of a child's chant.

## Commentary

The poem is a child's song, in the form of a question and answer. The first stanza is rural and descriptive, while the second focuses on abstract spiritual matters and contains explanation and analogy. The child's question is both naive and profound. The question ("who made thee?") is a simple one, and yet the child is also tapping into the deep and timeless questions that all human beings have, about their own origins and the nature of creation. The poem's apostrophic form contributes to the effect of naiveté, since the situation of a child talking to an animal is a believable one, and not simply a literary contrivance. Yet by answering his own question, the child converts it into a rhetorical one, thus counteracting the initial spontaneous sense of the poem. The answer is presented as a puzzle or riddle, and even though it is an easy one—child's play—this also contributes to an underlying sense of ironic knowingness or artifice in the poem. The child's answer, however, reveals his confidence in his simple Christian faith and his innocent acceptance of its teachings.

The lamb of course symbolizes Jesus. The traditional image of Jesus as a lamb underscores the Christian values of gentleness, meekness, and peace. The image of the child is also associated with Jesus: in the Gospel, Jesus displays a special solicitude for children, and the Bible's depiction of Jesus in his childhood shows him as guileless and vulnerable. These are also the characteristics from which the child-speaker approaches the ideas of nature and of God. This poem, like many of the Songs of Innocence, accepts what Blake saw as the more positive aspects of conventional Christian belief. But it does not provide a completely adequate doctrine, because it fails to account for the presence of suffering and evil in the world. The pendant (or companion) poem to this one, found in the Songs of Experience, is "The Tyger"; taken together, the two poems give a perspective on religion that includes the good and clear as well as the terrible and inscrutable. These poems complement each other to produce a fuller account than either offers independently. They offer a good instance of how Blake himself stands somewhere outside the perspectives of innocence and experience he projects.

### "Holy Thursday"

'Twas on a Holy Thursday their innocent faces clean
The children walking two & two in red & blue & green
Grey headed beadles walk'd before with wands as white as snow
Till into the high dome of Pauls they like Thames waters flow

O what a multitude they seem'd these flowers of London town
Seated in companies they sit with radiance all their own
The hum of multitudes was there but multitudes of lambs
Thousands of little boys & girls raising their innocent hands

Now like a mighty wind they raise to heaven the voice of song

Or like harmonious thunderings the seats of heaven among
Beneath them sit the aged men wise guardians of the poor
Then cherish pity, lest you drive an angel from your door

**Summary**

On Holy Thursday (Ascension Day), the clean-scrubbed charity-school children of London flow like a river toward St. Paul's Cathedral. Dressed in bright colours they march double-file, supervised by "gray headed beadles." Seated in the cathedral, the children form a vast and radiant multitude. They remind the speaker of a company of lambs sitting by the thousands and "raising their innocent hands" in prayer. Then they begin to sing, sounding like "a mighty wind" or "harmonious thunderings," while their guardians, "the aged men," stand by. The speaker, moved by the pathos of the vision of the children in church, urges the reader to remember that such urchins as these are actually angels of God.

**Form**

The poem has three stanzas, each containing two rhymed couplets. The lines are longer than is typical for Blake's Songs, and their extension suggests the train of children processing toward the cathedral, or the flowing river to which they are explicitly compared.

**Commentary**

The poem's dramatic setting refers to a traditional Charity School service at St. Paul's Cathedral on Ascension Day, celebrating the fortieth day after the resurrection of Christ. These Charity Schools were publicly funded institutions established to care for and educate the thousands of orphaned and abandoned children in London. The first stanza captures the movement of the children from the schools to the church, likening the lines of children to the Thames River, which flows through the heart of London: the children are carried along by the current of their innocent faith. In the second stanza, the metaphor for the children changes. First they become "flowers of London town." This comparison emphasizes their beauty and fragility; it undercuts the assumption that these destitute children are the city's refuse and burden, rendering them instead as London's fairest and finest. Next the children are described as resembling lambs in their innocence and meekness, as well as in the sound of their little voices. The image transforms the character of humming "multitudes," which might first have suggested a swarm or hoard of unsavory creatures, into something heavenly and sublime. The lamb metaphor links the children to Christ (whose symbol is the lamb) and reminds the reader of Jesus' special tenderness and care for children. As the children begin to sing in the third stanza, they are no longer just weak and mild; the strength of their combined voices raised toward God evokes something more powerful and puts them in direct contact with heaven. The simile for their song is first given as "a mighty wind" and then as "harmonious thunderings." The beadles, under whose authority the children live, are eclipsed in their aged pallor by the internal radiance of the children. In this heavenly moment the guardians, who are authority figures only in an earthly sense, sit "beneath" the children.

The final line advises compassion for the poor. The voice of the poem is neither Blake's nor a child's, but rather that of a sentimental observer whose sympathy enhances an already emotionally affecting scene. But the poem calls upon the reader to be more critical than the speaker is: we are asked to contemplate the true meaning of Christian pity, and to contrast the institutionalized charity of the schools with the love of which God—and innocent children—are capable. Moreover, the visual picture given in the first two stanzas contains a number of unsettling aspects: the mention of the children's clean faces suggests that they have been tidied up for this public occasion; that their usual state is quite different. The public display of love and charity conceals the cruelty to which impoverished children were often subjected. Moreover, the orderliness of the children's march and the ominous "wands" (or rods) of the beadles suggest rigidity, regimentation, and violent authority rather than charity and love. Lastly, the tempestuousness of the children's song, as the poem transitions from visual to aural imagery, carries a suggestion of divine wrath and vengeance.

"The Divine Image"

To Mercy Pity Peace and Love,
All pray in their distress:
And to these virtues of delight
Return their thankfulness.

For Mercy Pity Peace and Love,
Is God our father dear:
And Mercy Pity Peace and Love,
Is Man his child and care.

For Mercy has a human heart
Pity, a human face:
And Love, the human form divine,
And Peace, the human dress.

Then every man of every clime,
That prays in his distress,
Prays to the human form divine
Love Mercy Pity Peace.

And all must love the human form,
In heathen, turk or jew.
Where Mercy, Love & Pity dwell,
There God is dwelling too.

**Summary**

The personified figures of Mercy, Pity, Peace, and Love are listed as the four "virtues of delight." The speaker states that all people pray to these in times of distress and thank them for blessings because they represent "God, our father dear." They are also, however, the characteristics of Man: Mercy is found in the human heart, Pity in the human face; Peace is a garment that envelops humans, and Love exists in the human "form" or body. Therefore, all prayers to Mercy, Pity, Peace, and Love are directed not just to God but to "the human form divine," which all people must love and respect regardless of their religion or culture.

## Form

The poem is comprised of five ballad stanzas—quatrains in which the lines have four and three beats, alternately, and rhyme ABCB. This stanza form, in English poetry, conveys a sense of candor and naturalness, and it is common in songs, hymns, and nursery rhymes. The lilting rhythm and the frequent repetition of words and phrases combine with a spiritual subject matter to create the poem's simple, hymn-like quality.

## Commentary

This is one of Blake's more rhetorical Songs. The speaker praises both God and man while asserting an identity between the two. "The Divine Image" thus differs from most of the other Songs of Innocence, which deal with the emotional power of conventional Christian faith, and the innocent belief in a supreme, benevolent, and protective God, rather than with the parallels between these transcendent realms and the realm of man.

The poem uses personification to dramatize Christ's mediation between God and Man. Beginning with abstract qualities (the four virtues of Mercy, Pity, Peace, and Love), the poem makes these abstractions the object of human prayer and piety. The second stanza explains this somewhat strange notion by equating the virtues with God himself. But the idea is still slightly unorthodox, suggesting as it does that we pray to these abstract virtues because they are God, rather than praying to God because he has these sympathetic qualities. The poem seems to emphasize that Mercy, Pity, Peace, and Love are not God's characteristics but his substance—they are precisely what we mean when we speak of God.

The speaker now claims that Mercy, Pity, Peace, Love are also equivalent to Man: it is in humans that these qualities find a kind of embodiment, and they become recognizable because their features (heart, face, body, clothes) are basically human. Thus when we think of God, we are modeling him after these ideal human qualities. And when people pray, regardless of who or where they are, or to what God they think they are praying, they actually worship "the human form divine"—what is ideal, or most godly, in human beings. Blake's "Divine Image" is therefore a reversed one: the poem constructs God in the image of man rather (whereas, in the Bible, God creates man in his image). The implication that God is a mental creation reflects Blake's belief that "all deities reside in the human breast."

The poem does not explicitly mention Christ, but the four virtues that Blake assigns alternately to man and God are the ones conventionally associated with Jesus. Because Christ was both God and man, he becomes the vehicle for Blake's mediation between the two. But the fact that he is given an abstract rather than a human figuration underscores the elaborate intellectualization involved in Christian doctrine. Blake himself favours a more direct identification between what is human and what is divine. Thus the companion poem in Songs of Experience, "The Human Abstract," goes further toward exposing the elaborate institutions of religion as mental confabulations that obscure rather than honor the true identity of God and man.

"The Little Black Boy"

My mother bore me in the southern wild,
And I am black, but O! my soul is white;
White as an angel is the English child:
But I am black as if bereav'd of light.

My mother taught me underneath a tree
And sitting down before the heat of day,
She took me on her lap and kissed me,
And pointing to the east began to say.

Look on the rising sun: there God does live
And gives his light, and gives his heat away.

And flowers and trees and beasts and men receive
Comfort in morning joy in the noon day.

[illegible] we are put on earth a little space,
[illegible] we may learn to bear the beams of love,

And these black bodies and this sun-burnt face
Is but a cloud, and like a shady grove.

For when our souls have learn'd the heat to bear
The cloud will vanish we shall hear his voice.
Saying: come out from the grove my love & care,
And round my golden tent like lambs rejoice.

Thus did my mother say and kissed me,
And thus I say to little English boy;
When I from black and he from white cloud free,
And round the tent of God like lambs we joy:

I'll shade him from the heat till he can bear,
To lean in joy upon our fathers knee.
And then I'll stand and stroke his silver hair,
And be like him and he will then love me.

## SUMMARY

A black child tells the story of how he came to know his own identity and to know God. The boy, who was born in "the southern wild" of Africa, first explains that though his skin is black his soul is as white as that of an English child. He relates how his loving mother taught him about God who lives in the East, who gives light and life to all creation and comfort and joy to men. "We are put on earth," his mother says, to learn to accept God's love. He is told that his black skin "is but a cloud" that will be dissipated when his soul meets God in heaven. The black boy passes on this lesson to an English child, explaining that his white skin is likewise a cloud. He vows that when they are both free of their bodies and delighting in the presence of God, he will shade his white friend until he, too, learns to bear the heat of God's love. Then, the black boy says, he will be like the English boy, and the English boy will love him.

### Form

The poem is in heroic quatrains, which are stanzas of pentameter lines rhyming ABAB. The form is a variation on the ballad stanza, and the slightly longer lines are well suited to the pedagogical tone of this poem.

## Commentary

This poem centres on a spiritual awakening to a divine love that transcends race. The speaker is an African child who has to come to terms with his own blackness. Blake builds the poem on clear imagery of light and dark. The contrast in the first stanza between the child's black skin and his belief in the whiteness of his soul lends poignancy to his particular problem of self-understanding. In a culture in which black and white connote bad and good, respectively, the child's developing sense of self requires him to perform some fairly elaborate symbolic gymnastics with these images of colour. His statement that he is "black as if bereav'd of light" underscores the gravity of the problem. The gesture of his song will be to counteract this "as if" in a way that shows him to be as capable and deserving of perfect love as a white person is.

The child's mother symbolizes a natural and selfless love that becomes the poem's ideal. She shows a tender concern for her child's self-esteem, as well as a strong desire that he know the comfort of God. She persuades him, according to conventional Christian doctrine that earthly life is but a preparation for the rewards of heaven. In this context, their dark skin is similarly but a temporary appearance, with no bearing on their eternal essence: skin, which is a factor only in this earthly life, becomes irrelevant from the perspective of heaven. Body and soul, black and white, and earth and heaven are all aligned in a rhetorical gesture that basically confirms the stance of Christian resignation: the theology of the poem is one that counsels forbearance in the present and promises a recompense for suffering in the hereafter.

The black boy internalizes his mother's lesson and applies it in his relations with the outer world; specifically, Blake shows us what happens when the boy applies it to his relationship with a white child. The results are ambivalent. The boy explains to his white friend that they are equals, but that neither will be truly free until they are released from the constraints of the physical world. He imagines himself shading his friend from the brightness of God's love until he can become accustomed to it.

This statement implies that the black boy is better prepared for heaven than the white boy, perhaps because of the greater burden of his dark skin has posed during earthly life. This is part of the consoling vision with which his mother has prepared him, which allows his suffering to become a source of pride rather than shame. But the boy's outlook, and his deference to the white boy, may strike the reader (who has not his innocence) as containing a naive blindness to the realities of oppression and racism, and a too-passive acceptance of suffering and injustice. We do not witness the response of the white boy; Blake's focus in this poem is on the mental state of the black child. But the question remains of whether the child's outlook is servile and self-demeaning, or exemplifies Christian charity. The poem itself implies that these might amount to the same thing.

"The Nurse's Song"

When the voices of children are heard on the green
And laughing is heard on the hill,
My heart is at rest within my breast
And every thing else is still

Then come home my children, the sun is gone down
And the dews of night arise
Come come leave off play, and let us away
Till the morning appears in the skies

No no let us play, for it is yet day
And we cannot go to sleep
Besides in the sky, the little birds fly
And the hills are all cover'd with sheep

Well well go & play till the light fades away
And then go home to bed
The little ones leaped & shouted & laugh'd
And all the hills ecchoed

**Summary**

The scene of the poem features a group of children playing outside in the hills, while their nurse listens to them in contentment. As twilight begins to fall, she gently urges them to "leave off play" and retire to the house for the night. They ask to play on till bedtime, for as long as the light lasts. The nurse yields to their pleas, and the children shout and laugh with joy while the hills echo their gladness.

**[SH]Form**

The poem has four quatrains, rhymed ABCB and containing an internal rhyme in the third line of each verse.

**Commentary**

This is a poem of affinities and correspondences. There is no suggestion of alienation, either between children and adults or between man and nature, and even the dark certainty of nightfall is tempered by the promise of resuming play in the morning. The theme of the poem is the children's innocent and simple joy. Their happiness persists unabashed and uninhibited, and without shame the children plead for permission to continue in it. The sounds and games of the children harmonize with a busy world of sheep and birds. They think of themselves as part of nature, and cannot bear the thought of abandoning their play while birds and sheep still frolic in the sky and on the hills, for the children share the innocence and unselfconscious spontaneity of these natural creatures. They also approach the world with a cheerful optimism, focusing not on the impending nightfall but on the last drops of daylight that surely can be eked out of the evening.

A similar innocence characterizes the pleasure the adult nurse takes in watching her charges play. Their happiness inspires in her a feeling of peace, and their desire to prolong their own delight is one she readily indulges. She is a kind of angelic, guardian presence who, while standing apart from the children, supports rather than overshadows their innocence.

As an adult, she is identified with "everything else" in nature; but while her inner repose does contrast with the children's exuberant delight, the difference does not constitute an antagonism. Rather, her tranquility resonates with the evening's natural stillness, and both seem to envelop the carefree children in a tender protection.

"The Tyger"

Tyger Tyger, burning bright,
In the forests of the night;
What immortal hand or eye,
Could frame thy fearful symmetry?

In what distant deeps or skies.
Burnt the fire of thine eyes?
On what wings dare he aspire?
What the hand, dare seize the fire?

And what shoulder, & what art,
Could twist the sinews of thy heart?
And when thy heart began to beat,
What dread hand? & what dread feet?

What the hammer? what the chain,
In what furnace was thy brain?
What the anvil? what dread grasp,
Dare its deadly terrors clasp!

When the stars threw down their spears
And water'd heaven with their tears:
Did he smile his work to see?
Did he who made the Lamb make thee?

Tyger Tyger burning bright,
In the forests of the night:
What immortal hand or eye,
Dare frame thy fearful symmetry?

**Summary**

The poem begins with the speaker asking a fearsome tiger what kind of divine being could have created it: "What immortal hand or eye/ Could frame they fearful symmetry?" Each subsequent stanza contains further questions, all of which refine this first one. From what part of the cosmos could the tiger's fiery eyes have come, and who would have dared to handle that fire? What sort of physical presence, and what kind of dark craftsmanship, would have been required to "twist the sinews" of the tiger's heart?

The speaker wonders how, once that horrible heart "began to beat," its creator would have had the courage to continue the job. Comparing the creator to a blacksmith, he ponders about the anvil and the furnace that the project would have required and the smith who could have wielded them. And when the job was done, the speaker wonders, how would the creator have felt? "Did he smile his work to see?" Could this possibly be the same being who made the lamb?

### Form

The poem is comprised of six quatrains in rhymed couplets. The meter is regular and rhythmic, its hammering beat suggestive of the smithy that is the poem's central image. The simplicity and neat proportions of the poems form perfectly suit its regular structure, in which a string of questions all contribute to the articulation of a single, central idea.

### Commentary

The opening question enacts what will be the single dramatic gesture of the poem, and each subsequent stanza elaborates on this conception. Blake is building on the conventional idea that nature, like a work of art, must in some way contain a reflection of its creator. The tiger is strikingly beautiful yet also horrific in its capacity for violence. What kind of a God, then, could or would design such a terrifying beast as the tiger? In more general terms, what does the undeniable existence of evil and violence in the world tell us about the nature of God, and what does it mean to live in a world where a being can at once contain both beauty and horror?

The tiger initially appears as a strikingly sensuous image. However, as the poem progresses, it takes on a symbolic character, and comes to embody the spiritual and moral problem the poem explores: perfectly beautiful and yet perfectly destructive, Blake's tiger becomes the symbolic centre for an investigation into the presence of evil in the world. Since the tiger's remarkable nature exists both in physical and moral terms, the speaker's questions about its origin must also encompass both physical and moral dimensions. The poem's series of questions repeatedly ask what sort of physical creative capacity the "fearful symmetry" of the tiger bespeaks; assumedly only a very strong and powerful being could be capable of such a creation.

The smithy represents a traditional image of artistic creation; here Blake applies it to the divine creation of the natural world. The "forging" of the tiger suggests a very physical, laborious, and deliberate kind of making; it emphasizes the awesome physical presence of the tiger and precludes the idea that such a creation could have been in any way accidentally or haphazardly produced. It also continues from the first description of the tiger the imagery of fire with its simultaneous connotations of creation, purification, and destruction. The speaker stands in awe of the tiger as a sheer physical and aesthetic achievement, even as he recoils in horror from the moral implications of such a creation; for the poem addresses not only the question of who could make such a creature as the tiger, but who would perform this act. This is a question of creative responsibility and of will, and the poet carefully includes this moral question with the consideration of physical power. Note, in the third stanza, the parallelism of "shoulder" and "art," as well as the fact that it is not just the body but also the "heart" of the tiger that is being forged. The repeated use of word the "dare" to replace the "could" of the first stanza introduces a dimension of aspiration and willfulness into the sheer might of the creative act.

The reference to the lamb in the penultimate stanza reminds the reader that a tiger and a lamb have been created by the same God, and raises questions about the implications of this. It also invites a contrast between the perspectives of "experience" and "innocence" represented here and in the poem "The Lamb."

"The Tyger" consists entirely of unanswered questions, and the poet leaves us to awe at the complexity of creation, the sheer magnitude of God's power, and the inscrutability of divine will. The perspective of experience in this poem involves a sophisticated acknowledgment of what is unexplainable in the universe, presenting evil as the prime example of something that cannot be denied, but will not withstand facile explanation, either. The open awe of "The Tyger" contrasts with the easy confidence, in "The Lamb," of a child's innocent faith in a benevolent universe.

"Holy Thursday"

Is this a holy thing to see,
In a rich and fruitful land,
Babes reduced to misery,
Fed with cold and usurous hand?
Is that trembling cry a song?
Can it be a song of joy?
And so many children poor?
It is a land of poverty!

And their sun does never shine.
And their fields are bleak & bare.
And their ways are fill'd with thorns.
It is eternal winter there.

**Summary**

The poem begins with a series of questions: how holy is the sight of children living in misery in a prosperous country? Might the children's "cry," as they sit assembled in St. Paul's Cathedral on Holy Thursday, really be a song? "Can it be a song of joy?" The speaker's own answer is that the destitute existence of so many children impoverishes the country no matter how prosperous it may be in other ways: for these children the sun does not shine, the fields do not bear, all paths are thorny, and it is always winter.

**Form**

The four quatrains of this poem, which have four beats each and rhyme ABAB, are a variation on the ballad stanza.

**Commentary**

In the poem "Holy Thursday" from Songs of Innocence, Blake described the public appearance of charity school children in St. Paul's Cathedral on Ascension Day. In this "experienced" version, however, he critiques rather than praises the charity of the institutions responsible for hapless children. The speaker entertains questions about the children as victims of cruelty and injustice, some of which the earlier poem implied. The rhetorical technique of the poem is to pose a number of suspicious questions that receive indirect, yet quite censoriously toned answers. This is one of the poems in Songs of Innocence and Experience that best show Blake's incisiveness as a social critic.

In the first stanza, we learn that whatever care these children receive is minimal and grudgingly bestowed. The "cold and usurous hand" that feeds them is motivated more by self-interest than by love and pity. Moreover, this "hand" metonymically represents not just the daily guardians of the orphans, but the city of London as a whole: the entire city has a civic responsibility to these most helpless members of their society, yet it delegates or denies this obligation. Here the children must participate in a public display of joy that poorly reflects their actual circumstances, but serves rather to reinforce the self-righteous complacency of those who are supposed to care for them.

The song that had sounded so majestic in the Songs of Innocence shrivels, here, to a "trembling cry." In the first poem, the parade of children found natural symbolization in London's mighty river. Here, however, the children and the natural world conceptually connect via a strikingly different set of images: the failing crops and sunless fields symbolize the wasting of a nation's resources and the public's neglect of the future. The thorns, which line their paths, link their suffering to that of Christ. They live in an eternal winter, where they experience neither physical comfort nor the warmth of love. In the last stanza, prosperity is defined in its most rudimentary form: sun and rain and food are enough to sustain life, and social intervention into natural processes, which ought to improve on these basic necessities, in fact reduce people to poverty while others enjoy plenitude.

"The Human Abstract"

Pity would be no more,
If we did not make somebody Poor:
And Mercy no more could be,
If all were as happy as we;

And mutual fear brings peace;
Till the selfish loves increase.
Then Cruelty knits a snare,
And spreads his baits with care.

He sits down with holy fears,
And waters the ground with tears:
Then Humility takes its root
Underneath his foot.

Soon spreads the dismal shade
Of Mystery over his head;
And the Catterpiller and Fly,
Feed on the Mystery.

And it bears the fruit of Deceit,
Ruddy and sweet to eat;
And the Raven his nest has made
In its thickest shade.

The Gods of the earth and sea,
Sought thro' Nature to find this Tree
But their search was all in vain:
There grows one in the Human Brain

**Summary**

This poem offers a closer analysis of the four virtues—Mercy, Pity, Peace, and Love—that constituted both God and

Man in "The Divine Image." The speaker argues that Pity could not exist without poverty that Mercy would not be necessary if everyone was happy, that the source of Peace is in fear, which gives rise to only "selfish loves." The poem describes how Cruelty plants and waters a tree in "the human Brain." The roots of the tree are Humility, the leaves are Mystery, and the fruit is Deceit.

**Form**

The poem has six quatrains, each comprised of two rhyming couplets. The lines have none of the lilting quality so typical of Blake; the poem's didactic tone and austere subject matter occasion the harsh, severe rhythms he employs.

**Commentary**

This poem asserts that the traditional Christian virtues of mercy and pity presuppose a world of poverty and human suffering; so, too, do the virtues represent a kind of passive and resigned sympathy that registers no obligation to alleviate suffering or create a more just world. The speaker therefore refuses to think of them as ideals, reasoning that in an ideal world of universal happiness and genuine love there would be no need of them. The poem begins as a methodical critique of the touchstone virtues that were so praised in "The Divine Image." Proceeding through Pity, Mercy, and Peace, the poem then arrives at the phrase "selfish loves." These clearly differ from Love as an innocent abstraction, and the poem takes a turn here to explore the growth, both insidious and organic, of a system of values based on fear, hypocrisy, repression, and stagnation.

The description of the tree in the second part of the poem shows how intellectualized values like Mercy, Pity, Peace, and Love become the breeding-ground for Cruelty. The speaker depicts Cruelty as a conniving and knowing person; in planting a tree, he also lays a trap. His tree flourishes on fear and weeping; Humility is its root, Mystery its foliage; but this growth is not natural; it does not reflect upon the natural state of man. Rather, the tree is associated with Deceit, and its branches harbor the raven, the symbol of death. By the end of the poem we realise that the above description has been a glimpse into the human mind, the mental experience. Thus the poem comments on the way abstract reasoning undermines a more natural system of values. The result is a grotesque semblance of the organic, a tree that grows nowhere in nature but lies sequestered secretly in the human brain.

"London"

I wander thro' each charter'd street,
Near where the charter'd Thames does flow.
And mark in every face I meet
Marks of weakness, marks of woe.

In every cry of every Man,
In every Infants cry of fear,
In every voice: in every ban,
The mind-forg'd manacles I hear
How the Chimney-sweepers cry
Every black'ning Church appalls,
And the hapless Soldiers sigh
Runs in blood down Palace walls

But most thro' midnight streets I hear
How the youthful Harlots curse
Blasts the new-born Infants tear
And blights with plagues the Marriage hearse

**Summary**

The speaker wanders through the streets of London and comments on his observations. He sees despair in the faces of the people he meets and hears fear and repression in their voices. The woeful cry of the chimney-sweeper stands as a chastisement to the Church, and the blood of a soldier stains the outer walls of the monarch's residence. The nighttime holds nothing more promising: the cursing of prostitutes corrupts the newborn infant and sullies the "Marriage hearse."

## Form

The poem has four quatrains, with alternate lines rhyming. Repetition is the most striking formal feature of the poem, and it serves to emphasize the prevalence of the horrors the speaker describes.

## Commentary

The opening image of wandering, the focus on sound, and the images of stains in this poem's first lines recall the Introduction to Songs of Innocence, but with a twist; we are now quite far from the piping, pastoral bard of the earlier poem: we are in the city. The poem's title denotes a specific geographic space, not the archetypal locales in which many of the other Songs are set. Everything in this urban space—even the natural River Thames—submits to being "charter'd," a term which combines mapping and legalism. Blake's repetition of this word (which he then tops with two repetitions of "mark" in the next two lines) reinforces the sense of stricture the speaker feels upon entering the city. It is as if language itself, the poet's medium, experiences a hemming-in, a restriction of resources. Blake's repetition, thudding and oppressive, reflects the suffocating atmosphere of the city. But words also undergo transformation within this repetition: thus "mark," between the third and fourth lines, changes from a verb to a pair of nouns—from an act of observation which leaves some room for imaginative elaboration, to an indelible imprint, branding the people's bodies regardless of the speaker's actions.

Ironically, the speaker's "meeting" with these marks represents the experience closest to a human encounter that the poem will offer the speaker. All the speaker's subjects—men, infants, chimney-sweeper, soldier, harlot—are known only through the traces they leave behind: the ubiquitous cries, the blood on the palace walls. Signs of human suffering abound, but a complete human form—the human form that Blake has used repeatedly in the Songs to personify and render natural phenomena—is lacking. In the third stanza the cry of the chimney-sweep and the sigh of the soldier metamorphose (almost mystically) into soot on church walls and blood on palace walls—but we never see the chimney-sweep or the soldier themselves.

Likewise, institutions of power—the clergy, the government—are rendered by synecdoche, by mention of the places in which they reside. Indeed, it is crucial to Blake's commentary that neither the city's victims nor their oppressors ever appear in body: Blake does not simply blame a set of institutions or a system of enslavement for the city's woes; rather, the victims help to make their own "mind-forg'd manacles," more powerful than material chains could ever be.

The poem climaxes at the moment when the cycle of misery recommences, in the form of a new human being starting life: a baby is born into poverty, to a cursing, prostitute mother. Sexual and marital union—the place of possible regeneration and rebirth—are tainted by the blight of venereal disease. Thus Blake's final image is the "Marriage hearse," a vehicle in which love and desire combine with death and destruction.

### "THE SICK ROSE"

O Rose thou art sick.
The invisible worm,
That flies in the night
In the howling storm:

Has found out thy bed
Of crimson joy:
And his dark secret love
Does thy life destroy.

### Summary

The speaker, addressing a rose, informs it that it is sick. An "invisible" worm has stolen into its bed in a "howling storm" and under the cover of night. The "dark secret love" of this worm is destroying the rose's life.

**Form**

The two quatrains of this poem rhyme ABCB. The ominous rhythm of these short, two-beat lines contributes to the poem's sense of foreboding or dread and complements the unflinching directness with which the speaker tells the rose she is dying.

**Commentary**

While the rose exists as a beautiful natural object that has become infected by a worm, it also exists as a literary rose, the conventional symbol of love. The image of the worm resonates with the Biblical serpent and also suggests a phallus. Worms are quintessentially earthbound, and symbolize death and decay. The "bed" into which the worm creeps denotes both the natural flowerbed and also the lovers' bed. The rose is sick, and the poem implies that love is sick as well. Yet the rose is unaware of its sickness.

Of course, an actual rose could not know anything about its own condition, and so the emphasis falls on the allegorical suggestion that it is love that does not recognize its own ailing state. This results partly from the insidious secrecy with which the "worm" performs its work of corruption—not only is it invisible, it enters the bed at night. This secrecy indeed constitutes part of the infection itself. The "crimson joy" of the rose connotes both sexual pleasure and shame, thus joining the two concepts in a way that Blake thought was perverted and unhealthy. The rose's joyful attitude toward love is tainted by the aura of shame and secrecy that our culture attaches to love.

## Chapter 14

# William Blake: Songs of Innocence and Experience: Critical Analysis

Songs of Innocence and of Experience: Shewing the Two Contrary States of the Human Soul are two books of poetry by the English poet and painter, William Blake. Although Songs of Innocence was first published by itself in 1789, it is believed that Songs of Experience has always been published in conjunction with Innocence since its completion in 1794.

Songs of Innocence mainly consists of poems describing the innocence and joy of the natural world, advocating free love and a closer relationship with God, and most famously including Blake's poem The Lamb. Its poems have a generally light, upbeat and pastoral feel and are typically written from the perspective of children or written about them. .

Directly contrasting this, Songs of Experience instead deals with the loss of innocence after exposure to the material world and all of its mortal sin during adult life, including works such as The Tyger. Poems here are darker, concentrating on more political and serious themes. Throughout both books, many poems fall into pairs, so that a similar situation or theme can be seen in both Innocence and Experience.

Many of the poems appearing in Songs of Innocence have a counterpart in Songs of Experience with opposing perspectives of the world. The disastrous end of the French

Revolution caused Blake to lose faith in the goodness of mankind, explaining much of the volume's sense of despair. Blake also believed that children lost their innocence through exploitation and from a religious community which put dogma before mercy. He did not, however, believe that children should be kept from becoming experienced entirely. In truth, he believed that children should indeed become experienced but through their own discoveries, which is reflected in a number of these poems. Blake believed that innocence and experience were "the two contrary states of the human soul", and that true innocence was impossible without experience

Blake's Songs of Innocence and Experience (1794) juxtapose the innocent, pastoral world of childhood against an adult world of corruption and repression; while such poems as "The Lamb" represent a meek virtue, poems like "The Tyger" exhibit opposing, darker forces. Thus the collection as a whole explores the value and limitations of two different perspectives on the world. Many of the poems fall into pairs, so that the same situation or problem is seen through the lens of innocence first and then experience. Blake does not identify himself wholly with either view; most of the poems are dramatic—that is, in the voice of a speaker other than the poet himself. Blake stands outside innocence and experience, in a distanced position from which he hopes to be able to recognize and correct the fallacies of both. In particular, he pits himself against despotic authority, restrictive morality, sexual repression, and institutionalized religion; his great insight is into the way these separate modes of control work together to squelch what is most holy in human beings.

The Songs of Innocence dramatize the naive hopes and fears that inform the lives of children and trace their transformation as the child grows into adulthood. Some of the poems are written from the perspective of children, while others are about children as seen from an adult perspective. Many of the poems draw attention to the positive aspects of natural human understanding prior to the corruption and distortion of experience. Others take a more critical stance toward innocent purity: for example, while Blake draws touching portraits of the emotional power of rudimentary Christian values, he also exposes—over the heads, as it were, of the innocent—Christianity's capacity for promoting injustice and cruelty.

The Songs of Experience work via parallels and contrasts to lament the ways in which the harsh experiences of adult life destroy what is good in innocence, while also articulating the weaknesses of the innocent perspective ("The Tyger," for example, attempts to account for real, negative forces in the universe, which innocence fails to confront). These latter poems treat sexual morality in terms of the repressive effects of jealousy, shame, and secrecy, all of which corrupt the ingenuousness of innocent love. With regard to religion, they are less concerned with the character of individual faith than with the institution of the Church, its role in politics, and its effects on society and the individual mind. Experience thus adds a layer to innocence that darkens its hopeful vision while compensating for some of its blindness.

The style of the Songs of Innocence and Experience is simple and direct, but the language and the rhythms are painstakingly crafted, and the ideas they explore are often deceptively complex. Many of the poems are narrative in style; others, like "The Sick Rose" and "The Divine Image," make their arguments through symbolism or by means of abstract concepts. Some of Blake's favourite rhetorical techniques are personification and the reworking of Biblical symbolism and language. Blake frequently employs the familiar meters of ballads, nursery rhymes, and hymns, applying them to his own, often unorthodox conceptions. This combination of the traditional with the unfamiliar is consonant with Blake's perpetual interest in reconsidering and reframing the assumptions of human thought and social behaviour.

# Chapter 15

# Study Questions

**Q1. Write short notes on the poems of Songs of Innocence.**

**Or**

**Q. Briefly discuss Blake's Songs of Innocence.**

## Notes on The Age of Innocence

### Introduction

This 'Introduction' sets the tone for the Songs of Innocence as a whole, with its use of images of the child and the Lamb (Christ), together with the bright idyllic pastoral setting, establishing the tone of Innocence: guiltlessness, freedom from harm and sin. The full-page illustration, which accompanied this poem as frontispiece to the Songs of Innocence, shows a piper looking up at a child resting in the cloud, whilst sheep graze securely between the trees: the mutually complementary relationship between text and illustration is itself indicated in the final stanza, with the reference to the 'rural pen'.

Even in this apparently direct celebration of childhood innocence, laughter and joy, commentators have detected an anticipation of the darker tones of the Songs of Experience, and the sense that this Springtime vision is transitory. The phrase "wept with joy" is one indication, as is the reference to the staining of the "water clear". Yet the predominating tone of this lyric is happy and full of joy. It is worth comparing this poem with the 'Introduction' to the Songs of Experience.

### The Shepherd

Once again, as in the 'Introduction', we have a bright idyllic pastoral vision, but with perhaps more obvious allusion to the figure of Christ the Shepherd. It is worth noting that, in the poem, the Shepherd may watch over his flock, such that they are at peace and full of trust, but it is he who follows them, and is full of praise for their innocence and trust: the sense is one of mutual trust and responsiveness, rather than docile obedience.

### The Blossom

Many critics have pointed out the symbolic sexual connotations at play in this lyric, with its vision of the young Blossom anticipating the Sparrow's and Robin's embraces. These associations are there, but the poem can also be seen as an evocation of innocent love, merriment and growth within the natural order.

### The Schoolboy

This child-monologue, like The Little Black Boy and The Chimney Sweeper, expresses a less idyllic and sunlit feeling than poems such as The Shepherd. The boy complains at the constraints of education and the classroom, which deprive him of access to the joys of Nature, and force him prematurely into the world of adult cares and responsibility. His argument may be an innocent (unthinking) reaction, and thus represents one form of Innocence: - innocent complaint. However, it may also represent a view on childhood and education often associated with Rousseau, and developed by Wordsworth in the Lyrical Ballads and Ode: Intimation of Immortality, that childhood is a state of natural grace, and entrance into the adult world means loss and imprisonment in the artificial constraints of civilization ("shades of the prison-house begin to close / upon the dying boy", Wordsworth, Ode: Intimations). Within the Songs of Innocence it is probably right to view this as a 'transitional' poem, anticipating the darker vision of the Songs of Experience.

## Holy Thursday

This is probably the controversial of the lyrics in the Songs of Innocence. The problem is mainly one of identifying the tone and attitude of the speaker and the poem towards the procession of children. Like Holy Thursday: Experience the poem describes the annual service of thanksgiving held at St. Pauls in the 1780s and 1790s for Charity School children, where the children gave thanks for the charity they receive throughout the year. Should the children be so grateful for this charity, or are they so innocent that they know no better? It is clear that the children here are viewed as lambs, flowers and angels, traditional images of innocence, but what is the speaker's attitude to the "aged men, wise guardians of the poor"? Is the last line of the poem directed at them, (bearing in mind that Charity Schools were often accused of neglecting or mistreating their charges), or does it celebrate the ways that this young flock is taken in hand and arranged into serried ranks? Comparison with Holy Thursday (Experience) is illuminating.

## The Little Black Boy

In this child-monologue Blake's treatment of the little black boy's perspective on Christianity and salvation may well be ironic, forming the basis for a more savage attack on religious and social hypocrisy. The child's mother consoles the child with a vision of a better life to come, away from the prejudices and hardship of this life, and the child accepts this, encouraging him to a further vision of leading (rather than being led by) the little white English boy to God and Heaven. The mother's teaching may itself be a form of 'innocence', and the boy's vision of a Heaven, transcending the divisions of race, is certainly 'innocent'. The central question the poem raises, like Holy Thursday (Innocence) is what Blake's attitude is towards the child's (and the mother's) attitudes: does he see them as touchingly naive, or tragically misguided? Throughout the poem, in the references to 'black' and 'white', Blake plays around with the traditional associations between 'white' and 'good', but also, in the little black boy's views on

Soul/Body, makes the point that colour is skin deep, but colour is no indication of spiritual state. The poem should, perhaps, be approached in the light of British attitudes towards missionaries, and arguments about the abolition of slavery in the late eighteenth century.

## The Lamb

In this poem, like The Shepherd, Blake again brings out the traditional associations between the Lamb and Christ, in a simple lyric which relies on a pastoral setting. The speaker is presumably the child, which allows Blake to express a joyous state of protected innocence and harmony within and amongst creation. It is worthwhile to compare this poem with The Tiger.

## Night

In the first three stanzas of the poem we are presented with a view of a harmonious and protected creation, watched over by guiding angels. In the fourth stanza, however, there is an acknowledgement that even these angels cannot prevent 'wolves and tygers' from preying on the meek and mild, and the poem ends with a vision of the after-life, where the lamb and the lion lie down together, and the lion becomes shepherd. 'Innocence', in the poem, may be found in this life (symbolized by grazing lambs and the guardian angels), but ultimately is to be found in the after-life. The predominant tone of the poem as a whole, however, is one of idealism and of Christian celebration.

## The Chimney Sweeper

Once again, as in Holy Thursday and The Little Black Boy, this child-monologue uses the child's innocent perspective to present what could be a biting and savage indictment of social and psychic repressiveness: the child's consoling vision of the pastoral after-life may be a glorious and 'innocent' celebration of Heaven, or it may equally well show the extent to which the child-speaker has been conditioned into acceptance of his slavery in this life. The references to the 'blackness' of the children, together with the dualistic references to black body/ white soul, invites comparison with The Little Black Boy. The imagery within stanzas Four and Five, of leaping and laughing children, washing in rivers and children on clouds, recurs throughout the Songs of Innocence.

**The Divine Image**

This lyric expresses in abstract terms the cardinal Christian tenets of God becoming Man, and therefore of the human form as a manifestation of God himself: for that reason all men, regardless of creed or colour, should be seen as divine creations, and as manifestations of Love, Mercy, Pity and Peace. This 'innocent' multi-racial perspective is, perhaps, better expressed in lyrics such as A Cradle Song. the poem as a whole, however, should be compared with its counterpart, A Divine Image, the poem which initially appeared in the Songs of Experience,

**Q2. Write short notes on the poems of Songs of Experience.**

**Or**

**Q. Briefly discuss Blake's Songs of Experience.**

**Notes on the Age of Experience**

***Introduction (Experience)***

The Songs of Innocence begins with an 'Introduction' in which the poet is the Piper; here the poet is Bard, addressing the fallen and sinful Earth and asking it to return to Grace and God. Commentators have disagreed in their view of the Bard, whether he is a benevolent prophet, weeping over the fallen world, or an autocratic tyrant, jealous and possessive, full of the Holy Word. Furthermore, the Bard cannot wholly be seen as Blake himself, for the Songs of Experience show that the fallen world can also be a route to wisdom, understanding, and ultimately back to God.

## Earth's Answer

Our understanding of Earth's Answer depends on how we interpret the questions posed by the Introduction (Experience) and the Bard's motives for asking the Earth to return to Grace. If the Earth sees the "father of ancient men" as cruel, jealous and selfish (symbolised, for Blake, in the figure of Urizen), then she is right to turn away and attempt to remain free. However, because the Earth has fallen from Grace, then perhaps she does not see the truth behind the Bard's plea for her to return, and remains, as she sees it, a prisoner and victim of a jealous God. The elaborate form of personification in this poem, along with the imagery and its associations, allows Blake to express complex metaphysical and theological issues, of the Fall of Man from Grace and Good, in an apparently straightforward way. The figure of "Earth" here, might be loosely interpreted as the representative of Experience itself, but more widely as temporal physical existence.

## My Pretty Rose Tree

Some have seen this poem autobiographical, and as his reflections on a love passed over. However, it is probably wiser to read the lyric as the product of the' Experience' state of mind and soul, which has had to learn of thorns and jealousy from personal experience of love and life.

## A Poison Tree

This lyric is a subtle product of the voice of experience, using the figure of the poison tree as a vehicle for describing the psychological states of transferred hatred and anger. In an earlier draft of the poem the speaker gives the fruit of his anger to his foe, whereas here the foe is attracted to the apple because he knows it belongs to the speaker. Critical speculation surrounds the interpretation of both tree and apple in this poem: the most obvious association is with the apple on the Tree of Knowledge in the Garden of Eden, leading to identification of the speaker as the jealous God of creation. Clearly the poem raises issues of the tone and attitude of the speaker. Is he full of self-congratulation at the death of his foe? Can the poem be read as simply a warning over the dangers of repressed anger, for where is the remorse over the foe's death or the speaker's conscience?

**The Tiger**

Blake's most famous poem raises profound questions, but does not finally answer them. How could the creator make something as terrifying and awesome as the Tiger? Could the same creator also be responsible for making the Lamb (both Christ, and the creator whose meek and mild spirit dominates the Songs of Innocence)? Is the Tiger not created in God's own image? Is the Tiger a symbol of Evil, for elsewhere (as in The Marriage of Heaven and Hell) Blake praises energy as a form of good and delight. These speculations lead to wider questions, about the wisdom of a God who can create such terrifyingly destructive creations, and questions of God's creation of Good and Evil, or Good-and-Evil. Comparison with The Lamb in the Songs of Innocence is extremely illuminating here. The Tiger is personified as having been born from fire (stolen from the Gods by Prometheus?), forged rather than created, and characterised also in terms of its (metallic) coldness: note the effectiveness of the poem's imagery in creating associations of fire, coldness and darkness. Interpretation of the poem is complicated by the fact that we cannot assume the speaker of the poem to be Blake himself, but perhaps any poet, who has created this Tiger out of his own imagination ("forests of the night").

**The Sick Rose**

Many have seen this poem as directly sexual, in its references to venereal disease and to the corruption of the innocent Rose by the masculine "invisible worm" of sexual experience. Certainly the poem draws on these, but it should also be read less literally, relying on the traditional associations of the Rose (Love, the young girl) in its depiction of an altered state of psychological (and spiritual) awareness. The sickness, however, may well be an internal psychological sickness that comes from unacted desires within the Rose ("Sooner murder an infant in its cradle than nurse unacted desires", from the 'Proverbs of Hell' in The Marriage of Heaven and Hell) rather than corruption forced from outside. This is a recurrent theme in the Songs of Experience

**Infant Sorrow**

The counterpart to 'Infant Joy', in the Songs of Innocence. Here the child leaps into the "dangerous world", helpless as in the songs of Innocence, but here imprisoned by the parents and the world, and sulking at the breast. The infant describes himself as "fiend", having that energy and instinct which Blake praises in poems such as the Marriage of Heaven and Hell, but we are a long way in this poem from the innocence of the infant characterised in poems such as A Cradle Song and other lyrics in the Songs of Innocence sequence. It is worth noting, however, that the sense of constraint experienced by the Schoolboy in the Songs of Innocence begins at birth in this poem.

**The Chimney Sweeper (Experience)**

A very much darker and more savage vision here than in the counterpart poem in the Songs of Innocence. The references to a church which is complicit in the repression of the child, together with the treatment of the negligent parents, make this one of the most bitter poems in the sequence, with its emphasis on a whole system (God, Priest and King) which represses the child, even forcing him to conceal his unhappiness (a reference to being "clothed"), psychologically as well as physically). Comparison with the Songs of Innocence poem The Chimney Sweeper is valuable.

**Holy Thursday (Experience)**

As might be expected, the perspective in the Experience poem is much darker and more savage than in the Songs of Innocence counterpart poem. Here the tone, from the opening lines onward, is openly questioning of the 'usurous' system of charity which represses the children, and of the hypocritical un-Christian religion which refuses to do something more positive for them. It is far less descriptive than Holy Thursday (Innocence), but it still raises questions of the speaker's attitude and tone, particularly as to the status of the final lines: is this the speaker's vision of the after-life, or an ironic portrait of the vision of Heaven which is being offered to the children at this service?

### London

This provides a bitter and harsh view of the city, which is characterised in terms of repression, regimentation, disease, hypocrisy and death. London is dominated by the spirit of "Reason", the "mind-forged manacles" which bind and restrain the natural spirit (symbolized in the regimented streets and the "charter'd Thames"), and the hypocritical Establishment ("church" and "palace") does nothing to prevent or speak out against injustice (symbolized in the cries of the young chimney sweepers, with reference here to the political agitation from the 1780s onwards to improve their working conditions of child). The new-born child, traditionally a symbol of hope and the promise of a new start, is here the child of an adolescent prostitute, blighted by venereal disease, and every marriage, in this city, is associated with Death (the hearse) rather than Life.

This portrait of a city of repression and death owes something, perhaps, to Old Testament portraits of Jerusalem prior to its destruction, but it is clear also that Blake was offering a perspective on contemporary London, and more particularly to the city under the counter-revolutionary regime of Pitt in the 1790s. Blake, like contemporary Romantic poets such as Shelley and the young Wordsworth, were highly critical of the political reaction to the French Revolution in England, and in this poem we have some insight into the colour of Blake's radical politics, and his attempt to provide a total snapshot of a reactionary culture in all its aspects.

### Ah! Sunflower

In this poem the Sunflower, which traditionally looks like the sun and always turns its face to the sun, yearns to escape, partly from the sun and from what the sun represents, Time. Where the sunflower seeks to go is not clear, except that it is to a region out of or beyond time, a place either of rest and completion, or of exhausted desire, or of cold virginity (associated here with death and unacted desire). The actual destination aimed for is perhaps less important than the fact that the sunflower, rather than joyously rejoicing in life (the spirit of the Songs of Innocence), is here tired and weary of life.

### The Fly

The speaker, in this poem, speculates on whether he is or is not like the Fly, carelessly swept away by the speaker's hand. The Fly may have little, if any, conscious awareness of himself and his mortality and, if the speaker shares that freedom from awareness, then life or death is of little consequence. If, on the other hand, the fly does have human awareness then it is a different story.

### The Clod and the Pebble

This poem provides two contrasting attitudes, one of selfless love for others, and the second, of Love as self-absorption and possessiveness. The first stanza seems to belong to the Songs of Innocence sequence, and the final stanza to Songs of Experience, and perhaps it is left to the reader to adjudicate between the two attitudes. However, as a poem in the Songs of Experience sequence, it is important that the final words are given to the selfish Pebble rather than to the down-trodden Clod, perhaps suggesting that it is the former's attitude which is seen to be the most insightful. An alternative view is that the poem presents both perspectives as equally valid, and mutually true.

### The Garden of Love

This Songs of Experience lyric deals with the repression of joys, desires and instincts by the church and by prohibitive morality. The speaker, presumably no longer a child, returns to the Garden of Love, and sees that earlier pastoral and natural vision of Love transformed by the influence of the Chapel, and by the 'Priests in black gowns'. Given that the poem deals with a vision of a journey into the "garden", it is worthwhile to see the poem as a commentary on the ways that conscience and guilt are imposed on the Imagination and on what is natural and instinctual, the 'mind-forged manacles' of London. In Freudian psychological terms this would correspond to the Superego's policing of the Id. It is also worth noting that the references to playing "on the green" hark back to a recurrent image in the Songs of Innocence sequence.

## The Voice of the Ancient Bard

Originally this poem belonged to the Songs of Innocence sequence, but was later transferred to the Songs of Experience, such that its final stance is uncertain. It is worth contrasting the figure of the Ancient Bard with that of the Shepherd-piper who speaks in the Introduction: Innocence. Here the 'Youth of Delight' is invited to participate in a vision of truth, and to cast aside doubt and folly. Possibly the poem is inviting the attitude of Innocence to cast aside its innocence and to learn from what is presented in the Songs of Experience. Alternatively, perhaps the poem is a kind of summative statement for the Songs of Innocence and Experience as a whole, with its summons to a new life and vision.

## A Divine Image

This poem was replaced by The Human Abstract in the Songs of Experience, as a counterpart to The Divine Image in the Songs of Innocence. As such it directly opposes the view of humanity presented in the Songs of Innocence poem: Man, created in God's image, is seen here in terms of Cruelty, Jealousy, Terror and Secrecy, and characterised by images of fire, emptiness and coldness. As a Songs of Experience poem, however, it is the human (and therefore divine) form as seen from the vantage point of Experience, rather than being Blake's last word on human nature!

**Q3. Critically analyse "The Chimney Sweeper", in Songs of Experience.**

**Or**

**Q. Unlike the one in Songs of Innocence, "The Chimney Sweeper", in Songs of Experience is very dark and pessimistic.Discuss**

Unlike the one in Songs of Innocence, "The Chimney Sweeper", in Songs of Experience is very dark and pessimistic. This poem also seems to be very judgmental and gives motives for everything, but unlike Song of Innocence, the sweeper in this poem does not free himself from his misery.

In the first two lines, Blake gives us an image of an anguished child in a state of agony or even in a state of corruption. The colour black seems to be very important because it is used to represent sin against innocence, the colour of the white snow. Blake also shows the same child weeping, when he really means to say sweeping, because that is what has that child in such grief. This stanza ends by someone asking him about his parents, which later end up being responsible for this child's state.

In the second stanza, the child is pictured in a very more happier and playful mood. This soon changes when he decides to tell the stranger more about his parents. They are showed to be punishing their child for being so happy by "clothing in clothes of death and teaching him to sing notes of woe." It is very obvious the sweeper's feels hate towards his parents for putting him in such sadness, but instead he chooses to hide it by making himself look happy and satisfied.

It is clear in the last Stanza that Blake's criticizing the Church, especially, and the state for letting a lot of these things happen. During this time many children were dying from being, either, worked to death or from malnutrition. Neither the state or the church did anything to stop this and is obviously why Blake feels so much anger towards them. The sweeper's parents are really no help towards their own child. This makes the reader wonder, if they are worshipping god, the source of good doings, why do they chose to ignore their own child. They would rather turn their heads the other way and instead find love at church.

I think this is a very striking poem. It clearly shows Blake's anger towards society at this time. I also think that he used many of his poems to make people aware of the suffering of people at this time. I also think That he wrote two separate books to give a fuller effect. Songs of Innocence, I think was how people thought that everything was okay. Songs of Experience, in my opinion was to open every ones eyes.

**Q4. Critically analyse and study the poem "The Lamb" by William Blake**

It's a poem that portrays three main Romantic themes: childhood, nature and spiritual truth. I would like to write mostly on the spiritual truth of the poem:

"Little Lamb, who made thee?

Dost thou know who made thee?"

This poem begins with a child asking a little lamb, "who made thee?" Blake leaves no room for speculation. "Who made thee?" is a question that all of us have asked. The question, of course, has taken different forms and has been the subject of philosophy since Socrates. Blake would answer that a creature could only exist because a creator has made them. In this poem, Blake leaves no other answer but that somebody made everything. It's a personal question, "who made thee?" Who is the who? It must be somebody. It can't be chance. It can't be an impersonal being. It must be a person who created the lamb and a little boy, according to Blake in this poem:

"Little Lamb I'll tell thee!
He is called by thy name,
For he calls himself a Lamb;
He is meek & he is mild,
He became a little child;"

What a beautiful analogy to the Christ of the New Testament. Blake affirms with the Protestants, Eastern

Orthodox, and Roman Catholics, that the God of the world and everything in it, who "Gave thee life & bid thee feed... Gave thee clothing of delight; Softest clothing wooly bright;" is the Lamb. Christ was called the Lamb many times in the New Testament, most notably in Revelation 5:8-13: "Worthy is the Lamb who was slain... Blessing and honor and glory and power Be to Him who sits on the throne, And to the Lamb, forever and ever!" Anybody who is familiar at all with the Old Testament realises that the Lamb (or Christ/Messiah) would take away the sins of His people by dying on a cross. This small poem gives us, not only, a great depth of knowledge about how the Old and New Testaments fit together, but how Blake really knew the scriptures. I personally find great comfort in The Lamb because it points all of us to the Creator, who has given us everything, "life... feed... [and] clothing." All of us should be just as thankful as Blake; we exist because of the Lamb. The next question that follows is "How does this Lamb want us to live?

**Q5. Critically analyse Blake's Songs of Innocence & Experience.**

**Or**

**Q. What do you consider to be the task or purpose of Songs of Innocence? In other words, do the songs teach us anything? If so, what?**

William Blake – Songs of Innocence and Experience - Analysis

Blake's Songs of Innocence and Experience (1794) juxtapose the innocent, pastoral world of childhood against an adult world of corruption and repression; while such poems as "The Lamb" represent a meek virtue, poems like "The Tyger" exhibit opposing, darker forces. Thus the collection as a whole explores the value and limitations of two different perspectives on the world. Many of the poems fall into pairs, so that the same situation or problem is seen through the lens of innocence first and then experience. Blake does not identify himself wholly with either view; most of the poems are dramatic—that is, in the voice of a speaker other than the poet himself. Blake stands outside innocence and experience, in a distanced position from which he hopes to be able to recognize and correct the fallacies of both. In particular, he pits himself against despotic authority, restrictive morality, sexual repression, and institutionalized religion; his great insight is into the way these separate modes of control work together to squelch what is most holy in human beings.

The Songs of Innocence dramatize the naive hopes and fears that inform the lives of children and trace their transformation as the child grows into adulthood. Some of the poems are written from the perspective of children, while others are about children as seen from an adult perspective. Many of the poems draw attention to the positive aspects of natural human understanding prior to the corruption and distortion of experience. Others take a more critical stance toward innocent purity: for example, while Blake draws touching portraits of the emotional power of rudimentary Christian values, he also exposes—over the heads, as it were, of the innocent—Christianity's capacity for promoting injustice and cruelty.

The Songs of Experience work via parallels and contrasts to lament the ways in which the harsh experiences of adult life destroy what is good in innocence, while also articulating the weaknesses of the innocent perspective ("The Tyger," for example, attempts to account for real, negative forces in the universe, which innocence fails to confront). These latter poems treat sexual morality in terms of the repressive effects of jealousy, shame, and secrecy, all of which corrupt the ingenuousness of innocent love. With regard to religion, they are less concerned with the character of individual faith than with the institution of the Church, its role in politics, and its effects on society and the individual mind. Experience thus adds a layer to innocence that darkens its hopeful vision while compensating for some of its blindness.

The style of the Songs of Innocence and Experience is simple and direct, but the language and the rhythms are painstakingly crafted, and the ideas they explore are often deceptively complex. Many of the poems are narrative in style; others, like "The Sick Rose" and "The Divine Image," make their arguments through symbolism or by means of abstract concepts. Some of Blake's favourite rhetorical techniques are personification and the reworking of Biblical symbolism and language. Blake frequently employs the familiar meters of ballads, nursery rhymes, and hymns, applying them to his own, often unorthodox conceptions. This combination of the traditional with the unfamiliar is consonant with Blake's perpetual interest in reconsidering and reframing the assumptions of human thought and social behaviour.

**Q6. Discuss Blake's use of auditory imagery in the poems, and cite one example.**

Blake's work shows a constant awareness of the ironies of publishing "songs" in written form—publishing poems that lay claim to an oral culture in a series of elaborately visual engravings. This awareness reflects the general Romantic preoccupation with the possibility of capturing in writing the rhythms, immediacy, and spontaneity of the spoken human voice. Blake seems, if not pessimistic, at least dubious about such a possibility, as can be seen in his Introduction to *Songs of Innocence*. Here, a child gives wandering bard three commands: first to play his pipe, second to sing his songs, and third to write them. This progression may imply a decline, from the purity of music (without linguistic meaning), to morality (bound by meaning but still spontaneous and fleeting), to literacy (without need for human presence and perhaps less personal). The speaker's pen, ambiguously, "stain[s] the water clear"; thus the image simultaneously implies both a purification (to "stain" it "clear") and a corruption (to "stain" the "clear" water). On which process does the emphasis lie? Is writing part of the descent into experience?

**Q7. Comment on Blake as a social critic.**

Blake wrote in an era of great social and political upheaval. The democratic ideals of the French Revolution of 1789—the year of the first publication of Songs of Innocence—

undoubtedly influenced him. But in politics Blake aligned with no particular system or idealism; he speaks always for the primacy of the individual and the imagination. Blake did attach importance to particular social reforms: one might extrapolate some of these from a poem such as "London," depicting great suffering and oblivious social institutions, or one might consider Blake's use of the plights of innocent children in a whole range of poems such as "Holy Thursday." But a reading of Blake as social critic should always keep in mind the transcendent, humane values of the imagination and of the self unrestricted by narrow social convention; for these values formed the core of his moral code. This code stringently opposes an impersonal, conventional transcendence, and rejects the consolation of a life after this world—both of which are offered by the Church. See in particular the irony of "The Little Black Boy" for evidence of this last point.

**Q8. Compare and Contrast Blake's Songs as presentation of two different perspectives.**

Blake's Songs of Innocence and Experience (1794) juxtapose the innocent, pastoral world of childhood against an adult world of corruption and repression; while such poems as "The Lamb" represent a meek virtue, poems like "The Tyger" exhibit opposing, darker forces. Thus the collection as a whole explores the value and limitations of two different perspectives on the world. Many of the poems fall into pairs, so that the same situation or problem is seen through the lens of innocence first and then experience.

Blake does not identify himself wholly with either view; most of the poems are dramatic—that is, in the voice of a speaker other than the poet himself. Blake stands outside innocence and experience, in a distanced position from which he hopes to be able to recognize and correct the fallacies of both. In particular, he pits himself against despotic authority, restrictive morality, sexual repression, and institutionalized religion; his great insight is into the way these separate modes of control work together to squelch what is most holy in human beings.

The Songs of Innocence dramatize the naive hopes and fears that inform the lives of children and trace their transformation as the child grows into adulthood. Some of the poems are written from the perspective of children, while others are about children as seen from an adult perspective. Many of the poems draw attention to the positive aspects of natural human understanding prior to the corruption and distortion of experience. Others take a more critical stance toward innocent purity: for example, while Blake draws touching portraits of the emotional power of rudimentary Christian values, he also exposes—over the heads, as it were, of the innocent—Christianity's capacity for promoting injustice and cruelty.

The Songs of Experience work via parallels and contrasts to lament the ways in which the harsh experiences of adult life destroy what is good in innocence, while also articulating the weaknesses of the innocent perspective ("The Tyger," for example, attempts to account for real, negative forces in the universe, which innocence fails to confront). These latter poems treat sexual morality in terms of the repressive effects of jealousy, shame, and secrecy, all of which corrupt the ingenuousness of innocent love. With regard to religion, they are less concerned with the character of individual faith than with the institution of the Church, its role in politics, and its effects on society and the individual mind. Experience thus adds a layer to innocence that darkens its hopeful vision while compensating for some of its blindness.

The style of the Songs of Innocence and Experience is simple and direct, but the language and the rhythms are painstakingly crafted, and the ideas they explore are often deceptively complex. Many of the poems are narrative in style; others, like "The Sick Rose" and "The Divine Image," make their arguments through symbolism or by means of abstract concepts. Some of Blake's favourite rhetorical techniques are personification and the reworking of Biblical symbolism and language. Blake frequently employs the familiar meters of ballads, nursery rhymes, and hymns, applying them to his own, often unorthodox conceptions. This combination of the traditional with the unfamiliar is consonant with Blake's perpetual interest in reconsidering and reframing the assumptions of human thought and social behaviour.

**Q9. Critically Analyse of Blake's London.**

**Or**

**Q. What effects do the poem's insistent particularity and totality have - i.e. "charter'd," "mark," every"?**

**Or**

**Q. Why is the reference to prostitution the most significant one to the speaker, as we see from the last stanza?**

In the formal approach method to critical analysis, it is essential to read William Blake's "London" mechanically. Blake uses his rhetorical skills of alliteration, imagery, and word choice to create his poem, but more importantly to express the emotional significance that is implied.

William Blake's poem, "London", is obviously a sorrowful poem. In the first two stanzas, Blake utilizes alliteration and word choice to set the mournful atmosphere. Blake introduces his reader to the narrator as he "wanders" through the "chartered" society. A society in which every person he sees has "marks of weakness, marks of woe." Blake repeatedly uses the word "every" and "cry" in the second stanza to symbolize the depression that hovers over the entire society. The "mind-forged manacles" the narrator hears suggests that he is not mentally stable.

In the third stanza, Blake utilizes imagery of destruction and religion. This imagery is a paradox, which implies some religious destruction like the apocalypse. The "chimney-sweeper's cry" symbolizes the society trying to clean the ashes that causes their state of depression. Blake uses the religious imagery of the "black'ning church" to represent the loss of innocence, and the society's abandonment of religion. The use of the soldiers creates an imagery of war. The "hapless soldier's sigh" symbolize how men are drafted into war and have no choice but to serve their country. As these soldiers unwilling march to the beat of the country's forceful drum, they know their lives will be taken, as their "sigh runs in blood down palace walls." Blake uses this sense of destruction to explain how people are forced to repair the "weakness" and "woe" of their society.

The fourth stanza of "London" unravels the complex meaning of the poem. The "youthful harlot's curse" symbolizes how the youth's sinful deeds will effect the next generation. Their "curse" causes the "newborn infant's tear" which exemplifies how the new generation will have to correct the mistakes of the previous generation. The "plagues" also symbolizes this curse, and the "marriage hearse" creates a paradox, which confuses eternity and death.

William Blake's "London" is a poem about a society that is troubled by the mistakes of the generation before. Blake uses the rhetorical components of imagery, alliteration, and word choice to illustrate the meaning of the poem. What exactly does this poem mean? Blake creates complexity by using his rhetorical skills, which in turn opens up the poem for personal interpretation.

**Q10. William Blake's poems, "The Lamb" and "The Tyger," show two opposite extremes. Do you agree. Discuss**

William Blake's poems, "The Lamb" and "The Tyger," show two opposite extremes: the ultimate good and the contrasting evil aspects of human existence. The ideas of innocence and experience show the different views of creation. These differences can be seen through not only the meaning of the poem, but also through word choice and imagery.

The first images that appear to the reader come right from reading the title. Most people see a lamb as being a sweet, innocent animal. The poem describes the lamb as having "a tender voice" and being meek and mild. The lamb can do no harm. However, the tiger is a fierce and ferocious creature. Its "fearful symmetry" makes the animal seem so exotic. These two contrasting animals first set the mood for the poems.

When reading these two poems aloud, one can notice the differences in the two poems just by the sound of them. "The Lamb" has a singsong nursery rhyme cadence to it. The lines flow together very smoothly and calmly. A sense of innocence can be heard from this poem. However, even though both poems use couplets to create that sense of rhythm and continuity, the several questions that are asked in "The Tyger" makes is seem more demanding. The lines are still regular and rhyming, but unlike "The Lamb," the rhythm, as well as the consonants, is heavy.

This leads into word choice and how they sound. Good and evil are conflicting aspects of everyman's nature. Without this, innocence and experience, man is not whole. These two states have to deal with creation, which is shown in these poems.

In William Blake's Songs of Innocence and Experience, the gentle lamb and the dire tiger define childhood by setting a contrast between the innocence of youth and the experience of age. The Lamb is written with childish repetitions and a selection of words which could satisfy any audience under the age of five. Blake applies the lamb in representation of youthful immaculateness. The Tyger is hard-featured in comparison to The Lamb, in respect to word choice and representation. The Tyger is a poem in which the author makes many inquiries, almost chant like in their reiterations. The question at hand: could the same creator have made both the tiger and the lamb? For William Blake, the answer is a frightening one. The Romantic Period's affinity towards childhood is epitomized in the poetry of Blake's Songs of Innocence and Experience. "Little Lamb who made thee/ Do After more interrogation, the question evolves to "who could create such a villain of its potential wrath, and why?" William Blake's implied answer is "God. "Burnt the fire of thine eye (Blake 6)," and "What the hand dare seize the fire (Blake 7)?" are examples of how somber and serrated his language is in this poem. " The Lamb's introductory lines set the style for what follows: an innocent poem about a amiable lamb and it's creator. The Lamb, from

William Blake's Songs of Innocence and Experience is a befitting representation of the purity of heart in childhood, which was the Romantic period. The Lamb is written in the frame of mind of a Romantic, and The Tyger sets a divergent Hadean image to make the former more holy. Jesus Christ is often described as a lamb, and Blake uses lines such as "he is meek and he is mild (Blake 15)" to accomplish this. The stanza closes with the same inquiry which it began with. Experience asks questions unlike those of innocence. Innocence has not yet experienced fiery tigers in its existence, but when it does, it wants to know how lambs and tigers are supposed to co-exist. William Blake's words have turned from heavenly to hellish in the transition from lamb to tiger. According to Blake, God created all creatures, some in his image and others in his antithesis

**Q11. What is the child's role in relation to the piper? What does the child want the piper to do?**

**Or**

**Q. Might the line "I stain'd the water clear" be read in two different ways? If so, how?**

Criticism of Blake's "Introduction" to the Songs of Innocence has generally evolved along two separate, but not mutually exclusive strains of thought. One group of critics read the poem as Blake's commentary on the process of poetic creation, while another group insists that Blake is primarily concerned in the "Introduction" with illuminating the qualities of the state of innocence. And of course critics within each group produce contrary readings. Critics of the first group have found the "Introduction" to contain either Blake's affirmation of the communicative power of art, or his lamentation of it as an inherently limiting form. Critics of the second group have read the vision of innocence inscribed in the "Introduction" as either wholly untainted by experience, or already penetrated by it.

Both groups, however, read the "Introduction" as crucial to an understanding of Blake's larger poetic vision. For the former, what the poem reveals is nothing less than Blake's conception of the powers and limits of poetry and art. For many critics of the latter group, the "Introduction," by illuminating the qualities of the state of innocence, reveals how we are to read the songs which follow.

The summary which follows will examine the critical debate within these two strains of interpretation. However, rather than examining these two strains exclusive from one another, my summary will proceed more or less chronologically. In this way I hope both to avoid a reductive approach which would sacrifice a complete annotation of each critic's work for the sake of narrative coherence, and to avoid implying that these two strains of criticism are mutually exclusive of one another. Indeed, several critics bestride both groups, and several cannot be understood without some knowledge of what has come before.

The first critic to read the "Introduction" as a Blakean commentary upon the process of artistic creation, Joseph Wicksteed claims that Blake's "main interest" in the poem is putting into exact and expressive imagery his own experience as the singer of the songs which follow. Thus the piper's experience mirrors the experience Blake has undergone in composing the Songs of Innocence. The piper begins upon the "wild" earth, is lifted momentarily into direct intercourse with a heavenly vision (the "child" on the "cloud"), and finally returns to earth to sing a note of "joy." This movement symbolizes Blake's—or any other poet's—own creative process: first the poet amuses himself with his craft, then becomes inspired by artistic vision, and finally transforms this vision into material art. Thus the "Introduction" expresses "the theme of all Blake's greatest work": however one explores the realms of vision, one cannot remain there, and must return to earth.

Howard Justin also reads the "Introduction" as Blake's recognition of the increasing materialization and humanization of art, or "the descent of Innocence into the world with the contingent loss of ideality". For Justin, the poem is an elucidation of a single, necessarily ambiguous line, "And I stain'd the water clear," which should be glossed as both "by dipping my pen in the water, I stained it," and "I stained the water into clarity." Justin interprets the "pen" as art, and the "water" as nature; thus Blake is claiming that art leaves a blemish upon nature, and that art (though itself a blemish) stains nature into clarity. Material art, then, is both a corruption of "Ideal art"—which is symbolized by the "child" on the "cloud" who is himself "piping down the valleys"—and a transformative medium with the power to clarify existence.

In a direct response to Justin's reading, William Bowden asserts that the "Introduction" describes not the descent of ideal art into corrupted, material poetry, but the ascent inherent in the creative process: "it is not the disparagement of art, but a proud poetic credo". Bowden insists that it is Blake, not the "child," who opens the poem by "Piping down the valleys wild". Thus the evolution of the piper's song from pleasurable tune, to a song infused with specific meaning, to written verse addressed to "every child" symbolizes the creative process in which Blake (and every artist) participates. Blake recognizes that each artist bears a responsibility to compose not only work which is pleasurable, but work which is fraught with meaning. Moreover, this art must be disseminated and preserved for posterity, so that all "may joy to hear."

The first critic to read the "Introduction" as not primarily an exploration of the artist's creative process, but as an elucidation of the state of innocence, Margaret Giovannini claims that Blake consciously employs the style of ballad verse as well suited to his purpose: to introduce the songs which follow. Giovannini reads the "child" as a symbol of happy innocence who understands the "Lamb" only as the infant Christ, and not as the tragic figure of the crucifixion. For the child's state is one of innocence untainted by the tragic knowledge of experience; he, like all the children present in the Songs of Innocence, reflects a joy which issues from a perfectly innocent faith.

Robert Gleckner's reading of the poem both disputes the claim that the state illuminated exists free from the looming presence of experience, and affirms that Blake is graphically representing the process of artistic creation. Concluding that in the "Introduction" the "shadow of experience constantly impinges upon innocence," Gleckner finds in the child's thoughts of the "Lamb"—which symbolizes the Lamb of God, Christ—a vision of loveliness which is tinged with sorrow by knowledge of the crucifixion. This provides a hint that innocence is a temporary state, knowledge of which demands either a retreat to infantilism, or an advance to higher innocence through experience. In the final two stanzas—the "introduction proper to the Songs of Innocence"—the piper faces just such a choice when the child who inspires his song disappears: he may return to the state of selfish glee in which he opened the poem, or he may crystallize his vague feelings of change into a creative act. By composing the songs, the piper chooses creation: "the most divine act a human can perform".

Donald Dike also perceives in the state of innocence illuminated in the "Introduction" an intimation of the state of experience which must inevitably come to pass. The celebrations of innocence are never complete; they are always disturbed by a sense of vulnerability which anticipates the coming of the state of experience. Even in the "Introduction" there exists a "faint elegiac strain": a clue that the freedoms present in the state of innocence cannot long be imagined.

Unlike Dike, John Holloway does not perceive the world of innocence described in the "Introduction" as being threatened by the coming of experience, but as a "world of harmonious oneness". And unlike Justin, Holloway reads the line "And I stain'd the water clear" not as ambiguous, but as the line from which the poem's harmonious oneness springs. The phrase "the water" refers back to the child's tears; thus, since these tears issue from a cloud, they are also to be read as "joyous showers of rain". The poem's harmonious oneness, then, exists in the dual image Blake inscribes: the spiritual image of a poet singing to the presence of the divine (the child), and, "different but not different," the natural image of a springtime landscape containing lambs in meadows and rain-bearing clouds above.

Like Wicksteed, Justin, Bowden, and Gleckner before him, E.D. Hirsch reads the "Introduction" as a Blakean commentary upon the process of artistic creation. More specifically, Hirsch reads the poem as a symbolic account of the way Blake was inspired to compose the Songs of Innocence. In the poem Blake examines both the moment of religious and artistic expression, and the process of making poetry out of this inspiration. And, although C.M. Bowra had earlier claimed that Blake makes a distinction between the lyric poetry of the Songs, which the poet feels compelled to sing, and the visionary prophecies, which are the words of a prophet summoning his generation to new life, Hirsch views the "Introduction" as both lyric and prophecy. The poem's form is simple and lyrical, but its purpose is prophetic: to directly reveal the "joy" of artistic creation that is divinely inspired to all who "may joy to hear."

Heather Glen reads Blake's attitude toward artistic creation as more problematic: rather than simply being infused with a sensation of "joy" in the moment of creation, the poet experiences a dual sensation of loss and empowerment. In the "Introduction," Blake reveals that shaping a book involves abandoning a form of communication which is constantly changing and directly heard for one which is fixed and visible. The work becomes abstracted from real life, and spontaneity and face-to-face communication are lost. However, such abstraction allows the poet to address a wider audience—allows for a potentially joyful relationship with not one, but "every child." Thus art is not a reified object, but an agent which possesses the potential to stimulate the faculties of other children. This dual moment of artistic creation is neither a paradox nor a contradiction: both attitudes are part of a "coherent poetic vision" whose implications are worked out in the following Songs of Innocence.

Stanley Gardner discovers evidence for reading the "Introduction" as a Blakean commentary on the artistic process in the poem's design. The figures within the looping tendrils of the vines which frame the plate's text illuminate "the care, the instruction, the elation, thee good seed, the inspiration, the mechanics of publishing". Throughout the Songs of Innocence and of Experience, the illustrations often refer back to a condition which gave rise to the poem, or provides an alternative depiction of the proposition introduced in the poem. In the "Introduction" the design accomplishes the latter function. The text describes the ways in which a divine vision (the child) motivates communication and transforms the piper's "songs of pleasant glee" into something more profound; the design reveals, by its references to publishing, that the text can be read as a commentary on the process of poetic creation.

Claiming that the piper's unhesitating response to the cloud- borne child implies that adults have something to learn from children, Zachary Leader admonishes critics who would ignore the example of the sympathetic piper and approach the "Introduction" with the "adult's instinctive desire to anatomize or abstract or categorize" (a group which would certainly include those who read the poem as a Blakean commentary on artistic creation). Leader emphasizes the poem's dramatic context, and claims that a proper reading of the poem should begin on the literal level, and not with an examination of the symbolic meaning of the poem (for which he admonishes Gleckner). Read in this way, the child can be seen as divinely human, not a divine agent inspiring the human piper.

Harvey Birenbaum also takes issue with critics who would approach the "Introduction" with an eye toward analyzing its symbolic meaning. Birenbaum claims that the Songs of Innocence define innocence through the song process; that is, innocence is not just the subject of the verses, but each poem is itself an innocent song which is not to be read ironically. Read properly, the "Introduction" allows the reader to experience what it is like to adopt the persona of one in the state of innocence. Thus the reader becomes the voice of the song, and can ignore the ironic implications of certain clusters of words.

In his claim that the "Introduction" encourages its reader to abandon analysis and realise the perspective of one in the state of innocence, Birenbaum is anticipated by B.H. Fairchild. Although earlier Alice Ostriker had claimed that the meter of the "Introduction" provides enough slight variation to prevent sing- song monotony, Fairchild argues that the Songs of Innocence all contain "time meter" which is characteristic of many nursery rhymes. This submerged, insistent tempo pulls the reader closer to a "child-like, 'innocent' sensitivity which appeals to the child's ear within the adult ear". The last stanza especially evinces the pull of this temporal regularity.

Unlike Leader and Birenbaum, Edward Larrissy claims that with the vine-like designs which often frame the text of the Songs of Innocence, Blake is depicting the personas of the poems as limited, and thus they require an extra-textual level of interpretation to explain them. In the "Introduction," the staining of the water, the disappearance of the child (the source of the piper's vision), and the contrast between voice and writing all suggest that in writing down the songs the piper has corrupted the original inspiration of the idea. This could indicate that the state of innocence which this poem evinces— as well as introduces— has already fallen.

By contrast, Harold Bloom insists that the child who inhabits this region of innocence exists as one as yet wholly untainted by experience. As yet, the child has no conception of one of the defining characteristics of someone in the state of experience: self-consciousness. Rather, the child's pure reactions to the piper are those of the spirit "as yet undivided against itself," and the natural world which surrounds the child participates in this unity.

**Q12. On what style does the Blakean's poetry work?**

**Or**

**Q. Comment on the style and structure of Blake's poetry.**

Verily I say unto you, whosoever shall not receive the kingdom of God as a little child shall in no wise enter therein. [S Luke, 18 (17)] The words are those of Jesus, who was neither unaware of reality, nor indifferent to suffering. The childlike innocence referred to above is a state of purity and not of ignorance. Such is the vision of Blake in his childlike Songs of Innocence. It would be foolish to suppose that the author of ^Holy Thursday and ^The Chimney Sweeper in Songs of Innocence was insensible to the contemporary social conditions of orphans or young sweeps, and that therefore the poems of the same names in Songs of Experience are somehow apologies or retractions of an earlier misapprehension. For the language and style of Songs of Innocence are so consistently naïve compared to Songs of Experience, that it is clear that the earlier poems are a deliberate attempt to capture the state of grace described in the Biblical quotation above - a celebration of the triumph of innocence in a world of experience. Often the words of the poem are spoken by a child. It would be impossible to imagine a modern child using language such as:

Gave thee such a tender voice, making all the vales rejoice.

And it is most unlikely that children spoke thus even in Blake's day.

Yet this is the language of children's hymns. I was personally acquainted with all the words in The Lamb, through Sunday school hymns, long before reaching school age. By using the vocabulary of the hymnals, Blake emphasizes for us the connection of which the child is instinctively aware:

I, a child, and thou a lamb, we are called by his name.

The syntax and tone, however, have the authentic simplicity of children speech. The first verse is a series of questions addressed to the lamb. The second stanza begins with the child triumph at being able to answer those questions:

Little Lamb, I'll tell thee.

Typically the questions are asked purely for the satisfaction it gives the child in answering. There is a great deal of repetition in all the songs: in The Lamb this takes the form of a refrain repeated at the beginning and the end of each stanza, once more reminiscent of children hymns. In contrast,

^The Tiger has an incantatory rhythm, far more like a pagan chant than a childish hymn. And the vocabulary is no longer within the understanding of a child:

What immortal hand or eye could frame thy fearful symmetry?

This song also asks questions. But in the world of experience, unlike the world of innocence, there are no longer any reassuring answers. The world of Innocence is a world of confident answers; in Experience the answers remain. Indeed, the questions themselves become more threatening. The slightly incredulous question above alters subtly during the progress of the poem until the word could is finally replaced by the far more menacing dare. There is no such progression in Songs of Innocence. Each song captures the moment in each day that Satan cannot find [Milton, II, Pl.35, 1.42]. Blake's innocence does not develop: it exists.

If we compare Songs of Innocence with Songs of Experience we see that this pattern is constantly repeated. The moment that the concept of Experience is introduced the simplicity of the language disappears. As affirmation gives way to doubt, the unquestioning faith of innocence becomes the intellectual argument of experience. In Infant Joy the baby is free even of the bonds of a name. In Cradle Song it is the Mother who speaks, not with the simplicity of infant joy yet with a Naiveté emphasized by the repetition of key alliterative words -Sweet/sleep/smile - with their connotations of joy. In Songs of Innocence moans are sweet and dove like [Cradle song] whereas in Songs of Experience the babies cry in fear [London].

In Songs of Innocence the narrative is as simple as the direct speech. The verbs are straightforward and unambiguous; God Appeared, He Kissed the child, led him to his mother. And although the bleaker Side of life is portrayed - poverty and discrimination for example - the overall vision is positive.

Blake believed that without contraries there could be no progression. In Songs of Experience we see Blake ^Walking naked, to use Yeats phrase, as he shouts angrily against social evils and religious manacles and hypocrisy. Songs of Innocence are far more carefully controlled, for all their apparent artlessness. In Songs of Innocence Blake's voice never falters: the language is consistently naïve, and when images of a less childlike nature do intrude they are always absorbed into the security that is innocence. Innocence is a state of faith that must preclude doubt. Blake's language is naïve and unambiguous. It is deliberately adopted to suit the subject and discarded later in the prophetic books. He may have considered experience as a necessary part of life, but Blake remained, supremely, a poet of Innocence.

**Q13. Blake's poetry carries a modern day message.**

**Or**

**Q. State the importance of Blake in today's world.**

William Blake, who lived in the latter half of the eighteenth century and the early part of the nineteenth, was a profoundly stirring poet who was, in large part, responsible for bringing about the Romantic movement in poetry; was able to achieve "remarkable results with the simplest means"; and was one of several poets of the time who restored "rich musicality to the language".His research and introspection into the human mind and soul has resulted in his being called the "Columbus of the psyche," and because no language existed at the time to describe what he discovered on his voyages, he created his own mythology to describe what he found there (Damon ix). He was an accomplished poet, painter, and engraver.

Blake scholars disagree on whether or not Blake was a mystic. In the Norton Anthology, he is described as "an acknowledged mystic, [who] saw visions from the age of four" (Mack 783). Frye, however, who seems to be one of the most influential Blake scholars, disagrees, saying that Blake was a visionary rather than a mystic. "'Mysticism'... means a certain kind of religious techniques difficult to reconcile with anyone's poetry," says Frye (Frye 8). He next says that "visionary" is "a word that Blake uses, and uses constantly" and cites the example of Plotinus, the mystic, who experienced a "direct apprehension of God" four times in his life, and then only with "great effort and relentless discipline." He finally cites Blake's poem "I rose up at the dawn of day," in which Blake states,

> I am in God's presence night & day,
>
> And he never turns his face away (Frye 9).

Besides all of these achievements, Blake was a social critic of his own time and considered himself a prophet of times to come. Frye says that "all his poetry was written as though it were about to have the immediate social impact of a new play" (Frye 4). His social criticism is not only representative of his own country and era, but strikes profound chords in our own time as well. As Appelbaum said in the introduction to his anthology English Romantic Poetry, "[Blake] was not fully rediscovered and rehabilitated until a full century after his death" (Appelbaum v). For Blake was not truly appreciated during his life, except by small cliques of individuals, and was not well-known during the rest of the nineteenth century (Appelbaum v).

Blake lived during a time of intense social change. The American Revolution, the French Revolution, and the Industrial Revolution all happened during his lifetime. These changes gave Blake a chance to see one of the most dramatic stages in the transformation of the Western world from a somewhat feudal, agricultural society to an industrial society where philosophers and political thinkers such as Locke, Franklin, and Paine championed the rights of the individual. Some of these changes had Blake's approval; others did not.

One example of Blake's disapproval of changes that happened in his time comes in his poem "London," from his work Songs of Experience. In "London," which has been described as summing up many implications of Songs of Experience, Blake describes the woes that the Industrial Revolution and the breaking of the common man's ties to the land have brought upon him (Mack 785). For instance, the narrator in "London" describes both the Thames and the city streets as "chartered," or controlled by commercial interests; he refers to "mind-forged manacles"; he relates that every man's face contains "Marks of weakness, marks of woe"; and he discusses the "every cry of every Man" and "every Infant's cry of fear." He connects marriage and death by referring to a "marriage hearse" and describes it as "blighted with plague." He also talks about "the hapless Soldier's sigh" and the "youthful Harlot's curse" and describes "blackening Churches" and palaces running with blood ("London").

"London" and many of Blake's other works dealing with a similar theme, particularly those from the Songs of Experience, strike a particular nerve for those who are living in a society where the cost of living compared with income is steadily increasing, where AIDS, Ebola, and other new and frightening diseases are becoming increasingly common, and where the public is becoming increasingly disillusioned about the reliability and trustworthiness of politicians. These works resonate for a generation which has to deal with exponentially increasing population problems and with rapidly increasing demands on our immigration facilities and resources. They strike a special chord with a nation that, due to the aforementioned problems, the rise of violent crime, and other considerations, is rapidly desensitizing itself to the "marks of weakness, marks of woe" that we are becoming accustomed to seeing on the faces of passers-by on the street.

Blake did, however, approve of some of the measures that individuals and societies took to gain and maintain individual freedom. As Appelbaum said, "He was liberal in politics, sensitive to the oppressive government measures of his day, [and] favourably inspired by the American Revolutionary War and the French Revolution" (Appelbaum v). According to Keynes, Blake wrote many positive and appreciative things about the revolutionary American political thinker Thomas Paine, for instance, such as "The Bishop never saw the Everlasting Gospel any more than Tom Paine" (Damon 318). As "London" shows, however, Blake did not entirely approve of the measures taken to forward the causes he longed to advance: "London" refers to how the "hapless Soldier's sigh/ runs in blood down Palace walls" ("London" 791). Among many other events which took place during the French Revolution, this could possibly refer to the storming of the Bastille or the executions of the French nobility.

Blake also espoused many other notions with which we are now familiar, and occasionally even believe to be self-evident. For instance, in Jerusalem, Blake proposes the Brotherhood of Man as the only solution to the world's problems, both individual and international (Damon 60). According to Blake, we are all brothers because we are all sons of the Father, and all have Jesus (who often symbolizes Imagination, Humanity, and the source of everything for Blake) in us (Damon 60; Damon 158-159). This is very similar to the fundamental rights of man espoused in the Declaration of Independence, which states that "all men are created equal" because they are "endowed by their Creator with certain unalienable Rights" (Declaration 10-20).

Blake also believed that all life was inherently holy; Damon says that his religion "became all-inclusive when he declared that every thing that lives is holy. This was a natural conclusion from the ancient belief that all things were created from the divine substance" (344). This becomes especially important and vital to us in an age where terrorist attacks are becoming increasingly common (witness the bombings at the 1996 Olympics in Atlanta and the Oklahoma City building and increased security on international airline flights), the debate over abortion has led some anti-abortion activists to begin shooting doctors who perform abortions (such as the shooting of Dr. David L. Gunn in 1993), and the major nations of the world have nuclear weapons enough to kill every person on the earth multiple times. Blake's views on religion are also particularly relevant to the modern world.

As Appelbaum said of Blake, "Blake replaced the arid atheism or tepid deism of the encyclopedias and their disciples with a glowing new personal religion" (Appelbaum iii). Besides rejecting "arid atheism" and "tepid deism," Blake also attacked conventional religion. In The Marriage of Heaven and Hell he wrote "Prisons are built with stones of Law, Brothels with bricks of Religion" and "As the caterpillar chooses the fairest leaves to lay her eggs on, so the priest lays his curse on the fairest joys" ("Proverbs" 19; "Proverbs" 20). Rather than accepting a traditional religion from an organized church, Blake designed his own mythology (based primarily upon the Bible and Greek mythology) to accompany his personal, revealed religion.

Blake's personal religion was an outgrowth of his search for the Everlasting Gospel, which he believed to be the original, pre-Jesus revelation which Jesus preached. As Blake said, "all had originally one language and one religion: this was the religion of Jesus, the everlasting Gospel. Antiquity preaches the Gospel of Jesus" (Damon 344). Blake's religion was based upon the joy of man, which he believed glorified God (Damon 344). One of Blake's strongest objections to orthodox Christianity is that it encourages the suppression of natural desires and discourages earthly joy; in A Vision of the Last Judgment, Blake says that "Men are admitted into Heaven not because they have curbed & governed their Passions or have No Passions, but because they have Cultivated their Understandings.

The Treasures of Heaven are not Negations of Passion, but Realities of Intellect, from which all the Passions Emanate Uncurbed in their Eternal Glory" (Damon 344). Blake also believes that the religion of this world is actually the worship of the entity that St. Paul calls "the god of this world" in II Corinthians 4:4: Satan. It should be noted here that Blake does not conceive of Satan as an incarnate horned quasi-deity, but rather as Error and the "State of Death"; Blake also explicitly says that Satan is "not a Human existence" (Damon 355).

Blake believes that orthodox Christians, in part because of their denial of earthly joy, are actually worshiping Satan, which is to say that they are in Error (Damon 344-345; Damon xi). Since the 1960s, more and more Westerners have joined faith movements which promote individuals deciding on their own ethics and beliefs, or to find their own way to salvation. Examples of these groups include some Eastern religions, such as Buddhism, and certain liberal Christian movements, such as Unitarian-Universalism (which can also be a non-Christian faith, depending on the individual follower). As more people begin to question traditional, dogmatic Western religion, Blake's vision of individual revelation and a personal mythology makes powerful sense to many people.

Blake cautions us, however, against deluding ourselves with our personal mythologies in his poem "The Little Black boy" from Songs of Experience. In "Black Boy," Blake describes a young black male, who is just becoming aware of the societal differences between himself and a white boy ("English child") and uses his mother's mythology (which he makes his own) to relegate the solution of the problems of racism to an imagined afterlife where

I'll shade him from the heat till he can bear

To lean in joy upon our father's knee (Mack.

Even more compelling to a modern audience (but definitely less important to Blake) is his emphasis upon science as a tool of understanding. The last line of his unfinished epic poem The Four Zoas is "the dark Religions are departed & sweet Science reigns" (Damon xi). Many modern individuals would accept science while failing to attempt to create a personal mythology, and this is not at all what Blake is looking for.

Does Blake provide a solution to the ills of this world? Is this solution as relevant to modern times as it was to his own? Emphatically, yes to both questions. The similarities between our own age and Blake's are striking. Blake had the Industrial Revolution; we are living in the age of the Information Revolution, which is, with the Internet, entering a new phase which will enable information to be distributed on a scale never before possible. Blake lived in a time when greedy upper-class capitalists exploited the working class for personal profit; we are living in an age in which the nuclear family, with its one working parent and its one parent staying at home to raise the children, is becoming less common and feasible even as the cost of living rises.

Blake lived in an age where Deism, a faith which denied any possibility of direct experience with God, had captured the minds of the more intelligent people of the West; we live in an age of doubt, searching, rejection of traditional dogmatic religion, and science with no mystical experience. Certainly Blake's vision of a personal mythology actualizing an individual, revealed religion can offer as much to our society as it did to Blake's. However, whether Blake's offering will save our television-oriented, fast-food, pop-culture society is another question altogether.

**Q14. Comment on "The Different Faces of God" as presented by William Blake**

As a child Blake had no formal schooling. He was apprenticed at the age of fourteen by engraver James Basire. In 1779 he began studies at The Royal Academy of Arts, but it was as a journeyman engraver that he was to make his living. When Blake was engraving his own designs, the general public envied him because they were not as creative as he was.

Most of Blake's support came from a small group of artists and friends. Throughout his life booksellers employed Blake to engrave illustrations for a wide variety of publications. Blake printed much of his poetry himself by using engraving methods he created. His method was to produce the text and illustrations for his books on copper plates. His greatest work as an engraver was his series of twenty-one illustrations to the Book of Job that was commissioned by his friend John Linnell. During the twentieth century Blake was one of the greatest engravers since the Renaissance.

During his lifetime, Blake's work received very little attention, and most of his poetry was never published. When his work was noticed the readers viewed Blake as weird, confused, or mad. One of the purposes of Blake's art was to change the way people " see " and to open up new worlds to them "one continued vision" of what had once been ordinary and common, but would become "imagination itself". To Kathleen Raine "William Blake is the only English poet whose central theme is the confrontation of imagination". Blake's most famous statement about his art is " I will create a system or be enslaved by another man 's". Blake also provided illustrations for most of his poems. William Blake first published the Songs of Innocence in 1789.

In 1794, these songs and the Songs of Experience were issued together in one volume, with a title page promising a demonstration of " the two Contrary States of the Human Soul". According to Blake's nineteenth-century biographer Alexander Gilchrist, " the poet and his wife did everything in making the book (Songs of Innocence)- writing, designing, printing, engraving- everything except manufacturing the paper...Never before surely was a man so literally the author of his own book" (Gilchrist). The state of "Innocence" is of genuine love and naive trust toward all humankind, accompanied by unquestioned belief in Christian doctrine. The state of "Experience" is the profound disillusionment with human nature and society.

In selected poems by William Blake, he explores two different sides of God as represented in the creation of a tiger, a lamb, and a fly. In " The Tiger", William Blake explains that there's more that meets the eye when one examines the Creator and his creation, the tiger. In "The Lamb", Blake explains that God can be like a child meek and innocent. In " The Fly", Blake questions the nature of God with his creation of the fly.

In "The Tyger," William Blake explains that there is more that meets the eye when one examines the Creator and his creation, the tiger. The persona is never defined. All throughout the poem the persona questions the Creator of the tiger to determine if the Creator is demonic or godlike. The poem reflects primarily the persona's response to the tiger, rather than the tiger 's response to the world. The persona is curious about the location of the Creator of the tiger when he says, " In what distant deeps or skies". In this quote the persona is trying to figure out where exactly the Creator is located He wants to know if he's in Hell or in Heaven. The words deeps or skies could have many meanings. According to Inder Nath Kher "...The images of "deeps" and "skies" indicate usual theological expressions for Hell and Heaven...This leads to the ambiguity of 'the double/ness of the tiger', and it suggests that either God or the Devil, or both, could have been responsible for Creation". The persona is also wondering what does the Creator looks like when he says, " And what shoulder, and what art,/ Could twist the sinews of thy heart?".

These lines speak of the power and strength of the tiger, and of its maker. Shoulders and art both carry responsibilities and burdens and sinews are the tendons that make the heart work, and they are also known as a source of strength and power. So if God is the Creator, he is a strong and powerful force. Also Inder Nath Kher agrees that the Creator must be a powerful force he says, " The Creator is shown to be the strongest of creatures and the greatest of artists...It is only He who can 'twist the sinews' of the heart of His Creation". He's simply referring to God as the Creator when he use the word He this is a word for Christ or God.

Because of the magnificence of God's creation the reader learns that the creator is omnipotent. Blake may have done this to get the reader to think who did make the tiger, " As so many of Blake's lyrics, part of the poem's strategy is to resist attempts to imprint meaning upon it 'The Tyger' tempts us to a cognitive apprehension but in the end exhaust our efforts" (McCann).

There's more than one answer to this question. If the reader was a religious person they would know that God created every living creature on this world including the tiger. So the answer to them would be that God created the tiger. The reader will also come to that conclusion from this quote, " Did he who made the Lamb make thee?". As the reader read this paper one will learn that the Creator in the poem "The Lamb" is God so the reader will know that the Creator of the tiger could be the same Creator as that of the lamb. Derek Furr writes, " On one hand this is a reference to the God of the Bible; but on the other, it could be a reference to Blake himself...Surely, the poem is as awe-inspiring as it is ambiguous." One that is of no religion would think other wise or maybe one wouldn't care who made the tiger.

Blake uses literary devices such as symbols, and imagery to develop his theme. Blake's style of writing in " The Tyger" contains six four-line stanzas, and uses pairs of rhyming couplets to create a sense of rhythm and continuity throughout the poem. The majority of the lines in this poem contain exactly seven syllables, alternating between stress and unstressed syllables (Poetry for Students).

An example from the poem is, "Tyger! Tyger! burning bright", the Ty, burn, and right is the stressed syllables and the rest of the word is unstressed this pattern is known as trochaic tetrameter. A trochaic tetrameter is four pairs of stressed and unstressed syllables even though the final trochee lacks the unstressed syllable. A trochee is one stressed syllable followed by one unstressed syllable. Derek Furr writes, "Strung together, trochees sound like a chant...Blake drops the unstressed syllable from the last foot of each line. We're stopped in our tracks, as it were, held in suspense-just as Blake's questions hold us in suspense". Another example of a trochee is, "In the forests of the night". This style of writing makes the poem exciting to read, it gets the readers attention. This style show how different Blake is from other poets during that time.

Blake uses symbols to express the strength of the tiger and its Creator. The main symbol in "The Tyger" is the tiger itself, "The tiger is formed on anvil of inspiration which is the eye of man and God, but it is also a symbol of the very same eye which created it" (Adams). A tiger is a large Asian carnivorous mammal of the cat family or a fierce, daring, or aggressive person or quality. The word "fire" is used to illustrate the aggressive personality of the tiger, "Burnt the fire of thine eyes?". The fire can be used to describe the way the tiger sees and is seen by other people. When a person see or come in contact with a tiger the person gets tense right away because one know that one false move the tiger may attack. This example shows how destructive/aggressive the tiger can be just like a wild fire. The Creator could also be described as a destructive person too because what kind of person would make an aggressive animal.

This might be a representation of himself. According to Inder Nath Kher "the symbol of fire is dominant in the structure of the poem...To know the source of the 'fire' is to know the origin of the Creator." Blake relates the tigers environment to one during the Industrial Revolution when he says, "What the hammer? What the chain?/ In what furnace was thy brain?". This symbolizes what Blake's childhood was like to him. It was like an industrial factory and that the tiger's thinking and his creation began in a furnace. This is so because when Blake wrote this poem it was during the French Revolution that was a time of suffering for so many people. Blake is interpreting his environment through the tigers environment.

Blake uses good choice of words to place an image in the reader's mind. Blake starts off the poem by making the tiger seem like it is glowing: "Tyger! Tyger! burning bright".The word "bright" gives the reader a picture of a tiger walking through the forest with a ray a light hovering over its body. Bright is a good word to picture a tiger most people wouldn't use the word bright to explain the image of a tiger but that's how Blake sees it. The word bright could also be the amount of energy the tiger has. The tiger's energy could be so strong that it has to shine out to the world. According to Mark Schorer, " Energy can be curbed but it cannot be destroyed, and when it reaches the limits of its endurance, it burst forth in revolutionary wrath". The reader can picture how the tiger comes to life, "And when thy heart began to beat,/What dread hand? and what dread feet?" (11-12). The tiger has a life of its own. The reader can picture the tiger taking its first steps into his destructive lifestyle.

In " The Lamb," William Blake explains that God can be like a child, meek and innocent. The young boy in this poem questions who made the lamb and he compares his characteristics to this Creator. The fact that the persona questions who makes the lamb confirms the existence of a single, powerful, inspiring creator one who dares to produce both the tiger and the lamb. The persona in this poem is a child who wants to know if God is like a lamb when he says, " He is meek, and he is mild/ He became a little child./ I a child, and thou a lamb". When one thinks of a child they see someone who is meek, pure, and unclear of the world. So a child is like a lamb someone who stands for purity. In this poem the young boy is explaining that God consider himself to be like a lamb, innocent and meek when he says, " He is called by thy name,/ For he calls himself a Lamb" (13-14). A person would never know that God has different faces until one really understands who God is and what he is capable of doing.

Blake use literary devices to further explain who the lamb represents in the poem. In "The Lamb" the lamb is symbolic of Christ, the Son of God, " The lamb human form is achieved by the conventional figure of Christ as a lamb " (Adams). The lamb also symbolizes the meek and innocent side of God when Blake writes, " For He calls himself a Lamb ". In comparison with the poem "The Tyger" this poem was written to show that God can be fierce and meek at the same time. Another symbol in the poem could be the word bright, " Softest clothing, wooly, bright; ". The word bright in " The Tyger " was used to bring out the energy that the tiger has and it was used to describe the aggressiveness of the tiger. In " The Lamb " the brightness of the lamb is one of purity itself, " The effect of bright in " The Lamb " is less dramatic" (Adams). Like when one see an angel on TV there's always a light around them cause an angel is a sign of pureness/holiness and that's just what the lamb symbolizes. Bright is also what closes the gap between the lamb and the tiger.

From Blake's diction, the setting is somewhere quiet like countryside. Blake use words to suggest that it's a countryside,

" By the stream and o'er the mead".When one picture a stream and a mead (meadow) one can imagine someplace peaceful where the grass is green and it's just that person and nature surrounding them. Plus where else would a lamb be besides on a field in the country with his master. Another quote that suggests that the setting is in the country is, " Making all the vales rejoice ".In these lines the word rejoice can be the lambs surroundings coming to a state of peace whenever the lamb is in its presence. Nature is accepting the presence of the lamb. According to Adams, the lamb's surrounding has some human aspects, " The lamb's surroundings are not natural they are human. The vales are alive, and the lamb's voice speaks to them" (Adams). Adams could be right but the lamb's environment could also be natural too so one can look at it from both perspective.

In "The Fly," Blake questions the nature of God with his creation of the fly. The persona is comparing himself to man and a fly, " Am not I/ A fly like thee" (5-6). The persona want to know if he is useless to people just like a fly is in the world. This can also be a referral to how people see God sometimes as an insignificance role in their life. The persona also wonder's if he is a man when he say's, " Or art not thou/ A man like me?" (7-8). The persona is confused about what and who he wants to be either he is a fly or man.

The reader/persona learns that to him he is a fly. The persona says, " Then am I/ A happy fly," (17-18) the persona is simply saying that he is a fly and that his significance in the world is not important to others. But the persona is happy like that until he dies, " If I live/ Or if I die" (19-20). Even though the persona doesn't play a big part in the world he's happy, that's how he wants it to be. The reader might ask why he wants to be considered a fly, maybe that's the only animal that the persona like and he's fascinated with it. When one is fascinated with an object one sometimes long to see what it's like in their life.

Literary devices also play a part in "The Fly". Blake uses personification to give the fly more life when he says, "For I dance/ And drink & sing" (9-10). When one think of a fly they can't imagine a fly dancing or singing instead they would see a human figure rather than this fly. But one could say that the dancing could be the flight/flying of the fly moving from place to place around the world.

The singing could be the buzzing noise that the fly makes, that could be the fly way of making music. Another use of personification is when the persona says, " And strength and breath ". Blake make the fly seem like it's powerful when he writes "strength" when one thinks of a fly they see a little insect with no type of strength. So how can a fly have strength, according to Hazard Adams, " It is not a direct perception that causes the speaker to find human form in the fly, but a deeper sense of the relatedness of their fates in nature". To Blake the fly has human like qualities unknown to man.

From Blake's diction the setting is a nice day during the summer. From the poem, " Thy summer's play " the word summer makes the reader believe that it's during the summer time and the children is outside having a nice time playing with friends. Blake place this poem during the summer time to give the reader a sense of relaxation or to give the poem more life to it. The persona give the reader that summer is a time to have fun and hang out when he say's, " For I dance/ And drink & sing ". The reader can picture a family or just a group of people having a cookout with music playing and everyone is just having fun dancing and drinking punch.

The overall perspective in Blake's poems is to show the reader that God can be powerful and meek as shown in " The Tyger " and " The Lamb ". Blake doesn't just question the strength of God but his weakness as well. Blake is one of the people who saw visions and devoted his life to worshiping God with his poetry and art, to him the world was filled with symbols. Blake gave each of his symbols a deep meaning that even his contemporaries could not understand. In these three poems the reader learns that God created the tiger, the lamb, the fly and everything else that's on this earth. When one gets to understand the poems one will find out that God has different personalities, Blake just writes about two of those personalities. Blake also gets the reader to learn how one can go from a state of innocence to a state of experience. During one's lifetime, one learns and experience new and different things therefore one becomes more aware of what's going on around them. Derek Furr writes, "

We are all born innocents, but when we begin to recognize evil or wrong, and are inevitably tempted by it, we pass into a state of experience..." (Furr). What really make Blake a unique writer is that most of his poems is express what he felt or experienced during the French Revolution. From this experience Blake published the poem " The Tyger" in the Songs of Innocence and of Experience. Blake is also unique in his style of writing his style is one of confusion but that's what makes reading it enjoyable he gets the reader to think about life through his words.

The one thing that make Blake different is that most of his poems is centreed around his faith in God. Blake was a man of creativity one that was widely misunderstood by society. To make poems about the faces of God is truly wonderful. He demonstrates to the world that as a writer he understands some of the faces of God.

**Q15. Songs of Experience challenges conventional thinking in the poetry of William Blake**

**Or**

**Q. Discuss the criticism of dominant middle-class thought that William Blake presents in Songs of Experience.**

In this essay will be discussed, context of my vague understanding of late eighteenth- and early nineteenth-century society in Britain, the criticism of dominant middle-class thought that William Blake presents in Songs of Experience. I understand that perhaps less than thirty copies of this were ever printed in Blake's lifetime, so any challenge to contemporary conventional thinking was largely unheard, but this does not invalidate exploring the social conditions and attitudes that provoke the poems. I would then like to discuss some of Blake's grander challenges to conventional thought and, in particular, the received truths of orthodox religion as put forth in The Marriage of Heaven and Hell. Here we find not only a challenge to conventional thought, but also a challenge to sanity, and I found it to be the case that after reading and re-reading, just when the poem appears to come into focus and some understanding is reached, the very line which seemed sensible becomes insane, and meaning is lost. This by no means detracts from the worth of the poem, and could be said to be its very argument: that my doors are in need of cleansing.

The latter half of the eighteenth-century saw increased antagonism between the upper classes, which believed the lower classes had become riotous and unruly, and the lower classes, which were questioning the authority of the upper classes to keep them in subservience. With the government playing a diminishing role in the economy, and since only wealthy landholders could elect Members of Parliament, the chief concern of the state was the consolidation of property. 'The great and chief end,' said John Locke, 'of men uniting into commonwealths, and putting themselves under government, is the preservation of their property.'

Between 1688 and 1810, parliament added around two hundred capital offences against property. The attitude towards the poor was generally that they were lazy, and so it was harsh treatment that was needed to solve poverty. So, only those wearing a 'P' for pauper could receive charity and workhouses were established to hide the poor from sight. Of over two thousand children who entered London workhouses between 1750-55, perhaps ninety percent died there, and an extreme example of the treatment of children was the hanging of a seven-year old girl for theft.

Growing prosperity amongst the middle class gave rise to a 'culture of comfort', and a desire for privacy and social segregation. The defining character of social order, as they saw it, was that 'nursery of virtue', the family, and the rising standard of living encouraged the development of concepts of 'childhood' and 'adolescence'. We see in Blake's Songs of Experience the spotlight cast on those who could not afford these ideas, who could not afford virtue and respectability. In 'Holy Thursday', Blake laments that a nation as rich as his should be so miserly and lacking in compassion:

Is this a holy thing to see, In a rich and fruitful land, Babes reduced to misery, Fed with cold and usurous hand? (1-4)Here, we have the mild suggestion that the rich are acting irreligiously. As Blake goes on, criticism of middle class virtue become more vigourous, as do his attacks on the established church.

"They think they have done me no injury: And are gone to praise God & his Priest & King Who make up a heaven of our misery." ('The Chimney Sweeper', 10-12)

Now, although there was, in the legacy of the Enlightenment, a cynicism towards organized religion, there was nevertheless an increase in religious practice amongst all social classes in the eighteenth-century. And, also, the virtue of Christian morality was never in question. Observation of religious practices and Christian morality endowed the middle classes with a sense of self-worth. It was a method of achieving nobility without a title, since they reasoned that it was not in status, but in virtuousness that nobility resided.

We can see these views propagated and reflected in the work of Jane Austen. There was a move to instill these middle class sensibilities into the working class, and John Wesley (1703-1791) preached a populist sermon on the equality of man before God. He aimed to teach the working class of the virtues of abstinence from vice, and the propriety of hard work. There was a move in the Church of England to indoctrinate the workers-especially children, with Sunday schools where food was provided for the poor. Of course, under this guise of do-Gooding, the real achievement of this all was to teach subservience, and respect for one's social superiors.

Blake's Songs of Experience really do pose a challenge to all the middle classes hold as virtuous, and what they consider to be the underpinning of all society. They expose the rottenness of imposing a set of rules upon a class of people, which have the effect of robbing them of any little pleasure they might have in an already tough life.

The Little Vagabond makes light of this point in his endearing wish that 'the Church... would give us some Ale, / and a pleasant fire, our souls to regale...' ('The Little Vagabond', 5-6), but it is a poignant exclamation of the vile cultural imperialism to which they are subjected. Blake returns to the point in The Marriage of Heaven and Hell, when he states 'One Law for the Lion and Ox is Oppression,' (Plate 24) and in the 'Proverbs of Hell', The apple tree never asks the beech how he shall grow, or the lion the horse how he shall take his prey Although the language used throughout the Songs is one of innocent sentimentality, and one that encourages sympathy and pity (the most challenging of these in 'London', where Blake would have the reader feel pity for a prostitute), 'The Human Abstract' puts forth that it is not the pity of the reader he wishes for. Pity would be no more, If we did not make somebody Poor: And Mercy would no more be, If all were happy as we; (1-4).

Pity and mercy, it is suggested, are inventions of the rich to affirm their position in society. How could they be bad people if they feel such compassion for those worse off? In fact, they reason, it is precisely because they have such a capacity for human emotion and virtuous thoughts that they are above the common, vulgar classes. It is in these ways that Blake subtly challenges religious ideology, aiming to persuade and influence the reader, rather than engaging in an indignant, all out attack on conventional sensibility.

I think that a problem with Blake's work, here particularly The Marriage of Heaven and Hell, is that it is hard to criticize it. Apart from his apocalyptic use of language, and his persistent abstinence from any elucidation of ideas so that any intended meaning of his is always questionable, he includes many Freudian loopholes that ensure he cannot be proven wrong. When he states that 'a fool sees not the same tree that a wise man sees,' ('Proverbs of Hell', 8) he is surely saying that if his work looks, to you, madness then it could be you are a fool. And, 'Listen to the fool's reproach! It is a kingly title!' While definitely having elements of truth in these observations, if we consider them as a defence of his work, this surely rings of Emperor's New Clothes Syndrome, does it not?

This is, then, perhaps Blake's most challenging proposition, since it cannot be reasoned with and requires a blind faith and firm persuasion that you are the wise man and not the fool. It is impossible to tell, other than by being judged against common-sense, since 'Man by his reasoning power can only compare & judge of what he has already perceived.' But it is this type of perception that Blake challenges. So, it can be seen that this is a very difficult idea to reconcile with modern thought, one that requires we give ourselves up entirely to a belief that cannot be proven.

That is, a religious belief. Blake obviously does not see this as similar to the blind faith and received truths of the church, because it is blind faith in our own imagination that he stresses-not acceptance of others' beliefs. I cannot put faith in something that can never be proven or disproved, and see such behaviour as leading only to insanity. Again, Blake's argument is such that this statement can be turned against me. Perhaps some argument can be made against Blake on the grounds that imagination is definitely organic, and of the body, and is in no way a portal to the infinite universe, which I believe, though I cannot give this argument.

In There is No Natural Religion, Blake dismisses that idea, still beloved by many today, of common sense. He recognizes that morality is not absolute truth, but received in education-this coming from the church-and tells us that 'Reason, or the ratio of what we have already known is not the same that it shall be when we know more,' (b, II) so, that which seems reasonable today may not tomorrow. Slavery, of course, is a good example. He persuasively argues that we cannot rely on our five bodily senses, on the grounds that: if we did not have, for example, a sense of smell, we would never know of the existence of smell; it does not follow that because we cannot sense it, it does not exist. This is challenging in its implications, yet perfectly valid. He goes on to state that since men are capable of experience other than the purely physical, that is, spiritual, then perception must not and is not limited to (bounded by) that of the five senses. Imagination is the perception of infinite capacity, and 'He who sees the Infinite in all things sees God.' (Application, p. 15) This is the idea Blake would expand on greatly in The Marriage.

Blake begins his Argument with a bold statement: that, in the traditional sense at least, there is no Good and Evil; these terms do not exist in the sense that one is the aim of mankind, while the other should be eliminated. The two are 'contraries', and 'Without Contraries is no progression.' (Plate 3)

Goodness, we are taught, is Reason, restriction, and passivity. Evil is Energy, physical desire, and activity. Reason is Heaven. Energy is Hell. Blake challenges this with a magnificently vivid symbolization of the true natures of Reason and Energy. Reason, virtue in abstinence, is not of the soul while Energy is earthly temptation. Both are, in fact, of the body. Energy is the very driving force of life, 'is the only life... and Reason is the bound or outward circumference of Energy.' (Plate 4) The image is that of a sphere of Energy, surrounding man, and encased in Reason.

This accompanies his statement, in There is No Natural Religion, that if man limits himself to perceiving only through the bodily senses, then he limits himself to bodily desires and can never know God. He goes on to talk of 'Those who restrain desire because theirs is weak enough to be restrained,' (Plate 5) whom we can take to be priests. This, wickedly, carries connotations of phallic pride, and is suggestive of the sexual impotence of priests and the like. His argument is, that no desire should be unfulfilled, because we can only desire what is within our Reason. 'No bird soars too high,' he says in the 'Proverbs of Hell', 'if he soars with his own wings.' His theory on the effects of imposing false limits on Energy are similar to what Freud would later state in his theory of repression, that whatever desire is repressed will re-emerge in a corrupted and ugly form. This is the subject of 'The Poison Tree', in Experience, and of the 'Proverb of Hell': 'Expect poison from the standing watei.'

Blake's argument is that God 'reside[s] in the human breast' (Marriage, Plate 11), but what does he mean by this. It is not meant in the Nietzsche Ian sense that we are our own Gods, but in the sense that every man has the capacity to commune with God. God is not in any of the words of priests, or in the church. The Memorable Fancy on Plate 12 of The Marriage is an objection to the orthodox idea of God, and the Prophet Isaiah states that he 'saw no God, nor heard any, in a finite organically perception.' Blake's explanation of why religion strays so far from original meaning, however, is similar to the explanation that Nietzsche would offer on morality:

A morality at length enters consciousness as a law, as dominating-And therewith the entire group of related values and states enters into it: it becomes venerable, unassailable, holy, truc; it is part of its development that its origin should be forgotten-That is a sign that it has become master. We a see the comparison in The Marriage: The ancient poets animated all sensible objects with Gods... [And] a system was formed, which took some advantage of & enslaved the vulgar by attempting to realise or abstract the mental deities from their objects; thus began Priesthood. (Plate 11)

And in his earlier work, All Religions Are One. In this, viewed with There is No Natural Religion, and The Marriage of Heaven and Hell, we come close to understanding the real essence of what Blake means when he states, perhaps incomprehensibly, that 'The desire of Man being Infinite, the possession is Infinite, & himself Infinite.' (There is No Natural Religion, b, VII) He speaks of the Poetic Genius, those with 'enlarged & numerous senses' (Marriage, Plate 11), he who has cleansed the 'doors of perception' and to whom all things appear, as they are, 'infinite' (Plate 14). It is Blake's (questionable) belief that it is from the Poetic Genius that all knowledge springs, and without whom 'the universe would soon become a mill with complicated wheels' (There is No Natural Religion, b, IV). Without whose vision, the progress of humanity would halt, since 'none, by travelling over known lands can find out the unknown, So from already acquired knowledge Man could not acquire more' (All Religions Are One, Principle 4). This is the challenge of Blake, to become true Men:

**Q16. William Blake's Songs of Innocence and Songs of Experience were great literary examples that describe the conflict between innocence and experience**

One author that has influenced this positive experience was William Blake. William Blake's Songs of Innocence and Songs of Experience were great literary examples that describe the conflict between innocence and experience. In "The Lamb" of Songs of Innocence, Blake presents someone who receives an answer to his question and believes the answer without reservation. "Little Lamb who made thee...Little Lamb I'll tell thee/He is called by thy name/For he calls himself a Lamb". "The Lamb" describes someone with a child-like faith that does not question many things, but simply believes what is presented to him by faith. In Songs of Experience's contrasting piece, "The Tiger," Blake describes someone who is much more confused than this child-like figure in "The Lamb." This character seems to question everything and anything. "What the hammer? what the chain/In what furnace was thy brain?" This character has had more exposure to life and through his experiences he is unable to accept things for the way that they are, as a result, he questions their existence and the reasons for their existence.

These two pieces from Blake remind me of the phrase "ignorance is bliss." One idea is that the character in "The Lamb" was able to enjoy life because of his ignorance and, therefore, he was not bothered by their existence. On the other hand, however, the character with life experience in "The Tiger" was irritated with the curiosity of why things are as they are. Because of this character's knowledge, he was unsatisfied with life until he knew the answers to all of his questions, but even more questions were revealed with every answer that he received.

For me, the benefit of reading this work was that it made me consider ignorance versus knowledge. Today, in our society, the more you know the better off you will be, seems to be the view of the majority. Reading some of Blake's work, however, has made me wonder if life is more fulfilling with knowledge or with ignorance. Considering these works has made me see the value in knowledge because it allows us to understand more about our world, yet knowledge also seems to raise more questions than it answers.

Ignorance offers the same dilemma between enjoyment through simple faith or stupidity from living by this simple faith. Although knowledge is a useful tool in today's world, I think that you can have too much of a good thing and it can cause you to have a negative view of the world. This exposure to Blake's writing is significant to me because it teaches me how to evaluate the information that is presented to me by seeing both the innocent and the experienced sides. From Blake's writings I have learned that sometimes you need to take a closer look at things to learn about them but other times you can just take things as they are by faith.

I also found Chinua Achebe to be a valuable asset to the literature in this class. There are many things that we can learn from his piece Things Fall Apart. One idea that made a strong impact on me was the surprising opportunity I had to learn about another culture that is very different from our American society. Reading Achebe's Things Fall Apart, I was able to see the importance of knowing where these people are coming from before I judge their way of life. Although the Igbo culture is very different from our culture, the people are still people. by "listening to the weak" (handout) we can see how important their culture is to them. I think that this reading experience can teach almost any reader something. By reading this pie, we can learn about another culture and this new knowledge can help us understand these people and stop our racial judgments against them. When Okonkwo's son converted to the missionaries' religion, "a sudden fury rose within him" (1483). Okonkwo's saw how these missionaries were splitting the tribe and his family apart. From this I learned that forcing my beliefs on someone in a place that has not welcomed me, can harden the hearts of the people I am trying to witness to because my actions have displayed my racial prejudices against the people and their way of life.

English 109 has been important to my education because it has helped teach me evaluation skills. This class has proven to be an important tool for learning to understand other people and the reasons that cause them to feel the way that they do. Through studying Western world literature and reading literature from William Blake and Chinua Achebe I have learned that knowledge is a powerful tool but simple faith and understanding can also be valuable in evaluating the world around you.

**Q17. What is Blake's State of Mind in the Songs of Innocence and Experience?**

"When you put two minds togetner, there is always a third mind, a third and superior mind, as an unseen collaborator." William S. Burroughs and Brion Gysin, "The Third Mind" We are symbol-using primates in search for an ultimate Truth. No poet has understood and exploited this idea more successfully than William Blake, and this was solely due to his mysticism, the fact that his doors of perception were cleansed. What is his world like, then?

In the "Songs of Innocence and Experience" we are apparently presented with two different worlds, narrated by two different narrators. A more careful reading will present several interesting correspondences between the two. For example, the meek "Lamb" becomes the fiery "Tyger". The former appears to foster a syllogistic reasoning, a format of simple questions and easy answers in the midst of it's catatonia, we are unnerved by what we as readers bring to the text, inserting our alien (to the pastoral scene) phantoms of our experience. The latter poem, although pounding us with unanswered questions and awe-inspiring images, is, curiously, a more comfortable read in that it is a better fit into our perception. It seems that the open prairie and the dark forest belong to two entirely different worlds, but it is my belief that it is not the Lamb or the Tiger per se, that make the difference but the way they are treated, that is, narrated. Both "Chimney Sweeper" poems appear to be about the same situation. What clearly changes is the narration.

The narrator of the experience poem present a more complex understanding of reality. The child in the innocence poem is incapable of comprehending his situation, as he lacks the experience to do so. The poignant sense of injustice in our reading is clearly due to what we bring to it. The same sense, less biting but rather more bitter, is achieved by the amazing realization the child has come to posses: "because I am happy, & dance & sing, / They think they have done me no injury." Here we also bring our experience to the text, but not as pity for the child, but as guilt for our own actions, realizing that we often side with "God & his Priest & King / Who make up a heaven of [the child's] misery." Blake is clearly exploiting the infant archetype, in the first poem to lulls us into our traditional social roles as parent figures, and in the second to jolt us into re-examining these roles.

It is time to talk about the narrators as described in the two introductions, and to decide where Blake stands as the artist behind both of them. The first narrator is clearly a simple pastoral shepherd, young in age, truly innocent and untainted — unlike the water he dips his "rural pen" in. This is an interesting point: water is archetypal, and consistently so in Blake, associated with chaos but also with fertility — or, in one word: creativity, the faculty of the Poetic Genius. Now, the introduction to experience is wrought in Biblical allusions, a clear sign of experience. The Bard is also capable of seeing "Present, Past &

Future," another such demonstration, as time is synonymous with decay, thus, it's dominion is inherently associated with the post-lapsarian world. This made obvious by such references as "lapsed Soul" and "Fallen light renew". Therefore, the Bard, is surely capable of replicating the Shepherd, and we must thus assume that Blake can, too.

Blake, as the author, knew that his audience (had there been one, in his time) would me mature — or experienced — and therefore, would not read the songs of innocence as a child would. Therefore, we may safely say that Blake intended the first section of his book to be read as an ironic bucolic. This the reason for which the Shepherd emphasizes that his "happy songs / Every child may joy to hear," when just a few seconds before, the aforementioned "rural pen," a patriarchal phallic symbol of order has entered the water, a feminine space of creative chaos. We see similar symbolism in "The Book of Thel:" "Can Wisdom be put in a silver rod? / Or Love in a golden bowl?"

But, although the Shepherd and the Bard are clearly distinct voices, the poems themselves melt and mingle into one another, as if they come from the same voice, which has visions of both states. This is the voice of Blake, which permeates the entire work. If this is the case, then what are we to make of Blake's own epigraph to the book, which runs: "Shewing the Two Contrary States of the Human Soul?"

My assumption is that, as a mystic, he had progressed in perceiving reality beyond duality. Or, in his own words, he achieved a condition where "every thing would appear to man as it is, infinite." It has been proven that language on language, or mathematics on mathematics escalates into near nonsense because there is an infinite regress at work. The same result occurs in consciousness when it is pondering consciousness. Eventually it all explodes into infinity, like Moby Dick, which means too many things to be meaningful. Blake's work is lulling the reader into thinking he is journeying from a perfect world of innocence, into a fallen world of experience. But, there aren't two worlds, only one. Therefore, what changes is perception. "When you put two minds together, there is always a third mind, a third and superior mind, as an unseen collaborator." (William S. Burroughs and Brion Gysin, "The Third Mind") So, after the 2nd step, there follows a logical 3rd, what has been called higher innocence. Higher innocence is the mystical state where one realises that we are "models of ourselves, making models of ourselves, smaking..." (Robert Anton Wilson, "Prometheus Rising") If there is any perfection to be found in Blake, it is this.

**Q18. Present A Comparative Study of "Infant Joy" And " Infant Sorrow".**

Comparative Analysis of Infant Joy and Infant Sorrow William Blake's Infant Joy from the Songs of Innocence and Infant Sorrow from the Songs of Experience are in direct contrast from one another. Infant Joy represents the celebration and joy felt at the arrival of an innocent baby, while Infant Sorrow is a poem of the despair and rejection at the birth of an unwanted child.

The former poem leaves one with the feeling of warmth and innocence; the latter only offers a bleak and dark existence that shall last a lifetime. Blake presents the reader with two aspects of the birth of life one that is softened by peace and purity, and another that is really no life at all. Infant Joy radiates happiness and love. It is an expression of the elation and wonder felt at the birth of a tiny baby. The scene is one of tranquility a mother gently cradling her child at her breast. Both the mother and baby are given a voice. The mother addresses her tiny infant, only thoughts of tenderness and love consuming her. She revels in the joy of her motherhood. Her precious infant is embracing his new life and surroundings, proclaiming to the world his arrival of only two days before. The tone is one of hope mingled with a glowing, radiant happiness.

The tiny infant is only two days old, and he has yet to be named. Without a name, the infant cannot be judged; his short life has only been one of unblemished innocence. Limiting factors do not exist for the baby. The innocence known to the infant only serves to emphasize the lack of evilness and corruption in his world. At this moment, the baby is goodness and all those things in life that are warm and giving. One is left with the hope his innocence will not be lost, and that a beautiful and uplifting aura will always come from him. The words chosen by Blake joy, happy, pretty, sweet, sing, and smile display a sense of contentment.

The words contribute to a feeling of radiance felt at the occasion of the infant's birth a timeless situation. The joy felt by the mother is many times experienced throughout life, one would hope every time a woman gives birth. The age of the child is important, as it emphasizes the innocence of the baby. The mother names her child "joy." She revels in his innocent smile. The infant is trusting, as his mother tenderly holds him to her breast. As she sings a lullaby to her tiny babe, she wishes for only joy to befall him. One may almost interpret this as a prayer a prayer from her heart and a wish that his babyhood be filled with warmth, loving and happiness. In his smile, she sees a reflection of her own contentment.

Her sleepy infant warms her, and she wants only to protect him from the cold world that exists outside the adoring embrace of her arms. One envisions this scene in the purity of white. White is innocence and incorruptibility. The baby is gently tucked in a white, fluffy blanket only his rosy cheeks, sparkling eyes, and sweet smile are left to peek from the cuddly bundle. The vision is hazy, the harsh angles smoothed into a gentle roundness. This is heaven, but not heaven in the pastoral sense. This is a heaven found on earth. This is a heaven created especially for an adoring mother and the purity of her new infant. This is a place one wishes to stay forever. In stark and glaring contrast, Infant Sorrow is the dark scene of an unwanted birth an infant born in a cold and unfeeling world. The infant is the only angry speaker of this poem. He addresses a world that will never listen to his downtrodden voice, no matter how loud his wails.

The world weeps for him, but offers no comforting embrace. The tone is sullen and mean, contributing to a sense of hopelessness and despair. Unlike his two day old counterpart, one is introduced to this infant at his birth. One is left to witness the agony of birth. Although he is given no name, one unerringly may guess this child is Despair. Already, the squalling babe is stained with corruption. He is left with no chance to encounter joy in his life. He will never be branded innocent. One is left with a feeling of hopelessness this infant's existence will only be comprised of dissatisfaction and helplessness.

The words chosen by Blake are stark, dangerous, helpless, naked, loud, struggling, bound, weary, and sulk. These words conjure a bleak existence and encumber the poem with tension. This is not an anticipated birth, as the father weeps at the sight of his child. Blake describes the child's push from his mother's womb as a leap into the world, not even to be cradled in his parents' unwelcoming embrace. This unwanted babe finds a cold welcome in his father's hands, as he thrust away from a breast that will never offer him comfort. His parents are the poor and downtrodden of the London streets. Life has soured them of kindness and charity.

This infant is only one more mouth to feed, and it will be years before he will be able to work as a slave of child labour. He is wrapped, struggling, in dingy and vermin-infested swaddling rags. Already he is bound and downtrodden. He will not have long to wait until his cheeks will be hollowed with hunger and despair, his eyes robbed of life for eternity. Brown and grey are the colours of this scene. These are the colours of dirt and death. This place is a deep pit extending to the bowels of the earth. Not quite hell, for the devil does not possess souls. There are no souls here. The eyes, the windows to the soul, are forever shuttered. From the moment he was born as Despair, this infant was tightly imprisoned in his baby clothes, so he may never struggle again.

He is weary, and in defeat he sullenly rests against his mother's thin breast a breast never to offer him sustenance. In writing Infant Joy and Infant Sorrow, William Blake has offered us a coin, one side gleaming golden, while the other is tarnished. The golden side of this coin creates an almost indescribable emotion an emotion so pure, so innocent, and so untouched that one is hesitant to even name this feeling for fear of destroying the moment of angelic purity. The image of the mother and her babe is eternal. Blake does more than warm the heart with this poem; he crafts the heart and gives it life. The tarnished side of the coin represents a child stained by the misdeeds of life and the knowledge of an adult. Just as he crafted a heart with Infant Joy, with Infant Sorrow, Blake displays his ability to cripple the same heart with his gift for words.

**Q19. What emotional progression does the poem imply in the speaker's contemplation of the Tyger?**

**Or**

**Q. What is the answer to the question in line 20, "Did he who made the lamb make thee?" Why does the speaker need to ask the question? Who is "he," i.e. the lamb's creator?**

**Or**

**Q. What is the significance of the poem's references to "fire," "burning," and the "furnace"? What does fire often symbolize?**

**Or**

**Q. Examine the plate on page 55 - describe the Tiger's attributes. What sort of "tiger" is this that Blake has engraved? What effect does the odd spelling "tiger" create?**

In order to look at William Blake's poem "Tyger! Tyger!" one must also look at "The Lamb." The lamb and the tiger show the two contrary states of the human soul with respect to creation while asking what kind of god could make both. Blake's questioning of God reflects the influence of the Enlightenment period.

God is represented in two different ways by Blake. In "Tyger! Tyger!," Blake asks what kind of god could make such a fearful creature. In this God, it is easy to insert the image of an angry, wrathful God, immensely powerful; one who does not always use his power for good. Paradoxically, in "The Lamb," God is described as being "meek and mild". This is the typical description of the Christian God: a forgiving and loving God who takes care of his "children". This God gives the Lamb "clothing of delight,/softest clothing, wooly bright".

The Tyger and the Lamb can be interpreted as the two contrary states of the human soul. The Tyger is the part of human nature that is not inherently good. This "tiger" state if being is fierce and terrible, with "fearful symmetry." Blake seems to be referring to the Tyger as being a sort of mirror image of the angry, vengeful God.

However, the Lamb is the part of human nature which Christians would like to believe mirrors God. The Lamb is also a prominent figure in the Christian religion, representing God's human "children". The Lamb is typically portrayed as being meek and in need of protection. Blake's "The Tyger" is a poem about the nature of creation, much as is "The Lamb." However, this poem takes on the darker side of creation, when its benefits are less obvious than simple joys. This poem is meant to be interpreted in comparison and contrast to "The Lamb," showing the two contrary states of the human soul with respect to creation.

There can be no brief summary of "The Tyger" or to what Blake scholars Robert A. Gleckner and Mark L. Greenberg call "'Tyger' studies". The rare cultural status the poem has achieved can be reduced at last to raw empirical terms: William Harmon ranks "The Tiger" [sic] first among The Top 500 Poems anthologized in English, a fact that reflects how closely, in popular imagination alone, Blake is tied to his creature.

"The Tyger" has also been one of the most frequently explained poems in English literature. In fact, the width and depth of attention the poem receives testifies to its ability to contain a multitude of plausible, if widely divergent, interpretations. And critics have gone even farther, subdividing the lyric into parts, so that many articles are devoted only to individual segments of the poem— the state of the speaker, the tiger's spiritual alignment, and certain memorable cruxes in the text. Indeed, one surveys the sheer acreage of "Tyger" criticism and no longer sees a mere lyric, but finally a kind of massively succinct lexicon for William Blake's intellectual, political and spiritual life.

**Contemporary Reactions: "The Tyger" until 1863**

Nineteenth-century readers who had at least a glancing familiarity with William Blake would have had known "that one about a tiger," as Charles Lamb remembered it when the name of the poem escaped him. The poem's pulse-like meter and its simple, suggestive lyrics fastened themselves to the memories of even Blake's most virulent attackers. William Beckford, for example, the aristocratic man of letters and contemporary of Blake's, left this nearly forgotten commentary: "'Tiger, tiger burning bright In the forests of the night etc.' Surely the receiver and disseminator of such trash is as bad as the thief who seems to have stolen them from the walls of Bedlam." While posterity has not yet supported his verdict, he stands at the head of a tradition that remembers Blake first and sometimes exclusively as the author of "The Tyger".

This was partly due, of course, to the poem's better exposure. Eva Rosebery, who records Beckford's remark, notes that "the disseminator of such trash" in question was Benjamin Heath Malkin, an early admirer and acquaintance of the poet. Malkin, as G. E. Bentley, Jr. notes in William Blake: The Critical Heritage, included "The Tyger" among five other poems in his volume, Father's Memoir for His Child, published in 1806.

Bentley also reports Allan Cunningham's comment in the 1831 Lives of Eminent British Painters that the "little poem called 'The Tiger' has been admired... by poets of high name." In reality, such contact was only brief and incidental, though the poem was in fact well received by a prestigious audience. William Wordsworth saw Malkin's volume and was "sufficiently impressed" to copy "The Tyger" and other of Blake's lyrics into a commonplace book in 1807. Charles Lamb, who had only heard the poem recited, found it "glorious" even as he misquoted it (Bentley reproduces Lamb's "Tiger" as: "Tiger, tiger, burning bright,/Through the deserts of the night"). In 1818, Samuel Taylor Coleridge reviewed the illuminated manuscript itself; he liked the poem, though it did not inspire any direct remark.

Aside from an illuminated, though largely ignored edition of the collected Songs of Innocence and of Experience in 1828, "The Tyger" spent much of its nineteenth century life in the conventional typescript of journals and anthologies. This period, Bentley shows, begins in 1811 with the publication of an article by Henry Crabb Robinson. Robinson's short biographical introduction of Blake re-printed "The Tyger" which he praised as a "truly inspired and original description" of the beast. Between 1847 and 1862, the lyric was the only one of Blake's works to be reproduced in all four anthologies that included him. Of the thirty-seven poems by Blake published during this time, Suzanne Hoover notes, "The Tyger" "was the most popular, having been printed as many as seven times." In fact, the presence of "The Tyger" was perhaps a leading reason that Blake's name escaped complete obscurity before Alexander Gilchrist's biography of Blake in 1863 brought Blake a wider, more respectful audience.

In 1954, David Erdman, in Prophet Against Empire, was the first to offer an account of the poem solely in terms of its contemporary background, and evidence for other, equally plausible sources of the poem, have steadily mounted. In the last twenty-five years alone, critics have clarified even more distinctly the poem's relationship to its own era.

Nick Shrimpton and Heather Glen have shown that the Songs of Innocence and of Experience owe in part their metrical models and topics from a whole current of children's' literature that had become available to a larger, literate English public. For a poet who was at home with blank verse and artistic experimentation, "The Tyger"- - with four beats evenly striking almost all of its lines— was very much an appropriation of this fairly new literature. Glen, in fact, places

"The Tyger" among those "verses about birds and animals, of which there was a whole sub-genre in the children's books of the late eighteenth century." One cause of the growing literacy for children was a strict Methodist ethic which reared children as much for their future salvation as their adulthood. No one person typifies this ethic better than John Wesley, perhaps the foremost leader of English Methodism, who wrote hymns and rhymes that prepared children to accept death, among other pains, as a consequence of the reward of salvation (a doctrine which, Shrimpton asserts, that "The Tyger" (in part) "questions the adequacy of.").

## Some Contemporary Sources of the Poem's Minor Imagery

Some critics trace the poem's minor imagery, particularly the stars and spears of its fifth stanza, to events or institutions familiar to Blake in his own lifetime. In 1990, for example, Marilynn Olson and Donald Olson suggested that meteor showers— especially one spectacular bolides on August 18, 1783— may have been the "spears" the "stars threw down" in line 17. Colin Morton D. Paley notes that the weeping stars in lines 17-18 may refer to the anonymous lyric "Tom of Bedlam," reprinted popularly in 1792. And in the Songs of Experience, "The Angel" offers a close parallel to the lines:

I dried my tears & armed my fears
with ten thousand shields and spears.

In a different vein, William Doxey demonstrates that rhetorical precedence exists for interpreting line two's "forests of the night" as a figure of speech meaning simply the night sky and its constellations. (Along the same lines, he maintains that the line's significance, if not the whole poem's, lies in just such astronomical sources).

Tigers as Blake may have known them in his time

Tigers, as many scholars have discovered, held a special terror for the eighteenth century imagination. John E. Grant, writing in the Iowa Review in 1989, reproduces two pages from Thomas Berwick's A General History of Quadrupeds (published 1790, 1811), describing the tiger as "the most rapacious and destructive of all carnivorous animals." Berwick's tiger is "fierce without provocation, and cruel without necessity, its thirst for blood is insatiable."

Not surprisingly, editorialists, particularly British conservatives, were not slow in realizing the tiger as an invective against Jacobin France. David Erdman notes that on January 7, 1792, The [London] Times declared that the French had become "'loose from all restraints, and, in many instances, more ferocious than wolves and tigers'."

The metaphor proved to be exceedingly durable. Judging from the word's frequency in this context, it is not hard to conclude that "tiger" had become a trope with conditioned reflexes, to be released any time discussion headed in the vicinity of revolutionary France. Wordsworth's familiar description of post- revolutionary Paris (which Erdman cites in Prophet Against Empire) as a place where Robes Pierre's enemies were as "Defenceless as a wood where tigers roam" (Prelude, X.82) merely draws on an already popular image of the tiger as a beast of insolent ferocity.

Or the English may have heard, as Morton D.Paley notes, Sir Samuel Romilly inflecting the low bestiality of the new French republic: "One might as well as think of establishing a republic of tigers in some forest of Africa." From comparisons of animals, conservative editorialists were not far from using the epithet the "tygerish multitude"— a variant of Edmund Burke's "swinish multitude"— against the lower and artisan classes of England and France, who, as Stuart Crehan remarks, were "daring to assert their own power."

But the word could be aimed at individuals as well. The London Times on 13 July 1793, Crehan notes, published a "eulogy" for the assassinated David Marat, remembering him as "a fine portrait of [a] chief murderer with eyes of a tiger cat, and... looks that corresponded to that animal." In 1793 as well, says Colin Pedley, the English public heard Robespierre (and his followers) described as "that Tiger, in human shape surrounded by the assassins whom he dispatched."

Robespierre, Pedley notes, later tacitly endorsed the epithet, demonstrating some of the ambivalent power the word that Blake could draw on for the poem. In the experienced world that followed the French Revolution, says Ronald Paulson in Articulate Images: The Sister Arts from Hogarth to Tennyson, words took on dual, but antipodal values: king, traitor and, as Robespierre demonstrated, tiger.

The tiger survived revolutionary France to become a figure of Napoleonic militarism as well. Grant uncovers a fairly obscure, if virulently Anti-Gallican, caricature by cartoonist James Gillray. In it, the allegorical skulls of European nations lie beneath a French coat of arms whose central symbol is a bloody guillotine flanked on one side by a tiger (and, on the other, an undoubtedly racist depiction of a monkey). Such was the context of tigers in post-revolutionary Europe and Grant insists that any honest reader will acknowledge that "Blake selected a beast that truly could not be confronted with equanimity."

But the tiger's prominence in the mental life of eighteenth century England also owes to "the great upsurge of natural history in the eighteenth century," says Coleman O. Parsons. He notes that illustrations of exotic and foreign animals were frequently included in texts like Linnaeus's compendium. The "tiger" literature of the day was large enough, says Parsons, to create "an ambience of fact, fable, and interpretation which nourished Blake's imagination."

More immediately, Paul Miner suggests, "Blake could have seen a real tiger in eighteenth century London." Travelling menageries came to the city, including one, Miner documents, with a Bengali tiger in 1791. Superstitions grew around these menageries' tigers as well. John Adlard does not mention "The Tyger" by name in his book The Sports of Cruelty, but relevantly he explains that among the superstitious it was believed that every seventh year lions bred, and this accordingly was called "The Lion Year". However, "apparently this seventh year was sometimes the Tiger Year, for... a strange, sudden fury of a tiger in a travelling menagerie was blamed by the manager on the presence of pregnant women."

Whether any of these were the source of Blake's poem, or their effect on him was composite, the animal clearly led a powerful imaginary life in Blake's audience.

**The Main Topics and Problems of the Poem**

Despite the volume of published work on the poem this century, "The Tyger", as a critical phenomenon, really only began after the Second World War. Before then, only a few critics like Joseph H. Wicksteed offered thoroughgoing accounts of the kind that would become more common later.

One great difference between pre-War "Tyger" criticism and the later more densely-argued criticism of the 1940s and after, lies in the number of footnotes each uses. Wicksteed's 1928 study of the complete Songs, not burdened with competing theories or abstruse extra textual sources, approaches "The Tyger" with uncluttered conviction: "The whole thesis of `The Tyger' is that he [the tiger] is a spiritual expression of the Creator himself" and the poem "is a tremendous treatise enunciating the nature of the God that does exist— the God that is mighty and terribly visible in his manifestations." (In 1957, however, D. W. Harding complains that "the parish-magazine quality of sentiment [Wicksteed] expresses... is totally foreign" to Blake.)

S. Foster Damon, in 1924, was among the first to interpret the poem as essentially a doctrinal problem: "how to reconcile the Forgiveness of Sins (the Lamb)... the Punishment of Sins (the Tyger)." (277) The final question, "Did he who made the Lamb make thee?" (l. 20), is therefore "not an exclamation of wonder but a very real question, whose answer Blake was not sure of."

The Portable Blake, published in 1946, edited by Alfred Kazin, which included a short commentary on the poem, can be taken as the official beginning of modern "Tyger" studies. Two years later, Roy P. Basler, within an embryonically

Freudian reading, saw in the ambiguous morality of the tiger "a challenge to orthodox theology" as well as to "the rational design" of the universe prevailing among the so-called Natural Theologians of the eighteenth century. (This critique had a distant echo almost three decades later in June Singer's Jungian psychobiography of Blake, The Unholy Bible (1970): "He who made the Lamb is worshipped in all the churches, [but] he who fashioned the Tyger... is also God.")

The year following Basler's work, C. M. Bowra published The Romantic Imagination, and found in the tiger a symbol "for the fierce forces in the soul that which are needed to break the bonds of experience." Also in 1947, novelist and critic Wolf Mankowitz offered that the poem was "a comment on the limited capacity of man to conceive of God at all."

These studies, however, seem brief surveys compared to the more systematic treatment of Jesse Bier. For Bier, writing in 1949, Blake's poem is a record of the struggle between energy and matter; the tiger is "the face of creation"— "not sheer unadulterated evil and perversity in the outer world, but like Moby Dick... the marvelous and the fatal together within each of us." The structure of this reading is revived and put to somewhat different ends by Anne Kostelanetz Mellor in 1975, who viewed the poem as "portraying the process through which Energy is given artistic form is thus enabled to survive in the world of Experience."

Two other critics of the 1940s, re-introduced and made important clarifications to the Christian eschatology latent in the poem. Northrop Frye, in Fearful Symmetry (1947) sees in the poem a Satanic accuser of the Fall, "who frightens us out of Paradise behind the menacing blaze of a tiger's eyes." Conversely, Jacob Bronowski, writing in 1944, interprets the poem as one guide-post on a road to a complex religious redemption. "Christ is become the Tyger, symbol of energy burning in a darkening world," he writes prophetically, "It is no longer enough for the innocent boy to go from false experience to true, by chance. Experience itself must learn, fasting in the desert, to follow a greater innocence, by choice."

**Some Emergent Concerns of the 1940s and 1950s**

Mark Schorer was another critic in the 1940s to produce a major book-length study of Blake, The Politics of Vision (1946). Unlike S. Foster Damon, for example, he seeks to answer the final question of the poem by describing tiger and lamb as aspects of the same historical process. After centuries of oppression, "the innocent impulses of the lamb have been curbed by restraints, and the lamb has been turned into the tiger," and the new animal "bursts forth in revolutionary wrath."

David Erdman extends Schorer's argument into Blake's own historical context. Erdman is careful "not to imply the "The Tyger" is a political allegory," but finds ample political resonance in the contemporary events of France and America. But the poem culminates in the fifth stanza when the counter-revolutionary "stars threw down their spears" like the surrendering armies at Yorktown and Valmy, long at their wars (in the American and French revolutions, respectively), and "seemed ready to coexist with the Lamb." The cycle is complete, when "the wrath of the Tiger"— both revolutionary and counter- revolutionary— "done its task."

Stuart Crehan, writing in 1984, follows Erdman in correlating the poem with the revolutionary mood of the 1790s. The honestly partisan Crehan compares the poem to Yeats's "Easter 1916" as it depicts the "terrible, new-born beauty of violent revolution." But the tiger acts out of— indeed, is created out of — misery and desperation. For if "the forests... are, on one level, oppressive and crowded cities such as Paris and London, then it follows" that it is such "degradation, not some unfathomable Creator in the sky, that have bred tigers."

The project of reconciling the lamb and the tiger also continued during the 1950s. Stanley Gardner, in his 1954 book Infinity on the Anvil, harmonizes the two, if only for stanza five, maintaining that the "stars [who] threw down their spears" were giving up "material power." With "instruments of strife cast aside, and pity assumed," the tiger's Maker "smiles upon the triumph of the Lamb." Gardner is especially vivid in his discussion of the tiger, which he decides is a product of fiery Los-like creation: "With its five finite senses, forged round the infinite mind, separates that mind from infinity," the body is created out of fiery separation. Hazard Adams, writing in 1955, locates this struggle internally, seeing in the tiger "a mirror image of man in his fallen state." In an article which anticipates his 1960 essay ("Reading Blake's Lyrics"), Adams interprets the tiger's "identification and confrontation by Blake and Los [as a] symbolical leap from the forest [of the night] into the light of day."

Warren Stevenson (1969) joins Gardner in identifying Los as the creator: "In forging the Tyger, Los is accomplishing that same victory over... darkness which he accomplished in The Book of Urizen." Also in the Los column is Harry Williams (1972) who sees the tiger as a realization of that "spirit of forgiveness" which itself is composed of equal parts wrath and pity (in the spirit of the hellish proverb, "The cut worm forgives the plow"). Fred Kaplan (also in 1972) regards the poem as a moment of the recognition of one's own claim to divinity. "Blake the artist," says Kaplan, "does not fear to record his immortality; in fact, he stands in awe before his own fearlessness."

Harvey Birenbaum, in his 1992 study Between Blake and Nietschze, never mentions Blake's god of labour by name, but the Maker he describes and Los have nearly the same personality and face many of the same problems. However, the two finally diverge, as Birenbaum sees in the poem a lack of ethical intent: "the only moral question remotely implied is whether the reaching mind ought to do all it dare."

Urizen, Blake's repressive lawgiver god, was also named the tiger's father during the 1950s. Kathleen Raine argued in Encounter in 1954, drawing on ancient Gnostic texts, which were, she argued, "beyond question.... the inspiration and source of the 'The Tyger'." From Gnosticism's belief "that the creator of this world was a being different from the supreme God," Raine easily finds numerous distinct parallels from Blake's own Gnostic demiurge, Urizen. The tiger, then, is the representative of "a very Cruel Being" who was responsible for proportion and "symmetry"— clearly the work of Urizen. Furthermore, following the legacy of Urizen, she asserts (in what would become a frequently attacked phrase), "the tiger is a symbol of competitive, predacious selfhood."

(It should be noted that Margaret Rudd, a year before Raine, saw in the poem as a fragment of Blake's own religious struggle in which Urizen made laws, but not the tiger itself. For Rudd, "it is only an abstract law of Urizen which calls the Tiger, like sex, evil.")

While Raine's conclusion of Urizen as Maker was endorsed without alteration by S. Foster Damon, in his Blake Dictionary (1965), others offered variants of her interpretation. Robert F. Gleckner, in 1959, said the tiger belongs to "the finite world, ruled over by Urizen who caused its finiteness the world of experience and tygers." The creator's possible smile in fifth stanza ("Did he smile his work to see?) is the smile of spite, cynicism, cultivated by repressive experience. He elaborates this demiurgic universe further than even Raine had, describing "the forests of the night" as "the forests of experience in which roam fears and sorrows of the created universe."

Rodney Baine and Mary Baine seem to share Raine's thesis that the tiger belongs to Urizen, though they do not name the god as such. But, they say that Blake used "the tiger as symbol of fallen or brutalized man. Only when he is regenerated or redeemed does the tiger, like the other beasts, reassumes his unfallen creative vitality." (In 1986, Rodney Baine, intensifies his view and indeed begins to adopt Raine's familiar phrase: "Like the Tiger, Blake's subsequent tigers also exemplify man in the grip of selfhood— malevolent and stupid.") For Robert E. Simmons, writing in 1970, the tiger is an "illusion" which "amounts to a symmetrical précis of Urizen." Thomas R. Frosch (1974), in similar language, blames Urizen for the forests rather than for the tiger itself: "The forests of the night are Entuthon-Benython, the forests of illusion, the depths of the covered mind in which energy appears demonic... Urizen frightens us to his altars by showing us monsters."

As the above citations demonstrate, the criticism of the 1950s framed this question of identification so that it would be sustained well until the next three decades. But more importantly, this urge to name the tiger's maker points to a decisive change in "Tyger" literature. The joint significance the works of Erdman, Raine and Gardner share is in beginning a critical attitude, anticipated perhaps by Schorer that seeks to form some lasting conclusions about the symbols and concepts of the whole of Blake's poetry. But the successes of these authors were less in their positive assertions than in their methodology.

They initiated and fostered in "Tiger" commentary an abiding study of Blake's source material and of his intellectual life. In addition, Blake's work began to be thought of not as a disparate set of lyrics and mystical revelations, but as a broad and systematic oeuvre which represented a complex and distinct world-view. Later influential works by authors such as Hazard Adams, Morton D. Paley and numerous others have clear models in these earlier efforts.

Finally, in 1956, Martin K. Nurmi's article "Blake's Revisions of the 'The Tyger'" focuses Erdman's historical placement of "The Tyger" but more importantly represents the first consideration of the poem's textual development as a part of its meaning. Looking at different drafts of the poem alongside contemporaneous news of France, Nurmi argues that the poem matured with Blake's evolving sense of the moral ambiguities of the French Revolution. The "unified symmetry" Blake attains in his final draft, then, subsumes both the optimism of the National Convention of 1793 and the bloody massacres the previous September. In doing so, Blake "gives his symbol the comprehensive scope of an 'eternal principle'." (Tangentially, Nurmi cites H. M. Margoliouth's brief biography of Blake in establishing "The Tiger" as an occasional poem, though Margoliouth provides slender evidence for such a claim.)

Nurmi, approaching the poem in 1975, is more tentative: the poem, he says, "could be regarded as a providential creation for— not of or by— the fallen world of Experience," but only if the stars in the fifth stanza are defeated stars of oppression. Nurmi answers the penultimate question ("Did he who made the Lamb make thee?") with "a Yes of such deep ambivalence... as to leave the questions without definitive answers."

## The 1960s: Meet the Speakers

In Spring 1960, Texas Studies in Language and Literature presented two pivotal "Tyger" articles which introduce "the speaker" as a new character into "the forests of the night". Both John E. Grant in his "The Art and Argument of the Tiger" and Hazard Adams in "Reading Blake's Lyrics: `The Tiger'". The two critics radically altered the reception of the poem by insisting on the tiger as a created image, rather than a created thing. As Grant states, "the focus of interest in the poem itself is on the Tiger as percept, rather than object, and on the speaker as subject."

The speaker was imported from the New Criticism, which scrupulously divided poet from persona, and critics found in this difference a new, wealthy dimension of study. With this third party came a variety of new questions: what is the relationship between the speaker and the tiger? Between the speaker and the tiger's creator? This line of criticism has produced a speaker with a variety of spiritual, political and philosophical temperaments whose condition, more often not, needs careful diagnosis.

For Adams, the persona is less important as a speaker than as a viewer, or more specifically, as a visionary. Since it is the eye as much as the hand that "dares frame... fearful symmetry", it is not only "the tiger [that] is framed on the anvil of inspiration which is the eye of man and God, but [the tiger] is also a symbol of the very same eye which created it." It is therefore, in "the manner in which one beholds the tiger [that] is all important to its and one's own spiritual nature."

Grant identifies the speaker as the "awestruck voice of Experience, that of an average but also imaginative man, who is almost overwhelmed" by the mysteries of the Tyger. In the end, however, the speaker knows "that the Tiger was not created to improve his lot in the world, and he feels a holy dread" and finally, "indignity" at such a fate (his position does not change substantially after 29 years when writes again on the poem for the Iowa Review, "This is not Blake's `The Tiger'").

Grant's article also brought to the poem a new scrutiny to some oversights in the criticism. For example, his assertion that the "dare" in the earlier lines of the poem (as in "what dread hand dare seize the fire?") are in the present subjunctive tenses permits him "to bring these presumably past events into the imagination's present focus as the questioner meditates on them." Grant's suggestion, however, occasioned Fred Robinson's response, in 1964, which argued frequent precedence of the use of "dare" as a preterit. (Two years later, Grant and Robinson collaborated on the same issue in "Tense and the Sense of Blake's The Tiger.")

(Gardner, relies on a similar schism between the narrative time of the poem and the remote cosmic origin the speaker invokes. In 1986, in Retracing the Songs of Innocence and of Experience, he regards the poem as a short cosmic history "which takes the mind back through the poem and beyond... in a search of `his' identity, `he' who has been there all along, having created the tiger the poem invokes.")

Grant was also among the very first to closely study each grammatical molecule of the poem as it relates to the poem's overall meaning. His fastidious attention to syntax leads him to argue in favour of eliding identity of the tiger and its creator (as in, "what dread hand? & what dread feet?") and so, forbid any clean break between the identities of the two. The poem's "indeterminate syntax intimately relates [the two]. Any sharp division would constitute a `cloven fiction,' like the assertion that a good God can create evil." Leaving aside whether or not an indeterminate God creates an even more vexing theological question, it is sufficient to say that Grant's makes a subtle reading.

The speaker as a concept has produced a number of rival interpretations, most of which maintain that the speaker is somehow in error or is slowly awakening from it. Like Grant, E. D. Hirsch charts a transformation in the speaker, who begins the poem with a parody of the childish questions of "The Lamb". But the hardened cynicism of the opening stanzas modulates to "incoherent confusion" and then finally to incredulity by the final stanza, so that the speaker in the end is effectively "still close to the standpoint of Innocence." Similarly, for Martin Price (1964), the poem is a progression in the speaker from doubt to faith. The speaker, a "shocked doubter" frozen in his own spiritual "terror", gradually converts to "an assertion of faith (faith in the oneness of God, in the goodness of wrath, in the holiness of prophetic rage.)"

Likewise, other critics hold that the questioner, suffering from limited vision, does not, or cannot, understand the tiger. Leopold Damrosch, Jr. (1980), concluding that the tiger is a symbolic aspect of energy, says that "the speaker is right to fear the fires of energy," which, even if "creative", are obviously "purgative" and "tormenting" as well. Robert E. Simmons, writing in Visionary Forms Dramatic (1970), reads "The Tyger" "as an account of the growth of an illusion of terror" by a speaker who is conditioned by the symmetrical laws of Urizenic "fixity." John Beer brings in 'the fourfold vision', Blake's system of perfected consciousness, as an instrument of measuring the speaker. The loss of fourfold vision, common in the Fallen world, prevents the questioner from seeing that the "he who made the Lamb" also made the Tiger. But, Beer explains, terror and fascination are one in the speaker because "even while the twofold imagination in us is recoiling from the threat of the tiger, the lost fourfold in us is responding to the attraction of its energy and brightness." (Further, "because the horror is controlled by the harmonized energy of the poem," Beer observes memorably, "it appeals strongly to children, who enjoy the experience of controlled terror.")

In a lecture given in 1970, F. R. Leavis suggested that the poem's penultimate question ("Did he who made the Lamb make thee?") might stand in paradoxically as an epigram both books of Songs, for "the question is formidably complex, it is presented by the inclusive whole, which insists implicitly that there can be no pointing with epigrammatic neatness to any solution." The question, Leavis states "conveys no protest" against the divinity that created the tiger, but rather, with "profound awe," "it constates"— registers, simply acknowledges— the fact of the divine. But, he continues less clearly, this fact "is a value, and the problem constituted by the fact that there are other values gets its recognition in the poem itself."

**A Singular Opinion: Robert Graves's Reaction to the Poem**

Robert Graves's 1969 remarks ("Tyger, Tyger") are singular at least because of their categorical decisiveness. Graves makes a wide and largely original survey of issues within "The Tyger", discussing the poem's meter, its editing, and even (heretically) its "faulty craftsmanship." His conclusion, strangely, is not about the poem, but about how the poem demonstrates that "Blake was certainly in... a state of schizophrenia at the time" of its composition. It is a claim he further supports by citing its presence of tigers in the work of other tormented artists.

Paper Tygers: the poem as an instance of the false sublime (and still other disappointments)

Paul Miner, writing in 1962, is the first to write within a small set of readings in which "The Tiger" is posed as a philosophical hoax on the speaker, or as a moment of false sublimity. Miner sees in the poem as a deliberate and cosmic evasion: "What begins as a poem of pure ontology ends in metaphysical casuistry." Coleman O. Parsons (1968), feels that the "speaker has glimpses of reality," but receives "no vision" for his efforts. The final effect, says Parsons, is that "there is a feeling of enlargement, but no message, [and] no affirmation."

A less explicitly spiritual version of the poem's false sublimity exists in Harold Pagliaro's recent study (1987) of the poem charting a similar movement in the speaker. For

Pagliaro, the awe for the tiger dissipates in the asking of his questions, so that by the sixth stanza, he is beyond "the chief intensity of his vision of the fearful creature." The result is not much more than aerobic; the speaker arrives not at the spirituality of "poised enlightenment" but rather at a physically "heartened fatigue."

Another articulate case made for the poem's false (or failed) sublimity is in Harold Bloom's Blake's Apocalypse (1964). Bloom identifies the speaker as the Songs' own Bard of Experience, and characterizes him as a man who is typically liable to become "prostrate before a mystery entirely of his own creation." This cowardice of the divine reaches its height when, terrified of receiving a response to the question "Did he who made the Lamb make thee?", he "abandons the issue and plunges back into the affrighted awe of the sixth stanza."

**Against Interpretation**

Martin Nurmi observes that the "lyric in its powerful ambiguity approaches absolute art in poetry and stubbornly resists critical attempts to explain its meaning." The statement is in large part rhetorical, another laurel meant for the tiger's resilient, uninterruptible brow. Some critics, however, have taken that sentiment, or something close to it, at its word.

In his 1964 article "A Rhetorical Question Answered," for example, Philip Hobsbaum misanthropically states, "It is quite evident that the critics"— all critics, he attempts to show — "are not trying to understand the poem at all." The problem with them, he says, is that the poem's commentators demand answers to questions in a poem which are entirely rhetorical. Any answers to the question such as the one posed by Kathleen Raine, "Who Made the Tiger?," Hobsbaum says, "is going outside relevant enquiry." And in demanding such answers, what critics "seem to be looking for could be another poem, a mystical treatise, a philosophical dissertation" but "it cannot be a critique."

In a much lower key, Kay Parkhurst Long claims that "The Tyger" is a broad parody of "a major compulsion of mankind— the tendency to generalize, to label, to categorize." Long finds parallels between the eighteenth-century rationalists Blake attacked and the Blake scholars who limit his animal-poem by interpretation— both mind-forged manacles of "restrictive logic." And so, she concludes: "a tiger, or any creature, exists as evidence of the unending potentials of the universe and of man's imaginative perceptions of the universe."

Somewhat like Hobsbaum, Larry Swingle "looks to [the poem] as a positive phenomenon," an event from which the reader transforms and simultaneously, is transformed. Interpretation is not possible, says Swingle, for "our relationship with 'The Tiger' [and its questions] consists of 'We do not know' on nearly every matter." Since "one cannot reason things through and discover answers to "The Tiger"," he says, the reader must accept the text is a kind of spindle of meaning: "Like Los, the reader must say: "I will not Reason and Compare: my Business is to Create."

For Stanley Fish, the poem's critical legacy provides the opportunity to illustrate the possibly limitless horizons of "acceptable readings." In his 1980 book, Is There a Text in This Class?, he puts the contradictory interpretations of Kathleen Raine, and E. D. Hirsch, side by side. Both interpretations, he maintains, are not just right— in fact they are "obvious"— but only if one accepts the premises with which either begins. The equal "obviousness" of differing interpretations of "The Tiger" help Fish enunciate what has become a familiar interpretive problem: "it is assumptions, not the facts they make possible, that are at stake in any critical dispute."

(Taking this a step farther, he builds an "absurd" reading in which of the speaker of the poem regrets having eaten the tiger, a religiously forbidden meat. The poem, then, is a description of the food's course as it travels through his digestive system. Fish adds, in a parody of the breathless conclusions of so many "Tiger" articles: "The poem ends as it began, with the speaker paying the price of his sin and wondering at the inscrutable purposes of a deity who would lead his creatures into digestive temptation.")

## Smiling Tygers: Optimistic Views of the Poem

Whole-heartedly optimistic views of "The Tyger" are rare, which makes Dennis Welch's well-considered remarks on "'The Tyger' and Comic Vision" even more valuable. He finds the switch from the word "could" in the first stanza to the word "dare" in the sixth to imply "an admiration of such a power" that dazzles and fascinates the speaker. For Welch, the speaker sees in the tiger not a form of twisted energy (after Gardner's, for example), but rather "the limits of energy the Creator imposes on the tiger". This, in turn, calls to mind "the self-limitation of God— to become fallen in order to redeem the fallen." There should be assent to the question "Did he who made the Lamb make thee?", "because his plan is a divine and human comedy," about which "the speaker is on the verge of detecting."

It is the efficiency with which Raymond Lister dispatches the entire problem of the tiger's creator that deserves mention: "Blake himself could have supplied one answer to these questions if he had quoted his own words from America and elsewhere.... 'everything that lives is holy'— everything including the tiger." Therefore? "The answer is decidedly in the affirmative." And so, we are practically assured, the creator did in fact smile his work to see.

## Recent Interpretations of the Poem

Contemporary literary theory has not overwhelmed "The Tiger" with its customary interpretive zeal. Nevertheless, these new instruments have given the lyric new life and new contexts.

Critics favouring deconstructionist approaches to the lyric have been more frequent, though their work has been for the most part compact and incidental. Maybe because of this, their conclusions have not been entirely uniform, even if all of them bear the same theoretical turns of phrase.

For Graham Pechey, for example, "The Tyger" futilely attempts to carry out "a misdirected search for a transcendental signified," an "undivided divine subject" (i.e., God). Not finding one, the poem resolves not into a history of a Deity with an "indefinite past," but instead (rather anti-climactically) "a work of words that come together in that very moment." For Pechey, who offered this brief reading in 1981 for the collection 1789: Reading Writing Revolution, what finally emerges, like the French revolution itself, is the "profane historicity" of the signifier triumphing over the repressive signified.

Steven Vine (1993) replies that Pechey's reading "effectively eliminates the questions of the text." Vine clings, however, to Pechey's sense of a lost God, but he asserts that the transcendental signified "survives as a ghostly function," expressed as the silence meeting each of the speaker's questions. It is Nobodaddy, Vine says, Blake's sometimes risible figure of authority, who returns and "haunts" the poem (and others), "inscribing silence in the speech of performance." Michael Ferber's questioner, like Vine's, cannot receive answers from his tiger/auditor, and is left to wander "the forests of aporia."

Steven Shaviro's 1982 article in Boundary2, "Striving with Systems" is by far the most fully realised deconstructionist reading (though Shaviro places some distance between himself and Jacques Derrida). Shaviro assumes that a poem (and a poet) "so explicitly concerned with questions of origins" and contraries cannot hope to resolve its inevitable aporias. The result is a "Tiger" that exists in a state of impossible contraries that cancel one another as they strive to exist without each other; the poem becomes a "scene [that] is not a scene and not an origin, and can only be constituted as such, or be apprehended at all, by recourse to an act of interpretation or representation which it is advance disqualifies." Shaviro also explains some of the poem's convenience to psychoanalytic description; the poem becomes "the production or reproduction even as it is at the same time to the contrary, the repression, representation, and interpretation— of that pre-origin anxiety which precedes repression."

David Punter appears to agree with Shaviro on this point. "The tiger belongs," he says, "to a world before sublimation; he exists now as a haunting, flickering image of a dangerous world of instinct." The animal, "the unacceptable face of desire," is therefore a threat to those with "smooth notions of a divine plan." But "the tiger will not be kept in place," Punter says, "any more than we can refuse the manmade gifts which the hammer and the anvil will inevitably offer." The experienced world, therefore, must find a "path of manifesting energy lies not away from or round but through the jungle of developing human powers."

Susan Hawk Brisman and Leslie Brisman find in Lacanian psychoanalysis a productive means of re-naming the assumed roles in the poem. "The Tyger" and "The Lamb", they say, are ways of establishing a relationship to a Symbolic Other of order and authority (God) through an Imaginary Other (the animals addressed). While the speaker of "The Lamb" finds it very easy to incarnate God in the docile Lamb, "the incessant questions" of "The Tiger" fail "to call forth the Symbolic Other" that the questioner searches for. But if there is only silence from the tiger, there are "awesome thoughts that... take the place" of a direct reply. Instead of an emergence of a Symbolic Other, there is an elision of the two concepts: "The fearful symmetry of the tiger evokes from the speaker a response to this Imaginary counterpart that [he] desires to have from a Symbolic Other."

In the 1980 article "Spears, Spheres and Spiritual Tears", Nelson Hilton attempts to illuminate the perennially mysterious lines 17-18 ("When the stars threw down their spears/And water'd heaven with their tears."). First, Hilton begins, readers must recognize the associative logic which binds the words, rhymes and rhetorical imagery to one distinctly Blakean cosmogony of artistic creation. Further, an ideal reader will sense the "sub-vocalized paronomasia" of the poem, as in the word "tiger" itself, which is "in part the creature of wrath and anger and so associated with flames of fire; or the word "symmetry," which doubles, among other puns, as the exclamation "see me try." Words like "spears" and "spheres" of the fifth stanza set in motion other, more complex Blakean associations which spiral and enlarge the poem's meaning without any assurance of a comfortable closure. For Hilton, "the force of and desire for underlying, unending interconnections of language present in polysemous sub-vocalization are everywhere at work" in the poem. "The Tiger" then, is "a scene of writing" whose "real question" is "how the deadly terrors of language-overload are to be (mentally) grasped and (physically) clasped in words."

Stuart Peterfreund, writing in 1991, decides that the lyric is a direct, almost editorial, critique of the rationalist natural science that Blake so vehemently despised. Peterfreund's speaker is thoroughly Newtonian, searching with his questions for the identity of some Great Clockmaker of the Universe. Observing that the tiger is metonymically framed by the speaker's questions (which invoke each of its individual parts), Peterfreund finds that the tiger's relation to its Maker is rhetorically created by the speaker himself. "Tiger-as-effect," he says, "testifies to the existence of an artifice-as-cause that is the ultimate object of the speaker's knowledge." But the questioner is really only successful, he says, in creating "the illusion that the speaker is empowered to speak in place of the tiger's creator by insisting on the tiger as reified, naturalized effect of that first cause."

## A concluding Observation about "Tyger" Criticism and the Cold War

"The Tyger" has been Blake's most popular poem since almost its publication, a commonplace that everyone, from little children to retiring faculty, knows without hesitation. What, then, accounts for its sudden critical importance after the Second World War? And what has sustained that output for almost five decades? There is a respected interpretation of "The Tyger" that the poem records the French Revolution as an historical energy. Whether or not that moment should be one of wonder, beguilement or horror is a matter of principled judgment. Most critics are decided that the revolution, like the animal symbolizing it, belongs to a power beyond the control of human agents. In the same way, "The Tiger" came to speak for the dread energy belonging to the atomic bomb. Held together at a distance, critical responses to the poem after 1945 seem like a prismatic account of the self in the Cold War. An omnipresent and master less energy lurks in the most familiar critiques of the poem. Jesse Bier's tiger contains both "the marvelous and the fatal."

Even Nelson Hilton's "unending interconnections" of relatively innocent word play take on the nervous aspect of uncontrolled fission. Indeed, it is in this anxious context that Morton D. Paley (1954) and Harold Bloom (1976) looked for the source of sublime wrath in Job and Jacob Boehme. And it is the very evidence of this animal ("burning bright") that led Kathleen Raine and Stanley Gardner to find a creative (and potentially destructive) demiurge as its parent.

It is possible to date the true beginning of "Tiger" studies not simply from the emergence of the New Criticism, but from August 6, 1945. After that date, several millions in Europe, the United States, the Soviet Union and elsewhere faced collective annihilation as a casual possibility. And like the speaker of so many interpretations, this self, living in its petty world of experience, shrinks to an infinitesimal point when contemplating such a broadly statistical death. The "apocalyptic limelight" that critics like Northrop Frye saw the tiger bounding in was lit from the rising tower of a mushroom cloud.

Further, "The Tiger" seemed to be encoded with the same binary value systems that held the Cold War world in place: American capitalism in the West and Soviet communism in the East; the first world of the northern hemisphere and the third of the southern. The mutual exclusiveness of such an ethical world is mirrored in essays that seek to name the tiger as Los's or Urizen's, God's or the Devil's; good or evil.

Though it may risk trivializing forty-five years of scholarship, so much of this criticism has seemed to be a piece of Cold War magic; by naming the atomic beast, there existed a possibility of assimilating it, or least, turning it into a household demon, a more familiar nightmare.

With the passing of the Cold War (although not, as we often comfortably assume, nuclear weaponry) the "golden age" of "Tyger" criticism will also pass. Or at least one golden age, anyway. The questions of "The Tyger" will persist as long as possibility of the collective annihilation exists and, with it, the annihilation of the concept of the individual as well.

## Chapter 16

# Critical Studies on Blake's Poetry

In 1827 there died, undoubtedly unknown to each other, two plebeian Europeans of supreme originality: Ludwig van Beethoven and William Blake. Had they known of each other, they could still not have known how much of the future they contained and how alike they were in the quality of their personal force, their defiance of the age, and the fierce demands each had made on the human imagination.

It is part of the story of Blake's isolation from the European culture of his time that he could have known of Beethoven, who enjoyed a reputation in the London of the early 1800's. The Ninth Symphony was in fact commissioned by the London Philharmonic, who made Beethoven's last days a little easier. The artistic society of the day was appreciative of Beethoven. It ignored the laborious little engraver, shut off by his work and reputed madness, who was known mainly to a few painters, and held by most of them to be a charming crank.

It is hard to imagine Blake going to concerts or reading accounts of Beethoven's music. He never traveled. Except for one three-year stay at a cottage in Sussex, he hardly went out of London. Like his father and brothers, he lived the life of a small tradesman—at one time he kept a print shop. He was always very poor, and generally worked in such seclusion that at one period, near the end of his life, he did not leave his house for two years, except to go out for porter. Blake had instinctive musical gifts; in his youth and old age he spontaneously, when in company, sang melodies to his own lyrics. Musicians who heard them set them down; I wish I knew where. Even on his deathbed, where he worked to the last, he composed songs. But he had no formal musical knowledge and apparently no interest in musical thought. Self-educated in every field except engraving, to which he had been apprenticed at fourteen, his only interest in most ideas outside his own was to refute them. He always lived and worked very much alone, with a wife whom he trained to be the mirror of his mind. The world let him alone. He was entirely preoccupied with his designs, his poems, and the burden—which he felt more than any writer whom I know—of the finiteness of man before the whole creation.

Beethoven's isolation was different. He was separated from society by his deafness, his pride, his awkward relations with women, relatives, patrons, inadequate musicians. He was isolated, as all original minds are, by the need to develop absolutely in his own way. The isolation was made tragic, against his will, by his deafness and social pride. At the same time he was one of the famous virtuosos of Europe, the heir of Mozart and the pupil of Haydn, and the occasional grumpy favourite of the musical princes of Vienna. His isolation was an involuntary personal tragedy, as it was by necessity a social fact. He did not resign himself to it, and only with the greatest courage learned to submit to it. If he was solitary, it was in a great tradition. As he was influenced by his predecessors, so he became the fountainhead of the principal musical thought that came after him.

Blake's isolation was—I sometimes think it still is—absolute. It was the isolation of a mind that sought to make the best of heaven and earth, in the image of neither. It was isolation of a totally different kind of human vision; of an unappeasable longing for the absolute integration of man, in his total nature, with the universe. It was the isolation of a temperament run on fixed ideas; and incidentally, of a craftsman who could not earn a living. There are analogies to

Blake's position in a world which has so many displaced persons as our own; but they are inadequate. Blake's isolation may be likened to that of the revolutionary who sits in his grubby room writing manifestoes against a society that pays him no attention, with footnotes against other revolutionaries who think him mad. It was that of the author who prints his own books. It was that of the sweetly smiling crank who sits forever in publishers' offices, with a vast portfolio under his arm, explaining with undiminishable confidence that only through his vision will the world be saved. It was that of the engraver who stopped getting assignments because he turned each one into an act of independent creation. Blake was a lyric poet interested chiefly in ideas, and a painter who did not believe in nature. He was a commercial artist who was a genius in poetry, painting, and religion. He was a libertarian obsessed with God; a mystic who reversed the mystical pattern, for he sought man as the end of his search. He was a Christian who hated the churches; a revolutionary who abhorred the materialism of the radicals. He was a drudge, sometimes living on a dollar a week, which called himself "a mental prince"; and was one.

There are other points of difference between Blake and Beethoven, important to recognize before we can appreciate their likeness. With Beethoven we are in the stream of modern secular culture. Beethoven, the enduring republican and anti-Bonapartist, the social dramatist of *Fidelio,* the jealous admirer of Goethe, the celebrant of Schiller's call to the joyous brotherhood of man! is a central figure in *our* history, as Blake never has been. We remember Beethoven the moralist, the Beethoven who felt so gratefully at home in the world of Kant that he copied out a sentence, probably at second-hand, and kept it on his work-table—"The starry heavens above us and the moral law within us. Kant!!!" To Blake the "moral law" was a murderous fiction and the stars were in the heavens because man's imagination saw them there. Beethoven speaks to our modern humanity in tones we have learned to prize as our own and our greatest, as Blake has not yet; he is uneasily religious and spiritually frustrated, in a familiar agnostic way? where Blake is the "immoralist" and "mystic" by turns. Beethoven could not hear the world, but he always believed in it. His struggles to sustain himself in it, on the highest level of his creative self-respect, were vehement because he could never escape the tyranny of the actual. He was against material despotisms, and knew them to be real. Blake was also against them; but he came to see every hindrance to man's imaginative self-liberation as a fiction bred by the division in man himself. He was against society *in toto*: its prisons, churches, money, morals, fashionable opinions; he did not think that the faults of society stemmed from the faulty organization of society. To him the only restrictions over man are always in his own mind—the "mind-forg'd manacles."

With Blake, it would seem, we are off the main track of modern secular thought and aspiration. The textbooks label him "mystic," and that shuts him off from us. Actually he is not off the main track, but simply ahead of it; a peculiarly disturbed and disturbing prophet of the condition of modern man rather than a master-builder. From any conventional point of view he is too different in kind to be related easily to familiar conceptions of the nature of the individual and society. Blake combines, for example, the formal devotional qualities of the English dissenters with the intellectual daring of Nietzsche, the Marquis de Sade, and Freud. No Christian saint ever came to be more adoring of Jesus, and no naturalistic investigator was a more candid opponent of traditional Christian ethics. He was one of the subtlest and most far-reaching figures in the intellectual liberation of Europe that took place at the end of the eighteenth century. But he had no interest in history, and easily relapsed into primitive nationalism. To the end of his life his chief symbol for man, "the eternal man," was Albion; the origin of "natural religion" he located among the Druids; he hated Newton and despised Voltaire, but painted the apotheosis of Nelson and Pitt. Like so many self-educated men, he was fanatically learned; but he read like a Fundamentalist—to be inspired or to refute. He painted by "intellectual vision"—that is, he painted ideas; his imagination was so original that it carried him to the borders of modern surrealism. Yet he would have been maddened by the intellectual traits of surrealism: the calculated insincerities, the defiant disorder, the autonomous decorative fancy, the intellectual mockery and irreverence. That part of surrealism which is not art is usually insincerity, and to Blake any portion of insincerity was a living death. As he hated church dogma, so he hated skepticism, doubt, experimentalism.

He did not believe in sin, only in "intellectual error"; he loathed every dualistic conception of good and evil; the belief that any human being could be punished, here or elsewhere, for "following his energies." But he thought that unbelief—that is, the admission of uncertainty on the part of any person—was wicked. He understood that man's vital energies cannot be suppressed or displaced without causing distortion; he saw into the personal motivations of human conflict and the many concealments of it which are called culture. He celebrated in *Songs of Innocence*, with extraordinary inward understanding, the imaginative separateness of the child. He hated scientific investigation.

He could say in his old age, when provoked, that he believed the world was flat. He was undoubtedly sincere, but he did not really care what shape it was; he would not have believed any evidence whatsoever that there were many planets and universes. He did not believe in God; under all his artistic labors and intellectual heresies he seems to have thought of nothing else. He is one of the most prophetic and gifted rebels in the history of Western man—a man peculiarly of our time, with the divisions of our time. Some of his ideas were automatically superstitious, and a large part of his writing is rant. There are features of his thought that carry us beyond the subtlest understanding we have of the relations between man and woman, the recesses of the psyche, the meaning of human error, tyranny, and happiness. There are chapters in his private mythology that carry us into a nightmare world of loneliness and fanaticism, like a scream repeated interminably on a record in which a needle is stuck.

Yet Blake is very much like Beethoven in his artistic independence and universality. Like Beethoven, he is a pioneer Romantic of that heroic first generation which thought that the flames of the French Revolution would burn down all fetters. Like Beethoven, he asserts the creative freedom of the imagination within his work and makes a new world of thought out of it. There sounds all through Blake's poetry, from the boyish and smiling defiance of neoclassic formalism in *Poetical Sketches,*

> The languid strings do scarcely move!
> The sound is forced, the notes are few!

to the vision of man the divine in *Jerusalem* that lyric despair mingled with quickness to exaltation, that sense of a primal intelligence fighting the mind's limitations, that brings Beethoven's last quartets so close to absolute meditation and the Ninth Symphony to a succession of triumphal marches. What is nearest and first in both men is so strong a sense of their own identity that they are always reaching beyond man's conception of his powers. In both there is a positive assertion against suffering, impatience with forms and means. As Beethoven said of the violinist who complained of the difficulty of one of the Rasumofsky quartets—"Does he really suppose I think of his puling little fiddle when the spirit speaks to one and I compose something?"—so to Blake the forms he uses in his last Prophetic Books, even to their very narrative coherence, are nothing before the absoluteness of his vision. In both lives becomes synonymous with the will.

There, however, the resemblance ends. For Beethoven does not block our way by asking us to read him in symbols of his own invention. He is subtle, moving, reflective, in a language which we- share because he has made it possible for us to share in it. Out of a limited number of musical tones and devices, he has organized his thought and impressed his conception in such a way that his difference is all *in* his art. When we have grasped his meaning something has enriched our lives without dislodging them. Beethoven is as luminously human as he is creatively independent; he can be gay; he parodies; he introduces a little Russian tune to compliment a patron; he is fond of bearish jokes. He is often difficult, but never impossible. He does not challenge man's submission to the natural order; he finds his place in it, and often in such deep wells of serenity, of happiness in his own struggle, that the song that rises from him almost at the very end, in his last quartet, is for a dance. "Must it bed" he wrote on the manuscript. "It must be. It must be." He may have been thinking of something less than man's ultimate relation to life. But the idea that something *must be* is what is most hateful to Blake's mind.

For Blake accepts nothing—not the God who is supposed to have proposed it this way, or the man who is constrained to dispose it in any way he can. Blake begins with a longing so deep, for all that is invisible and infinite to man under the dominion of God, matter, and reason, that he tears away the shell of earth, the prison of man in his own senses, to assert that there is nothing but man and that man is nothing but the highest flights of his own imagination. With his little tradesman's look, his fanatical industriousness, his somber qualities of the English dissenter and petty-bourgeois, he begins with so absolute a challenge to the religion that was dying in his age, and to the scientific materialism that arose in it, that he transcends them both—into a world that is exalted and often beautiful, but of which he alone saw the full detail.

To understand this is to pass up the usual tags. Blake is seeking something which is analogous to mysticism, but he is not in any ordinary sense a mystic. He is very much in the stream of thought which led to naturalism, but he is not a naturalist. It is more important, however, to show what he shares with us rather than with the mystics. Only those who want to make a Blake easy to explain and apologize for, convenient for the textbooks, can see him as a queer and harmless "mystic." As D. H. Lawrence said of his work, "They'll say as they said of Blake: It's mysticism, but they shan't get away with it, not this time: Blake's wasn't mysticism, neither is this." Even at the end, when Blake celebrated Jesus as his great friend and deliverer, we have in "The Everlasting Gospel:"

> The Vision of Christ that thou dost see
> Is my Vision's Greatest Enemy:
> Thine is the friend of all Mankind,
> Mine speaks in parables to the Blind:
> Thine loves the same world that mine hates,
> Thy Heaven doors are my Hell Gates.

Christian mysticism is founded on dualism. It is rooted in the belief that man is a battleground between the spirit and the flesh, between the temptations of earth and God as the highest Good. The mystic way is the logical and extreme manifestation of the spiritual will, obedient to a faith in supernatural authority, to throw off the body and find an ultimate release in the Godhead. Christian mysticism is based upon a mortification of the body so absolute that it attains a condition of ecstasy. To the mystic, God is the nucleus of the Creation, and man in his earthly life is a dislodged atom that must find its way back. The mystic begins with submission to a divine order, which he accepts with such conviction that earthly life becomes nothing to him. He lives only for the journey of the soul that will take him away, upward to God. What would be physical pain to others, to him is purgation; what would be doubt to others, to him is hell; what would be death for others, to him is the final consummation—and one he tries to reach in the living body.

Blake has the mystic's tormented sense of the double ness of life between reality and the ideal. But he tries to resolve it on earth, in the living person of man. Up to 1800 he also thought it could be resolved in society, under the inspiration of the American and French Revolutions. Blake is against everything that submits, mortifies, constricts and denies. Mystics are absent-minded reactionaries; they accept indifferently everything in the world except the barriers that physical existence presents to the soul's inner quest. Blake is a revolutionary. He ceased to be a revolutionary in the political sense after England went to war with France and tried to destroy the revolution in Europe. That was less out of prudent cowardice—though like every other radical and free-thinker of the time he lived under a Tory reign of terror —than because he had lost faith in political action as a means to human happiness. Even in politics, however, his libertarian thought became a challenge to all the foundations of society in his time. Blake is not only unmystical in the prime sense of being against the mystic's immediate concerns and loyalties; he is against all accepted Christianity. He is against the churches,

Remove away that black'ning church;
Remove away that marriage hearse:
Remove away that place of blood:
You'll quite remove the ancient curse.

Against priesthood:
And Priests in black gowns were walking their rounds,
And binding with briars my joys & desires.

Against the "moral law." He denies that man is born with any innate sense of morality—all moral codes are born of education— and thinks education training in conformity. He is against all belief in sin; to him the tree in Eden is the gallows on which freedom-seeking man is hanged by dead-souled priests. He savagely parodied a Dr. Thornton's new version of the Lord's Prayer:

Our Father Augustus Caesar, who art in these thy Substantial Astronomical Telescopic Heavens, Holiness to Thy Name or Title, & reverence to thy Shadow.... Give us day by day our Real Taxed Substantial Money bought bread; deliver from the Holy Ghost whatever cannot be taxed....

He is against every conception of God as an omnipotent person, as a body, as a Lord who sets in train any lordship over man:

Thou art a Man, God is no more,
Thine own humanity learn to adore.

He believes that all restraint in obedience to a moral code is against the spirit of life:

Abstinence sows sand all over
The ruddy limbs & flaming hair,
But Desire Gratified
Plants fruits & beauty there.

Blake is against all theological casuistry that excuses pain and admits evil; against sanctimonious apologies for injustice and the attempt to buy bliss in another world with self-deprivation in this one. The altar is a place on which the serpent has vomited out its poison; the priest is a blind old man with shears in his hand, to cut the fleece off human sheep. Sex is life, and no one can be superior to it or honestly content with less than true gratification:

What is it men in women do require?
The lineaments of Gratified Desire.
What is it women in men do require?
The lineaments of Gratified Desire.

Restraint, in fact, follows from the organized injustice and domination in society:

The harvest shall flourish in wintry weather
When two virginities meet together:
The King & the Priest must be tied in a tether
Before two virgins can meet together.

He is against all forms of human exploitation, and all rationalizations of it in human prejudice:

And all must love the human form,
In heathen, turk, or few;
Where Mercy, Love, & Pity dwell
There God is dwelling too.

Against war, especially holy ones; against armies, and in pity for soldiers; against the factory system, the labour of children, the evaluation of anything by money.

In "London," one of his simplest and greatest poems, Blake paints the modern city under the sign of man's slavery, the agony of children, the suffering Soldier and the Whore:

I wander thro' each charter'd street,
Near where the charter'd Thames does flow,
And mark in every face I meet
Marks of weakness, marks of woe.

In every cry of every Man,
In every Infant's cry of fear,
In every voice, in every ban,
The mind-forg'd manacles I hear.

How the Chimney-sweeper's cry
Every black'ning Church appalls;
And the hapless Soldier's sigh
Runs in blood down Palace walls.

But most thro' midnight streets I hear
How the youthful Harlot's curse
Blasts the new born Infant's tear,
And blights with plagues the Marriage hearse.

"Charter'd" means "bound." In his first draft of this poem, Blake wrote "dirty Thames," but characteristically saw that he could realise more of the city's human slavery in describing the river as bound between its London shores. His own place in the poem is that of the walker in the modern inhuman city, one isolated man in the net which men have created. "I wander thro' each charter'd street." For him man is always the wanderer in the oppressive and sterile world of materialism which only his imagination and love can render human. In a more difficult poem, characteristic of his deeper symbolism, he speaks of the world of matter as

A Fathomless & boundless deep,
There we wander, there we weep;

In "London," however, the wandering is not a symbolic expression. In the modern city man has lost his real being, as he has already lost his gift of vision in the "fathomless and boundless" deep of his material nature. Blake here describes one man, himself, in a city that is only too real, the only city he ever knew—yet the largest in the world, the centre of empire. The city stands revealed in the cry of *every* Man, in *every* Infant's cry of fear. The wanderer in the chartered streets is concerned with a social picture and, in the face of so much suffering, with the social evil that some create and all permit. The extraordinary terseness of the poem stems from Blake's integral vision of the suffering of man and his alienation from institutions as one. His indignation gives him the power of movement; it also leads him into the repetitions which dominate the tonal order of the poem—the *every* cry of *every* Man, the Infant's *cry of fear*, till his tender vehemence swells into the generality of *in every voice, in every ban. Every* is magic to Blake. Poetically he cannot go wrong on it, for it carries such a kernel of glory to his mind, it points so immediately to his burning human solidarity, that in using it he knows himself carried along by what is deepest to him. The *mindforg'd manacles,* as central to his thought as any phrase he ever used, follows with a triumphant sweep right after it, and for an obvious reason. For he is one with every voice, every ban, and can now make his judgment. On this fresh creative impulse he leaps ahead to what is so complex, but for him so natural, a yoking of images:

> How the Chimney-sweeper's cry
> Every black'ning Church appalls;

The young Chimney-sweeper is always dear to Blake, especially when he is condemned to get the soot out of the churches—an impossible task. He is the symbol of the child who is lost. He works among the waste-dirt of the Church, itself black with dogma and punitive zeal, and his own suffering makes it even blacker. *Black'ning* is a verb of endless duration in present time for Blake. In his drawing to this poem, the Chimney-sweeper is shown in one corner struggling before a black flame. At the top of the page he stands in defiance before the blind and tottering old man, the fossilized Church, who seems to be pouring out fresh soot. The walls are the stone blocks of a prison. The whole page is marked, like the turn of the hand on a vehement signature, by a fierce black border. Pictorially and verbally we thus rise to a climax at the word *appalls*. The Church is not appalled by the Chimney-sweeper's cry; the cry of the child, out of the midst of the Church, makes the Church appalling. Blake's thrust is so swift and deep that he characteristically puts the whole burden of his protest, with its inner music, into four words. Every black and blackening Church is appalling, and in every way. The tone of *palls* to his ear, carrying the image of death, the grief and shame that will not rest, clangs with reverberations.

The unhappiness of the Soldier is not that of a man bleeding before a palace of which he is the sentry. Blake means that the Soldier's desperation runs, like his own blood, in accusation down the walls of the ruling Palace. Blake's own mind ran in so many channels at once, his vision of human existence was so total, that it probably never occurred to him that *blood* would mean anything less to others than it did to him. "Runs in blood down palace walls" is what Blake sees instantaneously in his mind when he thinks of the passivity and suffering of the Soldier. Blake is too much abreast of the reality he sees to use similes; he cannot deliberate to compare something to another. And he is equally incapable of using a metaphor with self-conscious daring. He saw the blood running down the ruler's walls before thinking of blood as a "powerful" image. There is no careful audacity in him, the preparation for the humour of T. S. Eliot's

I am aware of the damp souls of housemaids
Sprouting despondently at area gates.

Blake's poetic urge, it is clear, was not to startle, to tease the mind into fresh combinations, but to make tangible, out of the wealth of relationships he carried in his mind, some portion of it equal to his vision of the life of man. How swiftly and emphatically he turns, at the first line of the fourth stanza, to

But most thro' midnight streets I hear

*But most* stands for: what I have described thus far is not the full horror of London, my city; not anything like what I have to tell you! And he then gives back, in eighteen words, the city in which young girls are forced into prostitution; in which their exile from respectable society, like the unhappiness of the Soldier, expresses itself in a physical threat to another. The Soldier accuses the Palace with his blood; the prostitute curses with infection the young husband who has been with her; the "plague" finally kills the new-born child. The carriage that went to the church for a marriage ends at the grave as a hearse. Nothing can equal the bite of "blights with plagues," the almost visible thrust of the infection. And thanks to Blake's happy feeling for capitals, which he used with a painter's eye to distinguish the height of his concepts, Marriage stands above the rest in the last sentence of the poem, and swiftly falls into a hearse.

These are some of the poem's details, but they are not the poem. For the poem is to be grasped only by the moral imagination, as a shuddering vision of the mind. The title is a city, as the city is the present human world on the threshold of the industrial revolution. We are to read from the title to the last word, from London to its inner death, in one movement of human sympathy and arousal. This, in its simplest sense, is the key to Blake's meaning of vision. Vision is his master-word, not mysticism or soul. For vision represents the total imagination of man made tangible and direct in works of art. And as the metric structure of the poem encloses, in each line-frame of sharply enclosed syllables, the sight of man entering fully into the city with all his being—*hearing* "the mind-forg'd manacles," the harlot's disease *blasting* "the new born infant's tear," so the whole poem carries us along, in a single page, while the border designs meanwhile extend the vision by another art.

Blake was artist and poet; he designed his poems to form a single picture. Trained to engraving as a boy, he invented for himself a method of etching a hand-printed poem and an accompanying design on the same page. Only two of his works were ever printed—his first book, *Poetical Sketches*, most of which he wrote between the ages of twelve and twenty-one, and a long and declamatory celebration of the new world after '89 called *The French Resolution*. Neither of these works was ever published. *Poetical Sketches* was run do for him, with a patronizing and apologetic preface by a Reverend Mathew, who with his wife formed a provincial intellectual society that Blake burlesqued in *An Island in the Moon*. *The French Revolution* was printed by a bookseller, Joseph Johnson, who was the centre of a radical circle in London that included Blake, William Godwin, Mary Wollstonecraft, and Thomas Paine. After England became embroiled with France and a reactionary witch-hunt set after radical intellectuals and sympathizers with the French Republic, Johnson became panicky and left the book in proof. Some of Blake's greatest poem—"The Everlasting Gospel," "Auguries of Innocence," the lyrics that follow *Songs of Innocence and of Experience*—were found in "The Rossetti Manuscript," which was bought by Dante Gabriel Rossetti for ten shillings from an attendant at the British Museum. Blake's most famous works, *Songs of Innocence und of Experience* and *The Marriage of Heaven and Hell*, along with his Prophetic Books—*The Book of Thel, Visions of the Daughters of Albion, America, Europe, The Boot of Urizen, Milton, Jerusalem*, etc.—were done entirely by his method of "illuminated printing." Blake said he got the inspiration for this technique from the spirit of his dead brother Robert, the only member of his family with whom he had common sympathies. This may be true, but it is a pity that Blake had to say so, for it has given people the idea ever since that Blake's visions were of the kind limited to a séance.

Blake's general technique is now clear. He etched his poems and designs in relief, with acid on copper. He corroded with acid the unused portions of the plate— characteristically, this became a symbol in *The Marriage of Heaven and Hell* of the corrosion of dead matter by the visionary human imagination. Each print page as it was taken off the press was coloured by hand. Each copy of a work was planned in a different colour scheme. There are probably no handmade books in the world more beautiful. The only models for Blake were, of course, the illuminated manuscripts of the Middle Ages. But Blake worked in an entirely different spirit. The medieval manuscripts, impressive as they are, remain pictorial and remote; they were created by copyists, ornament lists and pious scribes who worked in a liturgical spirit. Blake's designs are the accessories of a single creative idea. His conception of the beautiful book, as Laurence Binyon said, was one of a complete unity, "in which the lettering, the decoration, the illustrations, the proportions of the page, the choice of paper, surpassed even the conceptions of the medieval scribes and miniaturists." Yet Blake was not aiming at a "beautiful book" for its own sake, or at the kind of isolated luxury product which we usually associate with book illustration by a master artist. To him all the arts were simultaneously necessary, in their highest creative use and inner proportion, to give us the ground essence of his vision and a stimulus to our own. What was most important to him was that he should get all his vision down, through all the arts open to him, in work done entirely in his own person.

Blake's search for unity began in his own hands, with his sense of craft. The symbolic synthesis to be created by his imagination was an image of man pressing, with the full power of his aroused creativity, against the walls of natural appearances. Each page of "illuminated printing" for him was a little world, in which the structure of the poem, the designs on the border, the accompanying figures on the page, the tints of the colour, the rhythm of the lettering, were joined together into the supreme metaphor.

The attempt to model some ideal unity in a single work is not unique in itself—it is the symbolic function of traditional religious art, and is to be found in the outer and inner architecture of the cathedrals, the structure of *The Divine Comedy*, and cruciformly printed poems of George Herbert. What is different in Blake is that he is not modeling after any symbols but his own. The symbols always have an inner relatedness that leads us from the outer world to the inner man. The symbols live in the ordered existence of his vision; the vision itself is entirely personal, in theme and in the logic that sustains it. What is before us, in one of his pages, has been created entirely by him in every sense, and the unimpeachable quality of his genius is shown in an order that is as great as his independence, and shows us how real both were. The characteristic of his genius is to lift his unexpected symbols for the inner world of the imagination into a world in which they stand apart from the natural world and defy it. When he designs illustrations to Gray's poems, the magnitude of his vision throws the lines he is illustrating off the page. But what impresses us in their magnitude is not their physical size, but the uncanny spiritual coherence which joins them together and gives them an effect of absolute force. Blake could never "illustrate" another man's work, even though it was pretty much the only way by which he could earn a living. Even if he respected the other man's work, as he did Milton and Dante, he created new conceptions of their subject in his own designs. When he did his twenty-one engravings to the Book of Job, he reversed the pious maxims of the Bible story to show a man destroyed by his own materialism and self-righteousness. Fortunately, he did not set his Job designs against a page reproduced from the Bible; he selected passages, and wrote new ones, and put both into the scroll-work of his border designs. His vision of Job is entirely his own work, as the Job is indeed the greatest of his "Prophetic Books." Where the words were created by him, as in his poems, the love of the word to the design is only one revelation of man's will to wed the contraries—like the marriage of Heaven and Hell. Blake's conception of union and of the infiniteness of union has no physical status. For him infinity is in man's passions and his will to know; it is a state of being.

Yet what has been designed is bound, much as Blake disliked all limits. So he carried the force and delicacy of his longing for the infinite into the subtle inwardness of everything he drew. In *Songs of Innocence and of Experience,* he designed his poems in such a way that the words on the line seemed to grow like flower heads out of a thicket. Each hand-printed letter of script, each vine trailing a border between the lines, each moving figure above, beside, and below the page mounts and unites to form some visible representation of the inner life of man—seen in phases of the outward nature. Yet Blake was not Peking to represent nature; he used it as a book of symbols. When he put down something "natural" and visible on his page—a bramble, a tree, a leaf, a figure moving mysteriously in its symbolic space—the effort seemed to dissolve his need to believe in its separate existence. The acid of the designer's imagination burned away the materials on which it worked. What he represented, for purposes of spiritual vision and imagery, dissolved its own exterior naturalness for him. The natural forms—from the arch of the sky to the stolid heroic figures he liked to draw—became a mold that would contain his symbolic ideas of them. This is what makes his gift so beautiful on one level, and often so unreachable on another. He brought a representation of the world into every conception; but he never drew an object for its own sake. He wrote and drew, as he lived, from a fathomless inner window, in an effort to make what was deepest and most invisible alterable by the mind of man. Then he used the thing created—the poem, the picture, joined in their double vision—as a window in itself, through which to look to what was still beyond. "I look through the eye," he said, "not with it."

In short, Blake was not looking for God. He shared in the mystic's quest, but he was not going the same way. But we can see at the same time that he was not interested in natural phenomena, in the indestructible actuality of what is not in ourselves but equally real. Spinoza once said that the greatest good is the knowledge of the union which the mind has with the whole nature. That is an exalted statement, but we can recognize its meaning through the work of naturalists of genius like Darwin, Marx, and Freud. The creative function of naturalism has been to establish, with some exactness, a measure of objective knowledge —whether in the description of matter and energy, man's own life as a biological organism, his economic society, or the life urges which civilization has pushed into a world below consciousness. Naturalism is a great and tragic way of looking at life, for with every advance in man's consciousness and in his ability to ascertain, to predict, and to control, he loses that view of his supreme importance which is at the centre of religious myth. Naturalism helps to postpone death, but never denies it; it cannot distort objective truth for the sake of personal assurance; it finds assurance in man's ability to know something of what lies outside him. There flows from its positive insights an advance in man's consciousness of his own power that is more fertile and resourceful than any anthropocentric myth can inspire. Naturalism declares limits, and discovers new worlds of actuality between them. It is tragic, for by showing that man's experience is limited it gives him a sense of his permanent and unremitting struggle in a world he did not make. But the struggle is the image of his true life in the world, and one he deepens by art, knowledge, and love. The quality of tragedy is not sadness but grave exhilaration; it defines the possible.

Blake is not a naturalist; he believes in apprehension, not in being; in certainty at the price of reality. He does not believe that anything is finally real except the imagination of man. He grasped one horn of the classic dilemma—"how do I know that anything is real, since I know of reality only through my own mind ?"—and pronounced that the problem was settled. He refused to believe the evidence of his senses that the human mind—however it may qualify or misread reality—is bombarded by something outside itself. We are eternally subjective; but there are objects. Indeed, it would seem to follow from our very ability to correct ourselves that we do measure our knowledge by some source. Our backs in Plato's cave are to the fire; but we know that the shadows on the wall before us are shadows, and not the fire itself. Blake assumed that what is partial is in error, and that what is limited is non-existent. But the truth is that he was not trying to prove anything philosophically at all; his greatness depends not on his conception of the world but on what he created through it. In defence of his own personality, and in defiance of his age, he imagined a world equal to his heart's desire. He refused to admit objective reality only because he was afraid man would have to share the creation.

It is here that Blake has perplexed his readers even more than he has delighted them. The reason lies in his refusal to concede a distance between what is real and what is ideal; in his desperate need to claim them as one. Blake is difficult not because he invented symbols of his own; he created his symbols to show that the existence of any natural object and the value man's mind places on it were one and the same. He was fighting the acceptance of reality in the light of science as much as he was fighting the suppression of human nature by ethical dogmas. He fought on two fronts, and shifted his arms from one to the other without letting us know—more exactly, he did not let himself know. He created for himself a personality, in life and in art that was the image of the thing he sought.

Like all the great enlighteners of the eighteenth century, Blake is against the *ancient régime* in all its manifestations—autocracy, feudalism, superstition. Though he loathed the destructive reason of the Deists, he sometimes praised it in the fight against "holy mystery." He was fighting for free thought. Yet he is not only a confederate of Diderot and Voltaire, Jefferson and Tom Paine; he is a herald of the "heroic vitalism" of Nietzsche and D. H. Lawrence, of Dostoevsky's scorn for nineteenth-century utilitarianism and self-contentment. Where the Encyclopedias were concerned with the investigation, on "natural principles," of man's place in society and his order in the universe, Blake—who hated the Church as much as Voltaire and was as republican as Jefferson—was concerned with the freedom of man from all restrictions, whether imposed by the morality of the Church or the narrowness of positivism.

Like Nietzsche, he considered himself an enemy of Socrates and of the Platonic dualism that became a permanent basis of Christian thought. What Blake said in so many of his early poems Nietzsche was to say in his autobiography: "All history is the experimental refutation of the theory of the so-called moral order of the world." Zarathustra, dancing mysteriously to the bacchanal of Nietzsche's imagined self-fulfillment, is prefigured in Blake's Los, the crusading imagination with the hammer in his hand. And like Nietzsche,

Blake writes in his masterpiece, *The Marriage of Heaven and Hell,* with the playful demonism of those who league themselves with the "Devil" because his opposite number restricts human rights:

> The reason Milton wrote in fetters when he wrote of Angels & God, and at liberty when of Devils & Hell, is because he was a true poet and of the Devil's party without knowing it.

With it there is the stress on heroic energy, on the rights of the superior that cannot be claimed under what Nietzsche called the "slave-morality":

> The eagle never lost so much time as when he submitted to learn of the crow.
>
> Damn braces. Bless relaxes.
>
> Improvement makes strait roads; but the crooked roads without Improvement are the roads of genius.

Destroy, Blake says, all that binds man to decayed institutions. But destroy as well man's obedience to moral precepts that hinder the full power of his creative will to assert, to love and to build. Desire is never vicious in itself; it is only turned to vicious ends when driven out of its real channel. Restraint in the name of the moral code is alone evil, for it distorts man's real nature. It is a device of the rulers of this world to keep us chained.

For life is holy. Energy is eternal delight. Jesus is dear to us not because he was divine, but because he was a rebel against false Law, and the friend of man's desire. He defied the Kings and Priests. He was against punishment. He was the herald of man's joy, not of his imaginary redemption. Joy is the only redemption and all suppression is a little death. Humility is an imposture born of cunning. Better wrath than pity. "The tygers of wrath are wiser than the horses of instruction."

> If he had been Antichrist, Creeping Jesus,
> He'd have done anything to please us:

Gone sneaking into the Synagogues
And not used the Elders & Priests like Dogs,
But humble as a Lamb or an Ass,
Obey himself to Caiaphas.
God wants not man to humble himself:

For he acts with honest, triumphant Pride,
And this is the cause that Jesus died.

In *The Marriage of Heaven and Hell,* Blake writes: "Opposition is true friendship." His drive is always toward creative self-assertion, toward man as a free creator. In *A Song of Liberty,* his vision of the old world burning in the fires of the French Revolution leads him to cry: "Empire is No More!"

Let the Priests of the Raven of dawn no longer, in deadly black, with hoarse note curse the sons of joy. Nor his accepted brethren— whom, tyrant, he calls free—lay the bound or build the roof. Nor pale religious letchery call that virginity that wishes but acts not!

So far Blake is a libertarian, an eighteenth-century radical more vehement, daring and imaginative in his conception of freedom than others, but sharing in a revolutionary tradition. Where he becomes truly prophetic and difficult is in his rejection of materialism. He denounces the Priest, in his "deadly black"; but he warns us not to "lay the bound or build the roof" with our anti-clerical freedom. He sets his thought absolutely against rationalism, skepticism, and experimentalism. He is with the Deists so long as they attack supernaturalism—detestable to Blake not because it is disprovable by reason, but because it implies obedience. He is against the Deists so long as they seek to submit the imagination to reason. Rationalism is dangerous because it leaves man in doubt. When the time-serving Bishop Watson wrote, at the request of the English Tory government, an attack on Tom Paine's *The Age of Reason*, Blake scrawled vehement attacks on the Bishop all over the margin of his *Apology for the Bible*.

It appears to me Now that Tom Paine is a better Christian than the Bishop.

I have read this Book with attention & find that the Bishop has only hurt Paine's heel while Paine has broken his head. The Bishop has not answered one of Paine's grand objections.

But in one of his most famous poems, he denounced Voltaire and Rousseau as the arch-Deists seeking to destroy man's capacity for visionary wonder:

Mock on, Mock on Voltaire, Rousseau:
Mock on, Mock on: 'tis all in vain!
You throw the sand against the wind,
And the wind blows it back again.

The sand is the dead particles separated by reason from the true unity of the human vision. Man under the domination of reason is to Blake a creature who has lost his integral nature and has become a dead fragment in himself. Separateness is death; doubt is the child of separateness; the portions which man separates by his reason, in the analysis of natural objects, or by thinking of himself as a natural object, are the mocking ghosts of his dead imagination.

This impassioned rejection of all that is analytical and self limiting in modern thought is central to Blake. It underlies all his conceptions, is the psychological background of his life, and falls, sometimes with a dead absoluteness, between his revolutionary thought and the modern world. It is only when we have understood that doubt and uncertainty stand to Blake's mind as the prime danger of modern life that we can see the main drives of his work, of his personal "queerness," and what led him to the artistic wreckage and incoherence of the later Prophetic Books. Blake's whole pattern, as man and artist, is that of one for whom life is meaningless without an absolute belief. He is like the nihilist Verkhovensky, in Dostoevsky's *The Possessed*, who "when he was excited preferred to risk anything rather than to remain in uncertainty." Freud spoke out of what is deepest and most courageous in the modern tradition when he said that "Man must learn to bear a certain portion of uncertainty." That is a great injunction which it is hard to follow: much harder than the authoritarian faiths of our time, the secular, sadistic religions, the phony ecstasy with which a Hitler's self-mortification is lost in vision of eternal conquest. But Blake is very much a man of our time: one who speaks to us with prophetic insight of our nihilism and insensibility. He was so frightened by what he could already see of it that he found his security only in an absolute personal myth. It is a trait that has become universal politics in our own time. Insecurity has become so endemic, in a society increasingly unresponsive to basic human needs, that men will apparently distort and destroy anything to find their way back to the mystical faith of the child in his parents, the medieval man in his God, and the Nordic in the pagan forest. Blake is peculiarly contemporary in his anxiety, his longing for a faith that will be absolute and yet insurgent, his fear of evidence that will destroy the fantasy of man as the *raison d'être* of the universe. He is as great as Dostoevsky in his understanding of our modern deficiencies; he is as self-deluding as Dostoevsky, who was so afraid of his own nihilism that he allied himself with all that was most obscurantists in Czarist Russia.

This does not make what is central in Blake's work any less prophetic and beautiful. He is not the enemy of society, any more than Dostoevsky was, or the D. H. Lawrence who succumbed to a silly literary Fascism. The very excesses of Blake's myth, like the golden quality in his best work, spring from his impassioned defence of human dignity. Far less than Blake have we solved the problem of restoring to modern man some basic assurance, of giving him a human role to play again. It is the mark of a genius like Blake, or Dostoevsky, or Lawrence, that what is purest and most consistent in his thought burns away his own suffering and fanaticism, while his art speaks to what is most deeply human in us. The distortions and flatulence of Blake's myth spring in part from the very abundance of his gifts—turned in on themselves, with the "fire seeking its own form," as he wrote in *The French Revolution*. Those who distrust reason are usually those who have not enough capacity for it to know why it is beautiful, and slander in advance what they are afraid will destroy their prestige. But there are also those, like Blake and Dostoevsky, who are supremely intelligent, and in whom the audacity and loneliness of genius, not to say social frustration, have led to the distrust of all that will not lead to personal security. Blake had one of the greatest minds in the history of our culture; and more fear of the mind than we can easily believe. He was a genius who from childhood on felt in himself such absolute personal gifts that, anticipating the devaluation of them by a materialistic society, he made sure that society's values did not exist for him. Yet one of his most distinguishable personal traits, weaving through his vehement self-assertion, is his need to defend himself against society.

This is not the view of many people who have written on Blake's life; but with the exception of writers like Alexander Gilchrist and Mona Wilson, who at least sought the basic facts about him, most of his biographers have had no understanding of him. The usual view is that he was a happy mystic, who sat like a gloriously content martyr before his work, eating bread and locusts with an idiotic smile on his face. Blake evidently did enjoy great happiness in many periods, for he was a man for whom life consisted in exploring his own gifts. But there is even more in Blake's total revelation of himself, a rage against society, a deeply ingrained personal misery that underlies his creative exuberance and gives it a melancholy and over-assertive personal force. He defends himself in so many secret ways that when he speaks of himself, at abrupt moments, his utterances have the heart-breaking appeal of someone who cries out: "I am really different from what you know!" To a Reverend Trusler, for example, who complained after commissioning some drawings that inspiration had led Blake too far, he wrote:

> I feel that a man may be happy in This World. And I know that This World is a World of Imagination & Vision. I see Every thing I paint in This world, but Every body does not see alike. To the Eyes of a Miser a Guinea is far more beautiful than the Sun, & a bag worn with the use of Money has more beautiful proportions than a Vine filled with Grapes. The tree which moves some to tears of joy is in the Eyes of others only a Green thing which stands in the way. Some see Nature all Ridicule

& Deformity, and by these I shall not regulate my proportions; & some scarce see Nature at all. But to the Eyes of the Man of Imagination, Nature is Imagination itself. As a man is, so he sees. As the Eye is formed, such are its Powers.

This is beautiful; as many of Blake's personal notes, in letters, marginalia, notebook jottings, and recorded conversation, are beautiful. But they are beautiful in the same way, just as most of *The Four Zoas, Milton*, and *Jerusalem* is ugly in the same way—as a series of passionately eloquent self-assertions, so burning in their exaltation that they seem to spring out of deep gulfs of private misery and doubt. That last word is always Blake's enemy. Just as he believed that

He who doubts from what he sees
Will ne'er Believes do what you Please.
If the Sun & Moon should doubt,
They'd immediately Go out

so he felt the antagonism of the age to his vision to be such a burden that he exceeded what is normal in the human longing for certainty and made his kind of certainty the supreme test of a man. Reading a contemporary work on mental disorder, he suddenly scrawled in the margin:

Cowper came to me and said: "O that I were insane always. I will never rest. Can you not make me truly insane? I will never rest till I am so. O that in the bosom of God I was hid. You retain health and yet are as mad as any of us all—over us all— mad as a refuge from unbelief—from Bacon, Newton and Locke."

Blake never wrote anything more important to himself. If he was mad, it was as a refuge from unbelief, and thus with the satisfaction of being firmly placed in the sense of his own value. His terrible isolation spoke in the need to defend his identity; if madness was the cost of this, it at least placed him "over us all." And he was higher than his age and over most of those who lived in it—higher not in a fantasy of superiority, but in the imaginative subtlety and resolution of his gifts; his faith that

we are put on earth a little space,
That we may learn to bear the beams of love.

Yet what is so marked in his history is his need to prove to himself that his genius could survive. For he was struggling with his own temperament in a time when society threatened his right to exist.

Blake's need of certainty, whatever its personal roots, is also one of the great tragedies of modern capitalist society; particularly of that loss of personal status that was the immediate fate of millions in the industrial England of the "dark satanic mills." Blake was only one of many Englishmen who felt himself being slowly ground to death, in a world of such brutal exploitation and amid such inhuman ugliness, that the fires of the new industrial furnaces and the cries of the child laborers are always in his work. His poems and designs are meant to afford us spiritual vision; a vision beyond the factory system, the hideous new cities, the degradation of children for the sake of profit, the petty crimes for which children could still be hanged. "England," a man said to me in London on V-E day, "has never recovered from its industrial revolution"; Blake was afraid it could not survive it; the human cost was already too great. He never saw the North of Britain, but the gray squalor of the Clydebank, the great industrial maw of Manchester and Liverpool, the slums, the broken families are remembered even in the apocalyptic rant of *Jerusalem*, where

Scotland pours out his Sons to labour at the Furnaces;
Wales gives his Daughters to We Loom.

The lovely poem at the head of Milton, beginning

And did those feet in ancient time
Walk upon England's mountains green?

is so intense a vision of a world other than the real industrial England that it has long been a Socialist hymn of millions of its working people.

Blake was an artisan; an independent journeyman living entirely on the labour of his hands, dependent on patrons in a luxury trade that was being narrowed down to those who could please most quickly. He lived as near the bottom of the English social pyramid as was possible to someone not sucked into the factories. His London is the London of the small tradesmen, the barely respectable artisans and shopkeepers who were caught between the decline of handicrafts and the rise of mass industry. He had to live by hackwork for publishers, but was so independent in his designs that he was forced more and more to engrave after others. One of the reasons why he delighted to make his own books is that he enjoyed complete liberty as an artist-engraver; they certainly would not have been printed by a commercial publisher. But his own prints went largely unsought. The stray copies of *Songs of Innocence and of Experience* and *The Marriage of Heaven and Hell* that now belong only to the wealthiest collectors were offered, often unsuccessfully, for a pittance. In 1809 he held an exhibition of his pictures, featuring his design of the Canterbury Pilgrims, and offering with it "a descriptive catalogue" that is one of his most personal documents. The exhibition, held under the grudging hospitality of his brother James, was a complete failure.

To measure the full depth of Blake's alienation from his age is impossible. Like Tharmas in *The Four Zoas,* he felt himself "a famished Eagle, raging in the vast expanse." But it may help us to see his predicament when we realise that he was an impoverished engraver, without any real class to which he could belong; a libertarian without continuing faith in politics—"something else besides human life"; an unknown Romantic poet and artist who felt suffocated by the formalized tastes of the age; a visionary without religion; an engraver after artists he often despised; a poet whose works were unprocurable. Even in his own trade, engraving, he seemed outmoded in competition with sophisticated craftsmen, especially from the Continent, who advanced beyond Blake's stiff techniques. Blake learned to engrave in a rigid and rather lifeless tradition; all his early training was under the direction of a master, James Basire, who set him to copy Gothic monuments. What makes his art so unique is his ability to design, with great formal inventiveness, his own intellectual visions; technically he was an anachronism even in his own day. He never resolved the twin influences upon his work of Gothic and Michelangelo's heroic grandeur. His human figures are always distinguished by a somnambulistic quality: they are mechanical actors in the spell of a tyrannical stage director. Their look on the page is always one of watchful waiting; they are symbols of ideas and states of being. Blake satisfied his own conception of design, but he very rarely satisfied anyone else. Naturally he resented more successful fellow-artists; particularly in oil portrait, for which he had no skill and which symbolized to him the effort of society artists to paint with ingratiating "realism."

It is no wonder that Blake's writing so often sputters out into furious protest against a world that would give him neither a living nor a hearing. In his own mind he lived in "a city of assassinations." He was a man who could be easily cheated; when defrauded by a shrewd "art-publisher" of the day named Cromek, he took out his revenge, after Cromek had brazenly hinted that it was easy to take advantage of him, since he was "one living in the wilderness," by writing in his notebook:

A Petty Sneaking Knave I knew—

O Mr. Cr(omek), how do ye do?

But his ability to hit back ended in his notebook. He hated Sir Joshua Reynolds—the ruling light of the Royal Academy from which engravers were excluded; the genial and obliging portraitist of the ruling aristocracy, the complacent Augustan mind counseling artists to follow the rules. But all he could do about it was to note his hatred of Reynolds and his intense opposition to the latter's theories in the margins of Sir Joshua's *Discourses*.

Having spent the Vigour of my Youth & Genius under the Oppression of Sir Joshua & his Gang of Cunning Hired Knaves Without Employment & as much as could possibly be without Bread, The Reader must Expect to read in all my remarks on these Books Nothing but Indignation & Resentment. While Sir Joshua was rolling in Riches... (he) & Gainsborough Blotted & Blurred one against the other & Divided all the English World between them. Fuseli, Indignant, almost hid himself. I am hid.

Henry Fuseli was a Swiss-born artist, famous in London, who liked Blake and was one of his few friends. He was successful, as Blake was not, and Blake seems to have exaggerated Fuseli's artistic solidarity in his joy at having found a friend in his own craft. Fuseli once said that he found Blake "damned good to steal from."

The vehement marginalia that contain so many of Blake's deepest resentments—against Bacon, against Reynolds, against Bishop Watson and Wordsworth's "atheistic" love of nature—are an obvious symbol of his protest against society. Not being part of it, he put his dissent into the margins. What is not so obvious, however, is that much of his vehement struggle to assert his independence was based on his marriage. The dissenting and small tradesman's class into which Blake was born was one tributary of our Puritan culture; on Blake it imposed poverty made drearier by genteel conformity.

Nietzsche, the lonely professor of Greek, became drunk on the vision of the all-conquering male, but the fantasy was his basic sex experience. Lawrence dreamed all his life of a sun-filled Mediterranean world, full of literary Indians and impossibly hospitable women, whose chief virtue was that they lacked the self-righteousness of Presbyterian miners and school-teachers in Nottingham. Blake in most accounts of his life is portrayed as the ideal husband, who taught his illiterate Catherine how to read, and even to see visions when he did. There is little doubt that he was the ideal husband; and apparently he could not stand it. Catherine Blake became the perfect amanuensis, to the man even more than to the artist. She even learned to write and draw so much in his style that her known contributions to his work would otherwise be indistinguishable from his own. She was the ideal wife of his artistic and intellectual alienation; she was the perfect helpmeet in his social and economic desperation. She starved with him, believed in him, and even saw visions for company. If visitors were shocked by the lack of soap in the Blake household, she explained that "Mr. Blake's skin don't *dirt*!" If Blake became completely indifferent to the lack of funds, she would gently remind him of the state of things by putting an empty plate before him for dinner.

Catherine Blake was an ideal wife; her only fault, apparently, was that she was not a person in her own right. The fault was most assuredly not in her but in Blake's annihilating need of her. He made an adoring servant out of her, and then evidently found that he longed for a woman. All the stories we have of them add up to very little, and those who drew upon her and Blake's friends for reminiscences after his death felt such veneration and excitement before their recovery of a neglected genius that they prettied up his domestic life as much as possible. But we do know that he proposed to her at their first meeting when, complaining that a girl had spurned him, she said: "Then I pity you." "Do you truly pity me?" he asked, in pleasure. Whereupon he found that he loved her. Yeats, who helped to doctor up the truth about Blake's life as much as anyone, thought this a lovely story and that they lived happily ever after. Unfortunately, Blake's own writing shows that he was tormented by her jealousy and that he thought marriage was the devil.

It is not necessary to find malicious confirmation of this in the famous story that he wanted Mary Wollstonecraft to join his household for a *ménage a trios*. Mary Wollstonecraft was a noble and deeply intelligent woman, more than a century ahead of her time, which believed in women's rights and took them. She was a tragic and courageous woman, far more attractive than the complacent bluestockings of London highbrow society, and much more interesting than her husband, William Godwin, or their daughter Mary, who became Shelley's second wife. She was the English type of the great Continental heroines of feminism, from George Sand to Alexandra Kollontai. But though Blake was a member of the same intellectual radical group, headed by Johnson the bookseller, it is not hard to imagine how incongruous she must have looked at his side—Blake, who was the imperial visionary of his meager household, but in the London world a curious and threadbare crank. A liaison between John Wesley and Isadora Duncan would not have been more strange— indeed, Wesley was a worldly and aristocratic figure; Blake was a lower middle-class drudge, more of a Wesleyan than Wesley himself. But he seems to have been of the type that makes history, partly because he is not very happy at home.

Blake's "immoralism" (a silly word made necessary by the fact that *moral* lies like a fallen giant across our discourse) is of two kinds: lyrical and poignant expressions of human longing, and a dark obsession in the "Prophetic Books" with sex as the battleground of human struggle and revolt. And however narrow and pitiful the experience from which his own search for fulfillment sprang, there is no doubt that in its psychological truth, its tenderness and passionate support of human dignity, 131ake's writing is one of the great prophecies of the love that is possible between man and woman.

He is not a writer of "erotica"—the honeyed crumbs of those who have no bread; he rages in his notebooks, but he is never sly. The very status of the dirty story in our society reveals a conception of sex as something one puts over on the conventions. It is the great betrayal of human sincerity. Blake's fight is against secrecy, unnatural restraint, the fear of life—the distortions in the personality that follow from deception and resignation to it.

There is implicit in all his attacks on the "moral code" an understanding that gratification is impossible without true union. In this, as in so much else of his thought, Blake painted not only the immediate consequences of a reactionary morality based on outward conformity—the anxieties, the subtle hostilities, the habit of lying. He also foresaw the danger that is exactly present in our modern eroticism, which has the same relation to the failure of love that totalitarian solutions have to the failure of society. When we compare Blake with an artist like D. H. Lawrence, or an oratorical rebel like Henry Miller, we can see how much the obsessive ness, the cringing over-emphasis on sex in the most advanced modern writing is due to the inability of these writers to treat sex naturally in the whole frame of the human organization. As the dirty story pays homage to Puritanism, so our modern eroticism wearily proclaims that the part which has been dislodged from the whole shall now be the key to all experience. The limitations of eroticism have exactly the same character, in life and in art: it divorces sex from human culture. As medieval men despised the body for the sake of the spirit and perhaps lost both, so we tend to forget that the body is above all a person. Every reaction in favour of some suppressed truth overshoots the mark. Hence, too, the dreary primitivism of so much advanced writing—as great a lie about our human nature as the genteel writing of the past.

Blake is not free of the characteristic modern obsessive ness; he was no more free than we are. But he always knows exactly what he is. His theme is always the defence of the integral human personality. His principal virtue is that he does not make a virtue of "frankness"; he is concerned with basic human desire, fear, longing, resentment; with the innermost movements of a human being in the world. He describes, in his great song cycle, the gulf between Innocence and Experience; he feels an inexpressible solidarity with those who are forever in it. For he knows that innocence and experience are not the faces of youth and age, but "the two contrary states of the human soul." He writes as a man, not as an "immoralist." One of the reasons why he is so supreme among those who have written of childhood is that he sees it as the nucleus of the whole human story, rather than as a state that precedes adult "wisdom." If he is afraid for the child, he pities the adult. In experience there is always the longing for "unorganized innocence: an impossibility"; in innocence there is the poignant foretelling of experience, which is death without the return to confidence and vision. Blake is utterly without cynicism. He never makes the characteristic modern mistake of devaluating a prime experience; he never throws out love with the love-affair. We may not agree with him that desire is infinite; we can never be sufficiently grateful to him for insisting that it is never cheap.

Blake is serious about sex, as he is serious about the child; and for the same reason. For he knows that as sex is the buried part of our civilization, so the child is the buried part of the man. His faith in the creative richness of love has the same source as his feeling for the secret richness of childhood: his ability to see through the dead skin of adulthood. He would have understood very well that our "child-psychology" shows the same guardedness toward the child that modern love and marriage reveal between men and women. The same guardedness and the same fear: for we "handle" children from the same negative fears and out of the same lack of positive participation and sympathy. Blake would have seen in our pedagogic carefulness the effort of caution to do the work of the imagination. In his own time, when children were regarded as miniature adults, or as slaves or pets to those who ruled by their maturity, he showed that a child is not an abbreviated version of the adult, but a different being. In our time he would have seen that the distance between a parent and a child is usually the distance between the parents as lovers. For him sex meant enjoyment framed in wonder: the full play of our life striving beyond all the distortions inflicted by respectable society and cynical experience. By the same token childhood was also a lost world—calling to us from our buried life.

Piping down the valleys wild,
Piping songs of pleasant glee,
On a cloud I saw a child,
And he laughing said to me:
"Pipe a song about a Lamb!"
So I piped with merry chear.

"Piper, pipe that song again;"
So I piped: he wept to hear.

Innocence is belief and experience is doubt. The tragedy of experience is that we become incapable of love. The tragedy of childhood is that we inflict our loveless ness upon it. Blake's thinking is always organic; it is always directed to the hidden fountains of our humanity. Having never lost the creative freshness of childhood, he challenged experience with it. Having, as I believe, no real love-affair of his own, he had it with childhood. In any event, he had no children of his own. He was a man who had to believe fully, at the highest pitch of being, to live at all; and he loved childhood because it was native in its certainty.

Human sensibility was so precious to him that he was ready to discard all its natural trappings to preserve it. Blake never deals with history, with the process and its reality; his search is only for the central and forgotten sources of human feeling, imagination, solidarity. To be certain of them, he conceived the world over again in the image of his desire. But it is like our desire, even if it is nothing like our real world. And our desire is always a portion of the reality we have, as it is always a shadow on the reality we have not. That is why Blake at his best is enchanting even in the smallest proportions—in fact, it is difficult to read him with the usual continuity, so much does he fill our minds at each step.

The central subject of *Songs of Innocence and of Experience* is that of the child who lost and found is. In its symbolism, it is the great theme of all Blake's work—the "real man, the imagination," that has been lost and will be found again through human vision. In Innocence, the little boy loses his father in the night, and God this Father leads him back to his weeping mother. The child is lost to its guardians, for in Blake's mind the child's nature is beyond the parents' comprehension, and is alone in a world the parents cannot enter.

The grief of the child is also the loneliness of the soul in its sudden prison of earth; he is protected by God the Father. In Experience, however, the little boy who demands of the priest the right to assert his own thoughts and desires is "burn'd in a holy place." The little girl who enjoys love, without shame or fear, is suddenly confronted with the earthly father whose "loving look, like the holy book," drives her into terror. One little girl is lost and yet found in Experience, however; for she enters lovingly into the world of the passions, where she lives in freedom from the "wolvish howl" and the "lions' growl."

Experience is the "contrary" of innocence, not its negation. Contraries are phases of the double ness of all existence in the mind of man; they reflect the unalterable condition of the human struggle. As hell can be married to heaven, the body seen by the soul, so experience lifts innocence into a higher synthesis based on vision. But vision is impossible without truth to one's deepest feelings. A lie is "the negation of passion." Life is thought and creation; it is to be had only in its fullness, for the "want of thought" is death. To enter fully into life we must go through the flame of disbelief, kill the fiction that man's desire is lawless and evil. In Innocence

Mercy has a human heart, pity a human face
In Experience
Cruelty has a Human Head
And jealousy a Human Face;
Terror the Human Form Divine,
And Secrecy the Human Dress.

The Human Dress is forged Iron,
The Human Form a fiery Forge,
The Human Face a Furnace seal'd,
The Human Heart its hungry Gorge.

That is what experience is for: to bring us from God the Father to the God that man alone creates. Experience is not evil; it merely shows us the face of evil as a human face, so that we shall learn that the world is exactly what man makes it, and that its ultimate triumphs occur within his understanding.

In the world of Innocence the child speaks to the lamb and marvels in its soft and bright goodness, over which stands the Jesus who is himself a lamb. In Experience we stare into the fiery eyes of the Tyger and think ourselves lost in the "forests of the night." But the Tyger is the face of the creation, marvelous and ambiguous; he is not evil. When Blake cries, in the most moving single expression in his work,

When the stars threw down their spears,
And water'd heaven with their tears,
Did he smile his work to see ?
Did he who made the Lamb make thee?

he does not find the thought abhorrent. But he does not answer the question; he keeps it as one, where a religious man would answer it consolingly. Never is he more heretical than in this most famous of his poems, where he glories in the hammer and the fire out of which are struck the "deadly terrors" of the Tyger. Blake does not believe in a war between good and evil; he sees only the creative tension presented by the struggle of man to resolve the contraries.

What has been created, by some unknown hand, is a fiery furnace into which our hands must go to seize the fire. "The Tyger" is a poem of triumphant human awareness; it is a hymn to pure being. And what gives it its power is Blake's ability to fuse two aspects of the same human drama: the movement with which a great thing is created, and the joy and wonderment with which we join ourselves to it. The opening and closing stanzas are the same, for as we begin with our wonder before the creation, so we can only end on it. It is the living eternal existence; the fire is, so long as we are. That is why Blake begins on the four great beats of "Tyger! Tyger!", which call the creation by a name and bring us in apprehension before it.

The poem is hammered together with alliterative strokes. *Frame* is there,

What immortal hand or eye
Could frame thy fearful symmetry?
because he wants fearful as well.

In what distant deeps or skies
Burnt the fire of thine eyes?
On what wings dare he aspire?
What the hand dare seize the fire?

begins the questioning. Blake goes straight to the poles; we are in the presence of a creation that can be traced from distant deeps to skies. What sustains the verse in our ear is the long single tone in which are blended the related sounds of *burnt, fire, thine, eyes*. By natural association—from the burning fire to the topmost eyes of the Tyger—and through the swell of the line, these words also form a natural little scale of four notes—a scale that ends in the crash of the question-mark. Blake's mind is darting between the mysterious unseen *he*, the maker of the Tyger, and the fire in its eyes.

The fire is central to his thought, so much so that it eclipses the maker as a person and turns him into the force and daring with which he creates. Blake does not write "He"; he is far more interested in the creation than in the creator. But so great is this creation that the creator grows mysterious and powerful in its light. What is so beautiful in the second stanza is the leap from the Tyger to the creator. Blake goes from the fire to the creator's wings. This is not because he has an image of a celestial being with great wings, but because the fire could be created only by someone lifted on topmost wings. Blake is as astounded by the creator as he is by the Tyger—and in the same way, for both are such revelations of absolute energy. The emphasis on the creator, in the last line of the second stanza, is thus on *dare*.

We are now in the midst of the creation—or rather, of the great tiling being created. The hammering, twisting, laughing strokes with which the creator works are not more decisive than Blake's own verse hammer. As usual, he has leaped ahead of us, and begins on a new question; a question that begins with *And* because it is like a man talking breath between hammer strokes:

And what shoulder, & what art, Could twist the sinews of thy heart? And when thy heart began to beat, What dread hand? & what dread feet?

The creator's shoulder, with terrible force, twists the sinews to make the Tiger's heart. *Twists* is powerful enough; but there is joined to it in Blake's mind what is "crooked" and off the main path for the genius-creator. The shoulder twisting the heart together has turned the creator's back away from us, even as we imagine him at his work. The hammer strokes now go faster and faster; the creation is so swift and final with each blow that Blake's mind rushes after the fall of the hammer, the movements of the creating hands and feet, the beats of the new heart. The poem now moves to the rhythm of the great work. Yet the poet must know whose dread hands and feet, working together before the anvil, could create this. Where does the creator's body and tools end and the Tyger begin?

What the hammer? What the chain?
In what furnace was thy brain?
What the anvil? what dread grasp
Dare its deadly terrors clasp?

The chains ring in the sorcerer's workshop. The questions now dart from the heart to the brain with the same instantaneous force with which brain and heart are being made. But *where* is this being done? Where is the furnace in which the fire of consciousness is being poured out into the Tiger's brain? What, in space and time, could even hold the Tyger as it is being created? Blake never answers, for the wonder with which he asks them is the wonder with which he beholds the Tyger.

But he leaps ahead, in the last phrase of the third line and the whole fourth line after it, to create the image of so dread a power that it can grasp the terrors of the Tyger. It is the long courageous movement with which the clasp is made—a great hand moving into the furnace to bring the Tyger to us—that gives the creation its final awesomeness. Blake creates this by the length of his question. Between the dread grasp and the clasp that holds the terrors in its hand is the movement between the creation and our being witness to it. Technically the thing is done by leaving a distance, a moment's suspense, between the end of the third line on *grasp* and the hard closing of the stanza on *clasp*. The assonance of those two words, like bones rasping together, joins us to the thing. The terror is in our hands.

But when Blake asks,

When the stars threw down their spears, And water'd heaven with their tears, Did he smile his work to see? Did he who made the Lamb make thee?

He has no answer—least of all the comforting religious explanation of the division between the Lamb and the Tyger. The stars throwing down their "spears" join in the generation. But did he smile his work to see ? Did *he*? Blake's answer is to bring us right back to the Tyger. He has no moral, and he will not let us off with anything less than our return to the fact that the Tyger exists—a fact that includes all its ambiguity and all our wonder and fear before it. The poem ends on the upbeat of man's eternal question of the world: where is its moral order? Blake offers no answer; he asks his question with the "fearful symmetry" of the creation straight before us.

Blake does not let us off with any conventional religious consolation; nor does he let the creator of. Had he believed in God, the contraries which are presented to man's mind by experience would have been easy to explain. The Christian explains them by the Fall—by that "happy guilt," as Augustine put it, which left man with a sense of original sin which only religion can cleanse away.

Blake is utterly opposed to this: man never fell, and there is no prime evil in him to redeem. For him the contraries exist not because God willed it so in his punishment of man's transgression—could a just God punish man for "following his energies" and for showing curiosity? They exist because man's gift of vision is blocked up in himself by materialism and rationalism. Every man, by the very nature of life, is engaged in a struggle, against the false materialism of the age, to find his way back to perfect human sight. Man is not a sinner—he is a weary traveller lost under the hill, a material "specter" looking for his "spiritual emanation." He is looking for his human centre. Man cannot help getting lost when he deludes himself that he is a natural body subject to a natural society, obeying the laws of a natural God.

Do what you will, this life's a fiction
And is made up of contradiction.

But vision restores his human identity. With the aid of vision, and through the practice of art, man bursts through the contraries and weds them together by his own creativity.

Blake's Prophetic Books are his attempt to explain how the contraries arose. They are his Greek mythology, his Genesis, his Book of Revelations. Blake is not Diderot or Stendhal; he does not take man as he finds him. He is a Bible-haunted English dissenter who has taken on himself the burden of proving that man is an independent spiritual being. This required the refutation of all existing literature. The tortured rhetoric of the Prophetic Books is not a lapse from taste; it is the awful wilderness into which Blake had to enter by the nature of his staggering task.

This was to give man a new Bible, and with it a new natural history; a new cosmogony, and with it his own version, supplanting Hebrew and Greek literature, of man's first self-consciousness in the universe. But this is not all he tried to do in the Prophetic Books. No one in his time, after all, could escape the influence of realism. To Blake the myth-maker the age required a new Bible. As a contemporary he could hardly escape the inspiration of neoclassical drama, of the historical chronicle, and even of the psychological novel. His Prophetic Books are in fact an attempt to create, on the basis of a private myth, a new epic literature that would ride the currents of the age. His chief model was *Paradise Lost*, and *Milton*, he tells us, was written because Milton came back to earth and begged him to refute the errors of his own epic. But Blake had an eye on Greek tragedy as well, and the Book of Job, and *The Divine Comedy*.

Blake was not a "*naïf*," a "wild man" piecing his philosophy together from "odds and ends" around the house. He was a very learned man who felt challenged and uneasy by what he had learned. One of the reasons why he labored so hard to create a new literature equal to his own vision is that he could never free himself of the models others had created. When we look at his first poems in *Poetical Sketches*, we can see solemn imitations of Shakespeare, Ossian, Gray, and Spenser; his first beautiful songs move slowly away from neoclassic form. His tracts, *There Is No Natural Religion* and *All Religions Are One,* imitate the geometrical order of philosophic propositions that was the carry-over from mathematics to natural philosophy. *The Marriage of Heaven and Hell* is a parody of sources to which Blake was deeply indebted for his form: Genesis, the Proverbs, the Apocalypse, and Swedenborg.

The Prophetic Books are an attempt to create a new classical literature, after all the sources. Nothing shows so clearly the tremendous inner conflicts in Blake as the ghosts of other men's books in his own. It is impossible, for anyone who has studied the Prophetic Books carefully, to see him as an enraptured scribe singing above the clouds.

His visions in these books were an attempt to force down his own uneasiness. He could find his peace only by creating an epic world so singularly his own that it would supplant every other. He never succeeded. His task was beyond all human strength and all art. He created myths endlessly and represented them as human beings in endlessly energetic and turgid postures of struggle, oppression, and liberation. *But he never gave up the myth*. The "mad" Blake, whose wildest sayings furnish so much biographical chit-chat about him, was the man who still believed the myth long after suffering and alienation had dulled in his mind the objects it represented. Without the myth he would have been entirely lost, intolerably isolated. So he went even further— John Milton believed in it, too; and— the significant last chapter of Blake's thought—Jesus was above all a Blakean.

The last Prophetic Books are a jungle, but it is possible— if you have nothing else to do—to get through them. What Joyce said so lightly Blake would have repeated with absolute assurance— he demanded nothing less of his readers than that they should devote their lives to the elucidation of his works. Yet there are whole areas of the first Prophetic Books that represent Blake's art and thought at their purest; the illuminated designs, even to a fantastic jumble like *Jerusalem,* are overwhelming in their beauty and power. To labour over works like *The Four Zoas, Milton*, and *Jerusalem* for the sake of intellectual exegesis is against the whole spirit of art. Where Blake does not write poetry, he orates; and when he orates it is "the will trying to do the work of the imagination." Yet his rhetorical resources were so overwhelming that they flow like hot lava over the stereotypes of the myth.

He obviously felt so little the consecutiveness of his "argument" that in at least one copy of *Jerusalem* he allowed misplaced pages to remain where they were. His concern is not with the coherence of his theme, but with his need to get everything in. Even within the assumed order of the myth the characters lose their symbolic references when they do not transfer them among each other. They came to represent so much of Blake's private life as well as his public vision that he interrupted himself at regular intervals to preach against jealousy and the domination of man by woman.

Blake was never jarred by the tumult of all the conflicts he revealed in his Prophetic Books. His loneliness as a man and thinker was so overwhelming that he took his gifts as the measure of human insight. He was a lyric poet of genius and a very bad dramatic poet; but he suffered from the illusion that his poetic gift was also a dramatic and representational one. The gift of creating character is inseparable from an interest in history. Just as the novel owes its principal development to the modern consciousness that society is man-made, so the ability to create character is impossible without an understanding of men in relation to other men; in short, of man as a creature of process and conflict. Blake's characters are names attached arbitrarily to absolute human faculties and stales of being.

The name of the character may have a Stunning or derived relation to the faculty he represents, as Urizen is the god of this world and its sterility who is "your reason," or Orc, Blake's first hero, may have been derived from "*cor*," or heart. So Albion is the central figure of man, "the eternal man," and Enitharmon is the "universal" woman. But when Blake sets them to orating against each other, their nominal identity is only the line which he must desperately hold on to bring up the deep-sea fish of human passions, errors, lamentations. The figure of Urizen is an of oppressor; Orc is the spirit of visionary emancipation; Los, who comes in later, is the spirit of time working to rejoin man to his lost unity, and the "Eternal Prophet." Through them, and many other characters, Blake is seeking to explain how man lost the gift of vision. Urizen is the false God, the Satan who separated himself from the prime unity and set in motion the divisions in man, the search after the analytical and the inhuman.

Blake is not interested in character. His figures are the human faculties at war with each other. He is trying to explain, in the form of a new Genesis, how the split in man occurred, and to show the necessary present struggle of man to unify himself back to an integral and imaginative human nature. He is also raging against all those who would hold him in—from the analytical God of Newton to the skepticism of Voltaire, from the successful painters of the day to "the shadowy female," who torments man by jealousy. But since he has no interest in history the beginning, the present, and the future dissolve into each other. What was begun in error is suffered through error now. He is fighting his own sorrows even as he is trying to impose the massive structure of his hazardously built myth onto the contemporary world: to bring himself to us, and the England he actually lived in. Hence the bewildering jump from Old Testament names to English streets, cities, and counties, in which Blake's own cries were never heard:

> O dreadful loom of death! O piteous Female forms, compelled
> To weave the Woof of Death! On Camberwell Tirzah's courts,
> Malah's on Blackheath; Rahab & Noah dwell on Windsor's heights,
> Where once the Cherubs of Jerusalem spread to Lambeth's Vale.
>
> Milcah's Pillars shine from Harrow to Hampstead, where Hoglah

On Highgate's heights magnificent Weaves over trembling Thames
To Shooter's Hill and thence to Blackheath, the dark Woof. Loud,
Loud roll the Weights & Spindles over the whole Earth, let down
On all sides round to the Four Quarters of the World, eastward on
Europe to Euphrates & Hindu, to Nile & back in Clouds
Of Death across the Atlantic to America North & South.
Hence, too, the poetic atrocities:
In torrents of mud settling thick
With Eggs of unnatural production

Which is dreadful, but only a paraphrase of the noble rant which deafens and dulls us all through the later books:

But in the Optic vegetative Nerves Sleep was transformed
To Death in old time by Satan, the father of Sin & Death:

And Satan is the Spectre of Orc, & Orc is the generate Luvah.

Blake cannot get away from the materialist trappings, the naturalistic "spectre"; no one can, and his collapse as an artist in the later Prophetic Books is due to his effort to dispel the natural forms by a mythological explanation of them. He crated his myth to contain his defiance, as it were; when he found it insufficient, he let it supplant life itself. On the subject of God, he even borrowed a thought from the Gnostic heresy, as he was indebted to the Jewish Cabala for his vision of the man who anciently contained all things of heaven and earth in himself.

The Gnostic heresy, as he was indebted to the Jewish Cabala for his vision of the man who anciently contained all things of heaven and earth in himself. The Gnostic heresy is one the Catholic Church understandably rooted out in furious alarm—for it held that the world was dominated by Satan. It is not hard to understand how comforting this thought must have been to Blake. If this world is a mere deception, and all its natural appearances a masquerade through which man must look for spiritual vision, it is because the "real" God has been supplanted by Satan. So all spiritual vision leads us back to the "real" God, who is now Jesus. Blake's Jesus is the defiant iconoclast, the friend of artists and revolutionaries. When one reads *Jerusalem*, one thinks of Nietzsche, who when he went mad signed himself "The Crucified One," and of that old cry from the defeated—"Thou hast conquered, O Galilean!"

Blake does not "yield" to Jesus; he creates Jesus in his own image.

The Son, O how unlike the Father! First God Almighty comes with a Thump on the head. Then Jesus Christ comes with a balm to heal it.

But not before he has shown us the inner thread in his snarled Prophetic Books—which is the lament against his owns "selfhood" and the appeal against the Accuser, "who is the God of this World." It is impossible to read Blake's vehement and repeated cries against the "Accuser" without being moved by the tremendous burden of guilt he carried despite his revolt and independence. The "Accuser" is Satan, who rules this world, which is "the Empire of nothing." It is he who tormented man with a sense of sin; who made men and women look upon their own human nature as evil; that plunged us into the cardinal human heresy, which is the heresy against man's own right and capacity to live. The "Accuser" is the age in which Blake lived and it is the false god whose spectre mocks our thirst for life. It is the spirit, to Blake, of all that limits man, shames man, and drives him in fear. The Accuser is the spirit of the machine, which leads man himself into "machination." He is jealousy, unbelief, and cynicism. But his dominion is only in you; and he is only a spectra

The Accuser is the prime enemy, yet he is a fiction; he need not exist. But Blake fought him so bitterly that he acknowledged how great a price he had paid for his own audacity. What was it that made him long at the end, above everything else, for "forgiveness" ? What was it he had to be "forgiven" for ?

And now let me finish with assuring you that, Tho' I have been very unhappy, I am so no longer. I am again Emerged into the light of day; I still & shall to Eternity Embrace Christianity and Adore him who is the Express image of God; but I have traveled thro' Perils & Darkness not unlike a Champion. I have Conquered, and shall go on Conquering. Nothing can withstand the fury of my course among the Stars of God & in the Abysses of the Accuser. My enthusiasm is still what it was, only Enlarged and confirmed.

We do not know—his only name for his "guilt" remains "selfhood"—that is, the full force of his individual claim to self-assertion. Blake was a prophet who was not delivered by his own prophecy. But if he succumbed at all to the "Accuser," he did more than anyone else to expose him. If he failed at the complete harmony to which all his own thought is directed, it is because man, though he is a little world in himself, is little indeed when measured against the whole of a creation that was not made for him alone—or for him to know everlasting certainty in it. Blake's tragedy was the human tragedy, made more difficult because his own fierce will to a better life prevented him from accepting any part of it. Laboring after the infinite, he felt himself shadowed by the Accuser. That is the personal cost he paid for his vision, as it helps us to understand his need of a myth that would do away with tragedy. But as there is something deeper than tragedy in Blake's life, so at the heart of his work there is always the call to us to recover our lost sight. Blake was a man who had all the contraries of human existence in his hands, and he never forgot that it is the function of man to resolve them.

Men are admitted into Heaven not because they have
curbed & governed their Passions, or have no Passions,
but because they have cultivated their Understandings

— *William Blake*

## The Romantic Movement and The Industrial Revolution

Throughout history, it has been repeatedly proven that developments and progressions of a society are a result of a tremendous event; the Industrial Revolution is an ideal example of such an event. During the 1770's and all through the 1790's, the Industrial Revolution opened way for more urbanized and entirely altered way of life for the population of the Western world. And from the revolution, emerged a movement that broke many of the traditional forms and styles of literature.

Romantic literature anspired at a time of a great deal of societal commotion and instability. Although the Revolution brought development to some aspects of society, many were still suffering. The hierarchy and classes of the society created conflict, and there was a great deal of economic anguish. Pollution and filth stained the streets of London due to the massive waste the factories dispensed.

Poets; William Blake, William Wordsworth and Samuel L. Coleridge, who are considered the landmark figures of romantic poetry, responded to the revolution through their literary works. All were especially critical of, what they believed was, a materialistic and hypocritical society.

Blake's resentment for his society is also stated in the last stanza "...I hear/How the youthful Harlot's curse/Blasts the new-born infants tear,/And blights with plagues the marriage hearse. The criticism is also mainly directed to the government. The diction and presentation of his poetry, was Blake's attempt to address the common man and influence some change in his society.

Through this poem, Blake comments on the despair, "weakness" and "woes" he sees on the faces of "London". acted works that reflected the society around them and were considered 'rebels' of their time. In London Blake provides his reader with his disturbance and resentment towards the hypocrisy of the church and society. From Songs of Experience, the poem The Lamb, is an illustration of Blake's use of simplistic language; "Little lamb who made thee? / Dost thou know who made thee,"(155). Blake blames the institutions for creating the city's 'woes', and for creating a system of enslavement.

The Songs of Innocence contrasts the themes of those in the Songs of Experience, in that it is the pureness and harmless of childhood against the real world of corruption.

The poem "London" is somewhat an 'open –letter of judgment' for the government of Blake's time.

Blake felt the limitations, restrictions and the 'mind-forg'd manacles" of the Church and the government, and expressed his beliefs as a "lesson" in his easy to read poetry. In the last line of the stanza, Blake compares marriage to a death and downfall.

Evidence of Blake's hatred for the institutions in his society is presented in the poem "London".

**Comparing London by William Blake and Composed Upon Westminster Bridge, by William Wordsworth:**

Both poems give their own, different accounts of London at around the same period. One is written with a happy and joyous mood and the other a completely opposite one - a dull and grim mood, which is given by Blake.

Starting with William Blake's background as a poet, I researched that he had a very eventful lifetime, which perhaps influenced his poems. For example, Blake was very religious. He lived by the bible and based some of his paintings (as Blake was also an artist) of the book of Revelation, such as his work "The Red Dragon and the Woman of the Sun". It is also said that he had been visited by angels at a point in his life. Is this to prove that he was somewhat deranged or is it his imagination? Blake's poem 'London' describes a London where everything has rules or boundaries.

We can see this where Blake tells us of the 'charter'd street' and the 'chartered Thames'. We can see the connection of this stanza and the fact that rules were pinning every body down, with the word chartered. Chartered means something is on the map, almost as if it is owned, owned by the king, perhaps. Blake is communicating the fact that there is a stamp of ownership on everything from a small street to the constricted

Thames, which being natural, makes the point more forcefully. It affects the way people live, work and play - people are not free. They are trapped in the prison of society, which is described by the line.

The mind-forg'd manacles I hear

What this simple phrase tells us is that people were not free to think. People were not free to think beyond the rules of society or beyond the rules of convention. The people of London had been brainwashed by society and they could not think for themselves because of that. Imaginary (mind forg'd) chains (manacles) were holding the minds of people down and they were struggling to break free (the sound that Blake hears). This did not only affect men, women, or infants, it affected all, as a city. In the next stanza, Blake goes on to describe the corruption of the Church of England (in one sense) or the dirtiness of all the buildings including the church, which is blackening (in another sense), with the line.

Every black'ning Church apalls

He sets the scene in this stanza by mentioning the chimneysweeper boys who cleaned the sooty chimneys of the houses of London at the time. It gives us a sense of filthiness in the everyday street of London and the fact that the job of the chimneysweepers was disgusting and dangerous. The air of London was not clean - the smoke of fireplaces filled the air and the pollution transformed the white stone of churches to jet-black. By talking particularly of the blackening church, the church can also be thought of as dirty or 'bad', or even corrupt. So is Blake telling us the church is corrupt and 'dark'? Or is it just physically dirty? There is no right answer, as both of these ways of thinking fit in to the context of the stanza. Further on, Blake writes about the 'hapless' or luckless soldier.

And the hapless soldier's sigh
Runs in blood down Palace walls.

His sigh runs in blood, signifying death, down palace walls, meaning the palace, or whoever lives in it, is to blame for his death. Which again, gives a thought of corruption. In the final stanza, Blake writes about the young prostitutes (harlots), who roam the streets of London, and how they are cursed with the consequences of their job. In the line of:

How the youthful Harlot's curse

Once again, Blake is playing a meaning game with the reader. This line, like the one about the blackening church could have two meanings. One meaning could be the curse on the Harlot of catching a deadly sexually transmitted infection. However the line could mean the curse of insufficient contraception measures, ending in the birth of a child, which itself would be quite painful and dangerous (as in those times childbirth could be so dangerous that the mother could die). Blake also makes a more 'shocking' comment in his remark about the marriage hearse and death. The way they have been written simply intertwines their meanings and become one shocking connotation of the start of a new life (marriage) and the end of a life (death). From the content alone, we can see what Blake is trying to depict here. London is a city where everything is owned, from the streets and buildings to the river and the inhabitants' minds.

This prevents them to break beyond the social rules and convention to make their own minds up. The people of London are brainwashed by society. Their minds are chained and controlled (quite like Aldous Huxley's 'Brave New World' where the people's futures, careers and social class are determined by how much oxygen is given to them during their IVF, and the drug soma is given out in church, rather than bread). At the same time, prostitutes 'infest' the streets of London and are cursed by S.T.I.s and the pains of childbirth. Swept over like a blanket, hangs the dank black cloud of pollution and corruption of the church and of the palace. Blake is describing a London where no one would want to live. The people of London were having their lives lived for them, where rules decided what people did everyday and they could not feel alive. Everything was stamped with ownership, and London was a dull and grim city. After looking at the content of the poem, we can see clear definitions of Blake's description.

However, looking more deeply into the poem, into the structure, we can see further ways Blake emphasizes his ideas. Firstly, the lines of the poem are short. This makes the poem more compact and gets to the point quickly. The short lines also make the rhymes more noticeable - they are just a line apart. This makes up a beat, which drives the message home. The compression makes the poem more complex and crowded, with a sense of anger and shock.

The name of this line-type in poems is called an Iambic Tetrameter. Secondly, The repetition of the words in the first and second stanzas gives us the notion that everything is the same, has an order and a rule, (which is also derived form the content). There is also a build up of emotion throughout the poem, slowly growing in intensity, stronger and stronger, to finally thrust the message home. It develops into a more dense and furious form, to give the reader a shock element. In the end, this poem gives us a view of controlled actions and motions via the content and the construction.

As for the second poem, 'Composed upon Westminster Bridge, September 3rd 1802' by William Wordsworth, we see an instantaneous difference of opinion to the City of London from Wordsworth. He has composed a poem with an awareness of the beauty of the conurbation. Wordsworth praises all the architecture, air and surroundings of the capital wonderfully. However, what is really interesting is that he is actually contradicting what Blake is saying in the previous poem (or vice versa). For example, the phrase 'smokeless air' does not support the account Blake gives the reader.

Every black'ning Church apalls

Blake's line, here, tells us that the air of London was so polluted with the smoke from the coal fires of the homes of the Londoners that it blackened the walls of the buildings. Why is it that two different poets, seeing and describing the city at roughly the same period have two different views?

The river glideth at its own sweet will

Furthermore, we see that Wordsworth says the opposite to Blake by saying the Thames is free and flows at its own accord, not owned as Blake is saying. Blake portrays the Thames as branded with a stamp of ownership, 'chartered'. Additionally, the mood of the poem is more 'bright' which helps picture the glittering ships, towers and domes - a complete opposite to Blake's mood. The dank and dirtiness of the buildings and the air creates a mysterious and eerie picture - like a dark alleyway, where a prostitute may loiter at night, whose mind was brainwashed by society. One final quality, as by the content, comes from the line

Open unto the fields and to the sky

Wordsworth illustrates the City of London as connected to the natural surroundings - the fields and the sky, and other elements of nature. After looking at the content of the poem, we can see clear definitions of Wordsworth's description. However, looking deeper into the poem, into the structure, we can see further ways Wordsworth accentuates his ideas. Firstly we can obviously see that the poem 'Composed upon Westminster Bridge, September 3rd 1802' is a sonnet consisting of 14 lines, but is also a special kind of sonnet, a Petrarchan Sonnet, where the rhyming couplets are closer in places than in others Secondly, by being a sonnet, the poem has a controlled but free form, showing emancipation and freedom. I think Wordsworth's writing style has a relaxed form. In contrast to Blake, Wordsworth uses longer lines, making the rhymes less closer together and so less obvious.

This makes the sonnet sound continuous and relaxed. The poem itself is also an Iambic Pentameter, unlike Blake's Iambic Tetrameter. Blake's style was more rhythmic and culminated in an ending with a shock element after an accumulation of emotion. We can see this too, in Wordsworth's poem. First there is the change in punctuation. There are more exclamation marks towards the end than in the start, which vociferates the implication of the poem, taking pride in the City of London, its great architecture, skyline, and, its free and open connection to nature. There is also another way Wordsworth makes a build up of emotion in the rhythm of the rhymes. I think that the message here is that London is a magnificent and glimmering city, in balance with human, natural and urban elements. To communicate this balance, Wordsworth personifies various objects to do with nature, making them more human. This includes: the river Thames, which does as it pleases, and the houses, which seem 'asleep'. Wordsworth does not usually write about cities, or about people, so he personifies them to talk about what nature teaches us.

In the end, we can see that this poem has given us a contrasting view of London in the nineteenth century to that of Blake's. Blake reveals that London is a rule-based society, teeming with unseemliness, corruption, and prostitutes, whereas Wordsworth communicates the idea of a superior metropolis coupled with nature, pure, and bathed in sunlight, just as if a piece of heaven had slipped off a cloud and landed on the earth.

By comparing these two poems, I have gained and understanding of how the writing styles of two different poets help describe a view of London. Blake used a short line and rhyming technique to create a beat, which was repetitive, controlled and inexorable, much like the portrayal of The capital being a place where everything was controlled and owned. Wordsworth used a long line and long word style to create a free yet controlled tune, much like the representation of the city open to the elements.

However, there is still a throbbing question unanswered. Why are they so different? Why is one saying everyone and everything is ensnared in a dirty and dark urbanization, while the other is saying everyone and everything is free in a sun-bathed metropolis on the edge of fusing with nature? One of my ideas as to why they are so reverse is that the poets may be seeing London at different points of time in the day. And this is why Blake's London is 'dull' and Wordsworth's, 'bright'. To support my idea, I have chosen a line from each.

'London' By William Blake
But most thro' the midnight streets I hear

'Composed upon Westminster Bridge, September 3rd 1802' By William

Wordsworth

The beauty of the morning; silent, bare

Here, we have clear proof that Blake's poem is narrating a view of London at night, from the excerpt above, including the word midnight. We also have clear proof that Wordsworth's poem is expressing a view of London in the morning, from the excerpt above, including the word morning. Midnight is a time when everyone is sleeping, all is dark, and the air is saturated with the smoke from people's fireplaces that have been turned on for warmth during the night. In the dark, there wonder mysterious figures, prostitutes, and the sound of the city. This is why Blake's London has a 'dark' side to it - it is written to describe London at night. Looking at Wordsworth's poem, morning is a time when again everyone is asleep (very early morning) and the sun is rising over the skyline, saturating the metropolis in illuminating sunlight, reflecting off the dew to create a shimmering effect.

The air is clean as all the smoke has been lifted over night and is fresh, clean and gleaming in the sun. This gives me a sense of pride for the city at its best - organic yet urbanized. Wordsworth is describing a 'London morning'. In question of which version is most like our London as we know it today, I would say a bit of both poems, but mostly Blake's. The reason being that the City of London in 2004 is a retro, beautiful city with towering skyscrapers, touching the sky (Wordsworth), however, the Thames is still controlled (Blake) by the Thames Barrier, St Paul's is a blackening church (physically - Blake) and the air of London is polluted (Blake). Not forgetting, finally the fact that there are still prostitutes (Blake) in the city. Furthermore, London is expanding out to the natural part of England, the rural area, where all the fields that Wordsworth is talking about are being consumed by the wave of concrete and tarmac of the modern city of London as we know it today. Additionally, the smog that Blake describes in his poem is not present anymore - of course there is the pollution from the cars of today, so we could assume that to be a connection to Blake's description. That is why I feel the London as we know it today fits in with Blake's portrayal as well as Wordsworth's, but in the end, the reason that London is such a beautiful city (in my point of view) is because there is an effort to save some greenery in the city, to balance the conurbation in aspects of both human and natural elements.

**Elizabeth Barrett Browning, and William Blake**

Elizabeth Barrett Browning, and William Blake both wrote poems concerning the suffering of children who were forced to do labour. The children were forced to work presumably to help their families survive in a time when everyone in the family who was able had to help support the family. Both Browning, and Blake obviously felt that the children were suffering from these circumstances, although they expressed their feelings from different perspectives and with different degrees of sympathy.

Elizabeth Barrett Browning had an extremely dramatic view of the suffering of working children. In her poem The Cry of the Children, Browning illustrates the extreme anguish of the children, "(The children) look up with their pale and sunken faces, and their looks are sad to see…" (Abrams, 1175). Browning tells us the horridness of the problem by having the children tell us that it is, "true—it may happen that we die before our time: little Alice died last year, her grave is sharpen like a snowball…"(Abrams, 1175). The tragedy is shown to us by the fact that the children, who are so young, are able to simply accept this fact. They are forced to see people their age worked to death, when perhaps they should be able to play.While Blake's Poems leave you with a sense that the children are not entirely suffering, Browning's poems leave you with an intense sense of dread and pity for the children.

William Blake, and Elizabeth Browning illustrate exceptionally different portrayals of the children's suffering. Blake's entire poem illustrates, as is intended, the innocence of the children. She tells the parents that they will, "explode with a deadlier blame than the worst of them all,". An adult would understand that if the child had no hair to spoil, he should not feel mollified that it will refrain from becoming dirty, as he has lost his hair already.

Both Elizabeth Barrett Browning and William Blake use theological references in their poetry concerning the suffering of the children who are forced to work. Blake shows us the children simply accepting their fate, and continuing on with their work almost happily as in the line, ."tho' the morning was cold, Tom was happy and warm; so if all do their duty, they need not fear harm," (Abrams, 47). This is shown again in their theological references; Browning's disbelief in God's help, and Blake's implication that God is what will help these children.

In Blake's Poem The Chimney Sweeper from Songs of Innocence the child says that his "father sold (him) while yet (his) tongue could scarcely cry ' 'weep! 'weep! 'weep! 'weep!'" (Abrams, 46). The poem goes on to chastise the parents for mistreating their child. He shows through the child's immature understanding that the children are too innocent to work. However, Blake felt that his feelings of theology were, "from spirits who visited him in dreams,"

**ON "Chimney Sweeper"**

William Blake's "The Chimney Sweeper", part of his Songs of Innocence, is about a young boy who was sold as a baby into the life of a chimney sweep. The boy has a dream about the child chimneysweepers' dreadful lives coming to an end, and finally being set free into God's arms.

The author of "The Chimney Sweeper," was also an English poet, artist, engraver, mythmaker and visionary. He was the earliest and most independent of the Romantics. Blake was born on November 28, 1757 in London, where he spent most of his life. "He taught himself Latin, Greek, Hebrew. French, Italian, and his English was often remarkably original" ("Blake, William"). Blake started writing when he was 12 and friends printed a few of his early poems in 1783. Blake's Songs of Innocence, wrote in 1789, expressed a happy image about the childhood of the soul in an everlasting world sustained by love. Later he wrote the Songs of Experience in 1794, which contained poems that challenged the assumed beneficence of God and society. After his death on August 12, 1827, Blake's works were dispersed and some may have been destroyed.

In this poem, it seems as though Blake, who uses the first person voice, is trying to make a clear connection between the exploitation

Their hopes and dreams could only be of the after-life that they would have, following the one they had to first endure. "Stanzaic form is the form taken by a poem when it is written in a series of units having the same number of lines". Blake uses a young orphaned boy to tell his story in "The Chimney Sweeper" and while there is no clear audience, it does appear that he is telling his story to anyone who will listen. Injustices like this no longer need to be feared. The rest of the world's children, in other countries, are not so lucky. Child labour was widely practiced in the years ending the Romantic Age. It helps to link the curls to something one can imagine, and gives the idea of the sacrificial lamb. It uses perfect rhyme at the end of each line as its rhyme scheme, for the most part, but also utilizes approximate rhyme in the lines 17-18:

"Then naked and white, all their bags left behind,
They rise upon clouds and sport in the wind;"
and also in 21-22:
"And so Tom awoke, and we rose in the dark,

And got with our bags and our brushes to work. The children had no choice to become slaves; they were just born into it. The shaving of his hair, which is also in line six, could also be a symbol, symbolizing the loss of innocence. " (13-16)

This really adds to the poem because one can actually visualize the boys being set free and running happily like they never have before in a wondrous new place.

"The Chimney Sweeper," written in the Romantic Age, thankfully cannot be considered a contemporary piece in the

United States today. The alliteration make the poem flow and sound good to the reader. This can be seen in lines of Innocence reading,

> "And got with our bags and our brushes to work," ...
> "So if all do their duty they need not fear harm" (22 and 24),
> while Experience shows its side with lines such as
> "They clothed me in the clothes of death,
> And taught me to sing the notes of woe" (7-8)

**T.S Eliot on William Blake**

T.S. Eliot once said of Blake's writings, "The Songs of Innocence and the Songs of Experience, and the poems from the Rossetti manuscripts, are the poems of a man with a profound interest in human emotions, and a profound knowledge of them." (Grant, Pg 507) These two famous books of poetry written by William Blake, not only show men's emotions and feelings, but explain within themselves, the child's innocence, and man's experience. A little over two centuries ago, William Blake introduced to the English literary world his two most famous books of poetry: the Songs of Innocence and the Songs of Experience. In his own day, he was widely believed to be "quite mad," though those who knew him best thought otherwise. Today, few of us take Blake's madness seriously, either because we don't believe in it or because it no longer matters. Blake's fundamental concepts speak mainly about the human condition and emotion; and within the realms of this paper, I would like to persuade my readers that William Blake uses simple language and metaphors to show the two contrary states of the human.

The mire was deep, & the child did weep The tears mentioned were hardly those of joy; they were tears of a child without his father - tears of sorrow. This entire poem, more or less, tells of unaccountable tears: Sleep sleep happy child. Northrop Frye once said of the experience world; "The world of experience is the world that adults live in while they are awake. Blake did not believe that all human woes are self-induced. With the above example, one can assume that there is a great deal of sorrow within Blake's 'world of innocence'; for most of the tears shed are not tears of joy. " Blake brings it to the readers attention in the last stanza of "The Shepherd": He is watchful while they [the sheep] are in peace, For they know when their Shepherd is nigh. the changes that occur in the world of experience are, on the whole. A writer once said of this, "Experience is the 'lapsed Soul' that is addressed in the 'Introduction' to Experience. The child, then, innocently, requested to hear the song again, but this time he 'wept to hear. He widened the world of innocence to embrace the ultimate in suffering; but he also kept it 'innocent', and rather obviously so. The "Introduction" points the readers towards the pastoral world and the pastoral idea to follow in the next couple of songs.

Among English authors there are probably few figures who present as many potential difficulties for an introductory volume as does William Blake. The breadth of Blake's talents as engraver, designer, printer, painter, and poet, as well as the notorious difficulty of his "system" and the composite nature of his illuminated books all conspire to make it tough to discuss Blake as simply or primarily a literary figure.

Add to these difficulties intrinsic to the study of Blake's work itself, the vast, diverse, and conflicting contemporary critical approaches to it and the dimensions of the problem begin to assume their proper proportions. All these difficulties ensure a certain number of shortcomings and dissatisfactions with Victor Paananen's update of his William Blake in the Twayne's English Authors Series.

The strength of Paananen's update of his book, first published in 1977 (but whose initial draft was completed in 1972), is that it brings his analysis out of the so-called "golden age" of Blake studies by adding a Marxist dimension to its earlier focus on Blake's Christian vision. Concentrating on the dialectical character of Blake's thought, the readings of his works emphasize their critique of the social-material basis of culture. Thus, Paananen's book offers a scholarly, if narrowly-based, introduction to the study of Blake. William Blake gives a first-time reader of Blake a clear approach to his works; one that is, from a critical point of view at least, an improvement on the old recipe of sympathetic and enthusiastic identification with the search for spiritual truth-through-Blake.

Paananen's new Marxist emphasis presents a Blake much more in touch with the material realities of the world, a Blake whose poetic vision is less an endlessly baffling elaboration of characters/symbols and geographical/mental regions, than it is an attack on the ideology machine of church and state, decoding their efforts to control the material and spiritual shape of lived experience.

To this extent, the update also better serves the purpose of introducing readers to a Blake with whom they can find a more direct connection than did the first edition of William Blake. Still, the limited theoretical scope of William Blake 's approach is also the revised work's greatest shortcoming in that it does little to give a reader an accurate idea of the shape of contemporary Blake studies.

The updated preface and bibliography indicate William Blake 's theoretical orientation and expose the gaps in the scholarship which informs it. After three pages in justification of his approach as reflecting the "Marxist turn" in Blake studies (ix), Paananen undermines his own point with the odd claim that "[d]despite my concern with explaining aspects within both Christian and Marxist thought, I do not feel that a book in this series should primarily argue a thesis" (xii). Despite this disclaimer, the book does argue for the significance, to the virtual exclusion of any other, of a Marxist approach.

Beyond this, the "Marxist turn" Paananen sees in Blake studies, while an important and vital approach to the subject, seems more a result of his failure to fully inform himself on the shape of contemporary Blake criticism. The studies Paananen cites as evidence for the Marxist Blake, while fine scholarly studies, are all sufficiently dated as to suggest that more or less direct comparisons of Blake and Marx are not the central focus of the most recent scholarship.He claims his approach is both confirmed and inspired by the appearance of E. P. Thompson's "Witness against the Beast:" William Blake and the Moral Law (1993). The reason for Witness ' importance seems to rest with it being "written from the point of view of one of the world's most respected Marxists" (xi), while noting in his bibliography the work's "disappointing feature is that Thompson...does not develop comparisons between Blake and Marx as thinkers". I would suggest that, rather than a limitation of Thompson's book, it is instead the limitations of the explanatory power of direct comparisons between Blake and Marx that has led Blake criticism in different directions.

This failure to acknowledge, incorporate, or even supply bibliographical entries for some key studies representative of the most currently productive directions in Blake criticism is the updated William Blake 's greatest shortcoming. Among the most startling omissions is any reference to recent influential studies emphasizing the importance of Blake's poetry within the context of an artistic process and the cultural conditions that shaped its appearance.

Most prominent among these studies are Robert Essick's William Blake, Printmaker (1980), Morris Eaves' The Counter Arts Conspiracy (1992), and Joseph Viscomi's Blake and the Idea of the Book (1993). Essick, Eaves, and Viscomi have also made their mark on both the Princeton/Blake Trust facsimiles and the on-line Blake archive. The omission of these writers and this particularly influential direction in Blake studies, not to mention that of any of the numerous, sophisticated studies of Blake's language or attempts to examine Blake in terms of poststructuralist thought, marks a serious limitation to the scholarship informing Paananen's update.

The limitations of William Blake 's scholarship are apparent in its approach to Blake's works. In making the distinction between the illuminated works and those in conventional printing, Paananen does little to suggest either the nature or the importance of the illuminated books as representative of a composite art. Paananen states that the non-verbal aspect of Blake's works "either illustrates the text or otherwise compliments it" (17). Not only are the illuminated books more highly ornamented than Blake's few early works in conventional printing and his manuscript poems, but they necessitate an interdisciplinary approach in order to account the dual nature of these works as both visual art and poetry. William Blake neglects a large body of scholarship on the complex intertextual relationships of word and image in the illuminated books.

William Blake begins with a short biography of the artist, one very little changed from the first edition. While performing the necessary function of giving a reader some idea of the shape of Blake's life, it follows in the unfortunate tradition of Blake biographies by presenting him as a purely autonomous visionary artist, insisting "[t]he source of Blake's art was never to be the external world or the models provided by the work of others; instead, his source was always to be his own vision". It is well known that Blake's art was quite alive to the influence of the external world both in terms of the thought that informs his visionary work and the form the visions take within the work. In this instance, I don't think the sentimental tone of this brief biography is so much a limitation unique to William Blake itself, as it is indicative of the generally unsatisfactory state of Blake biographies in their common dependence on Alexander Gilchrist's Life of William Blake.

Perhaps the best view of Blake's life is afforded by G.E. Bentley Jr.'s Blake Records, since it does not aspire to construct a narrative about Blake from a single or consistent point of view, rather it simply presents the extant views of Blake from his own age. William Blake proceeds by chapter through Blake's poetic works starting with The Book of Urizen, Poetical Sketches, The Marriage of Heaven and Hell. The French Revolution and America, Visions of the Daughters of Albion, Songs of Innocence and of Experience, The Four Zoas, Manuscript Poems, Milton, and Jerusalem. Frustratingly, Paananen quotes from The Complete Writings of William Blake edited by Geoffrey Keynes in 1966, an edition long since superseded by G. E. Bentley Jr's William Blake's Writings in 1978, and, by far the most popular serious edition of Blake's work, The Complete Poetry and Prose of William Blake edited by David Erdman, mostly recently revised in 1982. Paananen's choice not to update his citations renders the book considerably less useful than it might have been otherwise.

One of the most interesting features of Paananen's approach to the Blake canon is that it situates The Book of Urizen rather than The Marriage of Heaven and Hell as the best introduction to Blake's works:

Even though The Marriage of Heaven and Hell (c. 1793) is of particular value to anyone beginning the study of William Blake, it is perhaps unfortunate that this work has come to serve as almost the only one of Blake's, other than a few of his lyrics, that some students ever see. The work is hardly a characteristic production, as it is written largely in prose and contains only minimal poetry, and it is not mythic except in the appended "Song of Liberty" portion.

Paananen concludes of The Marriage of Heaven and Hell that "the form and the content of The Marriage bear too many signs of an occasional work that depends on a parody of the opponent's methods to make debater's points". This view of The Marriage is generated by paying too much attention to the Blake/Swedenborg relationship at the expense of a serious consideration of The Marriage 's treatment of the intrinsic relationship between the process of Blake's thought and his material methods of producing the illuminated books.

The analysis of The Book of Urizen as an attack upon empiricism and an exposition of the Blakean imagination is set up by way of a brief consideration of the tractates All Religions Are One and There is No Natural Religion. From these short didactic prose works, which are, in both spirit and form, precursors of The Marriage, Paananen deduces the essential tenets of the humanist vision he finds common to Blake, Marx, and Lenin. The treatment of There is No Natural Religion errs by reading the work as the total of the known plates from which Blake printed, rather than considering the work as an arrangement of the plates that he issued as an actual version of this work. Paananen chooses The Book of Urizen as "[t]he best work to introduce the reader to Blake's mythic figures and narrative method" because of its focus on "the limits we place on perception in our acceptance of the natural world". This choice makes a good deal of sense in comparison to the all too common strategy of introducing readers to Blake through the deceptively difficult Songs of Innocence and of Experience as a basic statement of Blake's principles. The Book of Urizen becomes a key to "the outlines of Blake's mythic system" and thus allows for the claim that it, like Blake's other minor prophecies, has "the same themes as the epics Blake later wrote".This position minimizes the considerable development of these themes in the later works, and it fails to consider Blake's radical experiments in narrative form in these later works.

One can only wonder why the treatment of The Book of Urizen is followed by a brief chapter on Poetical Sketches which reaches the disappointing conclusion that "[p]perhaps we are wisest...to concentrate upon his [Blake's] adult productions".Equally perplexing is the relatively large amount of attention Paananen gives to The French Revolution, a work known only through Joseph Johnson's proof sheets. While the chapter is supposedly on "The French Revolution and America," its last page simply comments that America, "needs less commentary than The French Revolution because it is a less difficult work". America, regardless of its supposed "difficulty," merits careful attention as the first of what critics now call Blake's "continental prophecies." Unfortunately, William Blake barely mentions these works in passing.

In his treatment of Songs of Innocence and of Experience, Paananen flatly rejects any potentially ironic readings of Innocence: "[a]attempts by critics to make the Songs of Innocence ironic, to suggest that Blake undercuts or even mocks the perspective and language of innocence, are based on an inadequate grasp of Blake's thought".Paananen paraphrases Stanley Gardner's argument in support of an exclusively innocent reading of Innocence, claiming "that at the time that these songs were written Blake shared the hope that childhood innocence was being protected and nurtured in the reformed charity school in the Parish of St. James". In discounting the potential for irony to emerge in Songs of Innocence, especially when it is placed into a shared context with Songs of Experience would suggest that Blake's vision of the work is inflexibly bound to the supposed circumstances of its creation. Paananen insists that we take even one of the most obvious opportunities for an ironic reading of Innocence at face value, claiming of "Holy Thursday" that "[a] sight such as is presented in this poem seems to justify the pious conclusion 'cherish pity lest you drive an angle from your door'". To read this line as advocating pity would go against all the negative connotations it carries in every other instance in which Blake employs it—excepting, of course, "The Divine Image". The visual dimension offered by the "Holy Thursday" of Innocence can easily be seen as supporting the argument for an ironic position. The stiff, dehumanized, ornamental wrought iron look of the design suggests the purely formal and institutional nature of the pity expressed in the poem. The design encourages a reader to see the Ascension Day event at St. Paul's as a moment of aesthetic satisfaction for the speaker of the poem. This is a satisfaction that does not allow the speaker to discern the individuality and the personal suffering of the children which compose the spectacle. To read the Songs of Innocence as having potentially ironic elements is not to deny the importance of innocence to Blake's artistic vision, it is merely to acknowledge the limitation of that state and the necessity to pass beyond it.

The discussions of Blake's longer, more complex works are predictably less useful than the treatment of the shorter works. The Four Zoas, Milton, and Jerusalem are probably impossible to present in a simplified form which doesn't grossly distort the richness of these texts in their seeming or actual chaos. Paananen situates The Four Zoas as the great achievement of Blake's mythic vision, calling it the poem which "comes closest to being the Romantic epic that every Romantic poet wanted to write. Blake's Milton and his Jerusalem lack this particular kind of success because of their concern with specific theological, even 'doctrinal,' issues". This high praise for The Four Zoas runs a serious risk of universalizing the importance of this work. The Four Zoas does have an extremely significant place in Blake's canon because of its tangle of revisions over many years and the possibility that these reflect changing and ultimately irreconcilable intentions on Blake's part. The Four Zoas may well be "the flowering of the germ of an epic that is in The Book of Urizen ", but, in view of the later and more fully realised epics, The Four Zoas seems more like a workshop of ideas and techniques than Blake's ultimate poetic expression. The Four Zoas is where Blake recasts and begins to redirect his prophetic vision in the new directions realised in Milton and Jerusalem. Despite Milton 's and Jerusalem 's possibly more "'doctrinal'" focus, they offer radical experiments in narrative that don't yield to the kind of linear plot summarization upon which William Blake depends.

Paananen's readings of Milton and Jerusalem tend to rest upon explicit and implicit comparisons to what is perceived as the coherency of The Four Zoas. For example, in the discussion of Milton it is simply noted that there suddenly exists in "Book the Second" "a systemization of levels of vision not found elsewhere in Blake" without any inquiry as to what such a strange occurrence might suggest for understanding the work on its own terms, rather than by comparison to the structure of visionary states as presented in other works. The chapter on Jerusalem, in its attempts to offer the kind of plot summary which might prove superficially relevant when looking at The Four Zoas, is probably more misleading than it is useful.

Among the conclusions William Blake offers is that, "[w]e must learn to trust the intuition of the Songs of Innocence that humanity belongs to a better world than this one",and that "political revolutions, like those in France and America, reveal that the human mind is expanding toward the freedom of Eternity" seem both naive and sentimental to a point that distorts the dynamic changes that took place in Blake's thinking in later years. Innocence is wonderful, but, as The Book of Thel so powerfully demonstrates, if it is not left behind when appropriate one never realises a spiritual or intellectual maturity. To highlight in Blake fervor for political revolution is to ignore much of his ambivalent treatment of revolution after the early 1790's when actual political revolution is only pure for a moment before it simply becomes another iteration of an eternal cycle of oppression. To say that this cycle of oppression is broken by "Blake's determination to reconcile subject and object before setting out on the revolutionary path" again distorts the issue as it appears in Blake's later works. In both Milton and Jerusalem what Paananen sees as the "reconciliation of subject and object" is the only revolution that we can expect from Blake. While the scope of this moment may aim at universal significance, the insights it yields never permanently efface the fallen world from which they came.

Unfortunately, what Paananen's updated William Blake gains in usefully bringing a Marxist perspective to an introduction to Blake's work, it more than loses by not adequately taking into account the considerable interdisciplinary depth present in many contemporary studies of Blake. In keeping with the Twayne series, Paananen attempts to cover Blake's major works, an introduction to Blake might benefit, however, from more modest aims, so that it need no be burdened with trying to address The Four Zoas, Milton, and Jerusalem in less than fifty pages.

A comparison of Songs of Innocence (1789) with Poetical Sketches shows that the promise of Blake's earlier poetry has, indeed, been fulfilled, but in a somewhat unexpected way. Naturally, the mature work is free from the juvenile habit of imitation; it is, however, of interest to note in passing the suggestion that the hint of the composition of these Songs may have come from a passage in Dr. Watts's preface to his Divine and Moral Songs for Children. 2 Moreover, the baneful Oceanic influence is suspended for a space. But the vital difference is that here, for the first time, Blake gives clear indication of the mystical habit of thought, which, though at first an integral part of his peculiar lyrical greatness, ultimately turned to his undoing. In Poetical Sketches, his vision of life is direct and naïve: he delights in the physical attributes of nature, its breadth and its wonders of light and motion, of form and melody.

But, in Songs of Innocence, his interest is primarily ethical. The essence of all being, as set forth in the piece called The Divine Image, is the spirit of "Mercy, Pity, Peace and Love"; and as, later, he uses the terms "poetic genius" and "imagination" to express his conception of this fundamental principle, so, here, the "Divine Image" is his vision of that spirit which is at once universal and particular, God and Man. Under the inspiration of this belief, the world of experience fades away: there is nothing of death, pain or cruelty, except in the opening couplet of The Chimney Sweeper, and, even then, the idea of suffering is almost lost in the clear sense of a sustaining presence of love in the rest of the poem.

Every other instance shows sorrow and difficulty to be but occasions for the immediate manifestation of sympathy. God, as the tender Father, the angels, the shepherd, the mother, the nurse, or even the humbler forms of insect and flower, as in The Blossom, or A Dream,—all are expressions of the same universal ethic of love. But, perhaps, the most remarkable illustration of this belief, particularly when contrasted with Blake's later criticism of public charity, is Holy Thursday. Clearly, in the world of these Songs there is not any suspicion of motives, any envy or jealousy.

To use a later phrase by Blake, it is a "lower Paradise," very near to the perfect time wherein the lion shall lie down with the lamb: as in the poem Night, the angels of love are always by, to restrain violence or to bring solace to its victims.The theological reference in this simple ethic is slight. God and Jesus are but visions of the love that animates all forms of being. Hence, at this period, Blake's position is distinct from that of mystical poets like Henry Vaughan, in whom a more dogmatic faith tends to overshadow the appeal of the natural universe. So, too, Blake's poetry has more of the instinct of human joy. Mercy, pity, peace and love, the elements of the Divine Image, are "virtues of delight," and nothing is clearer in these Songs than his quick intuition and unerring expression of the light and gladness in common things. In this, he returns to poems in Poetical Sketches like I love the jocund dance, rather than to the more formal pieces of nature-poetry. His delight in the sun, the hills, the streams, the flowers and buds, in the innocence of the child and of the lamb, comes not from sustained contemplation but as an immediate impulse.

There is not as yet any sign of his later attitude towards the physical world as a "shadow of the world of eternity." His pleasure in the consciousness of this unifying spirit in the universe was still too fresh to give pause for theorizing; and, perhaps for this reason, such pieces as Laughing Song, Spring, The Echoing Green, The Blossom and Night, sung in pure joy of heart, convey more perfectly than all his later attempts at exposition the nature of his visionary faith.

In Blake's later writings, there is a wide gulf between the symbol and the reality it conveys; so, the reader must first grapple with a stubborn mass of symbolism. But, in Songs of Innocence, this faculty of "spiritual sensation" transfigures rather than transforms. Thus, in The Lamb, pleasure in the natural image persists, but is carried further and exalted by the implication of a higher significance. It is the manifest spontaneity of this mystical insight that carries Blake safely over dangerous places.

A little faltering in the vision or straining after effect would have sunk him, by reason of the simplicity of theme, diction and meter, now the sources of peculiar pleasure, into unthinkable depths of feebleness. Contrast with the strength of these seemingly fragile lines the more consciously didactic pieces like The Chimney Sweeper and The Little Black Boy. These, indeed, have the pleasant qualities of an unpretentious and sincere spirit; but their burden of instruction brings them too near to the well-meant but somewhat pedagogic verse that writers like Nathaniel Cotton and Isaac Watts thought most suitable for the young. Blake regarded children more humanly as the charming "Introduction" to these Songs bears witness, or the poem Infant Joy, a perfect expression of the appeal of infancy. And, in The Cradle Song, almost certainly suggested by Watts's lines beginning "Hush! my dear, lie still and slumber," Blake's deeper humanity lifts him far above the common-place moralizing of his model.

The Book of Thel was engraved in the same year (1789), though its final section is almost certainly later in date. The regularity of its unrimed fourteeners, the idyllic gentleness of its imagery and the not unpleasant blending of simplicity and formalism in the diction, proclaim the mood of Songs of Innocence. It treats of the same all-pervading spirit of mutual love and self-sacrifice. In response to the "gentle lamentations" of the virgin Thel, to whom life seems vain, and death utter annihilation, the lily of the valley, the cloud, the worm and the clod, rise up to testify to the interdependence of all forms of being under the law of the Divine Image, and to show that death is not final extinction, but the supreme manifestation of this impulse to "willing sacrifice of self." Blake's original conclusion to this argument is lost, for the last section has not any perceptible connection in its context. In it, the whole conception of life is changed. This world is a dark prison, and the physical senses are narrow windows darkening the infinite soul of man by excluding "the wisdom and joy of eternity," the condition of which is freedom. The source of this degradation is the tyranny of abstract moral law, the "mind-forged manacles" upon natural and, therefore, innocent desires; its symbols are the silver rod of authority and the golden bowl of a restrictive ethic that would mete out the immeasurable spirit of love. Here, Blake is clearly enough in the grip of the formal antinomianism that produced the later "prophecies."

## William Blake's The Tiger, London, and the Little Girl Lost

William Blake's the Tiger is a reminiscent of when God questions Job rhetorically about his creations. The Tiger also uses a significant amount of imagery and symbolism, which contributes to its spiritual aspects. In the poem London, Blake is trying to dispel the myth of grandeur and glory. This associated with London and to show how 'real' people of London felt. London was seen and portrayed as a powerful city where the wealthy lived and socialized. However, Blake knew that London was really a dirty, depressing and poverty-stricken city filled with slums and the homeless and chronically sicks. To reveal the truth, Blake combines descriptions of people and places with the thoughts and emotions of the people. The poem "A Little Girl Lost," from Songs of Experience is the story of a naturalistic love between the sexes told as a tragedy. Blake addresses this poem to an idealistic future age. Apparently, Blake felt animosity towards how people viewed love during his own time (Lang ridge).

In the Tiger, there is a wealth of imagery in the first of two lines alone. The poem begins: "Tiger: Tiger: burning bright In the forest of the night," The reader conceives in their mind the image of a tiger with a coat blazing like fire in the bowels of a dark forest. This creates a negative impression of the tiger, so some might say that the tiger is symbolic of evil. Some people may even go farther to conclude that the tiger is a symbol of Satan. The same type of imagery and symbolism is used in the first two lines of the second stanza. The image of fire in connection with the tiger is conceived again, this time within the eyes. The fire in a tigers eyes can be seen as a symbol of ferocity, and it takes no stretch of imagination to look upon Satan in the same way as well (Vine).

In the poem London, Blake starts by combining the descriptions of the crying baby and man with the observation that people oppress their hopes and dreams, because they know that they will never be able to achieve their dreams. Another is in the third stanza when Blake describes the crying chimney sweep and then the "blackening church," but is it really saying that the church does not want to dirty its hands by helping the soot-covered chimney sweep. Therefore, a "blackening church," is one that helps the common, dirty people. Blake says, "every blackening church appalls," showing that the aristocracy and those in positions of power did not want the church that they supported associating with common people. Throughout the poem, Blake uses fairly simple language punctuated with the occasional obscure word, but generally the more common words. Probably, to appeal to the common people who he was supporting through this poem (Margoliouth).

In the first stanza of Little Girl Lost, Blake introduces the setting of the poem. It starts with 'In the Age of Gold' because he was addressing the poem to the 'future age' therefore beginning the poem in storytelling style. The tragedy begins in the fourth stanza where deception takes place. The two youths become weary, as their day spent together comes to a close. Realizing that it is almost evening and they soon must part, 'they agree to meet, when the silent sleep.' This lyrical poem is written in a distinctive form, excluding the introductory stanza. A rhyming scheme is incorporated throughout the entire poem. There is no distinct pattern in his work but he tends to only capitalize those words that should be emphasized. Blake also likes to use colons, especially in this poem. A missing period at the end of his poems is extremely conspicuous and questions the ending of this poem.

In conclusion, the spiritual aspects of the Tyger are apparent and undeniable. Equally so is Blake's use of symbolism and imagery which contributes to these. The Tyger just goes to show that literature need not be divinely inspired in order to be spiritually though provoking. All the things that happen in the poem London are not surprising, considering that Blake was born and lived in London poverty from 1757-1827. He was a republican and was against the monarchy and probably the aristocracy who supported them. It is said that Blake had his own version of Christianity. Knowing this in not surprising that he wrote such a poem as 'London,' because he was talking about things that he knew and understood. "The Little Girl Lost," is a tragic love between a girl and a boy and mainly a girl and her father. Blake conveys this tragedy through a structural six stanza lyrical poem that included a setting, characters, a plot, a climax, and a downfall

Chapter 18

# Further Study Questions

### Songs of Innocence, General Questions:

1. How is the title phrase "songs of innocence" capable of more than one interpretation?
2. Are adult limitations in understanding different in kind from a child's limitations? What bounds the perceptions of an adult? What bounds the perceptions of a child?

### "Introduction"

3. What is the child's role in relation to the piper? What does the child want the piper to do?
4. Might the line "I stain'd the water clear" be read in two different ways? If so, how?

### "The Echoing Green"

5. How do the poem's aged characters perceive the children's joyful play?
6. What interpretation of the passage of time does the child provide? In other words, how does the child-speaker view the cessation of play and the coming on of night? Does the child welcome the nightfall? If so, why?

### "The Lamb"

7. How are the child-speaker, the lamb, and Christ "the Lamb" set in relation to one another? Why is it so

easy for the child to identify the lamb's creator, and so easy to invoke God's blessing on the lamb?

**"The Little Black Boy"**

8. Where has the child learned that he is "bereaved of light"? How would you characterize his interpretation of his race?
9. How does the child's mother accommodate the boy's understanding and yet correct it? How does she view racial difference?

**"The Chimney Sweeper"**

10. Why does the child-speaker interpret his situation - practically a form of industrial-age slavery - in a positive light? Does the content of his narration undercut his innocent trust in God?
11. What is the child-speaker's relationship to little Tom Dacre? What does Tom's dream mean?

**"The Divine Image"**

12. Why are "mercy, pity, peace, and love" good attributes in this poem? (The poem's contrary is to be found in Songs of Experience, "The Human Abstract")

**"Holy Thursday"**

13. How does the speaker describe the movements of the children? Is this description ambivalent, and is the poem as a whole less innocent-sounding than some of the others? If so, why? What lines or phrases might lead us to that conclusion?

**"Nurse's Song"**

14. What is the difference in the way the Nurse perceives the children's playing and their own understanding of their day's events? How does an adult perceive time (and play) differently than a child?

**"Infant Joy"**

15. What happens to us when we transition from a nameless being to one that has been endowed with a name? What is gained? What is lost?
16. What is the significance of the fact that the child names herself?

**Songs of Experience**

To be in a fallen condition and not interpret it spiritually and in light of the doctrine of contraries is to compound and perpetuate human error.

**"Introduction"**

17. What is the difference between the "piper" of the introduction to Songs of Innocence and the "Bard" in Songs of Experience?
18. How do you interpret the symbolism of the introduction - its references to "Earth," light and darkness, and the "starry floor / watry shore"?

**"Earth's Answer"**

19. Who does Earth say prevents her from being regenerated? How does he do that?
20. What ideal relationship between nature and humanity does the poem imply? What is the relationship as it stands in the poem?

**"The Clod and the Pebble"**

21. Is the Clod's interpretation of love privileged? Is the Pebble's?
22. What view of love emerges when you try to put both interpretations of it together?

**"Holy Thursday"**

23. How has the speaker's perspective changed from the corresponding poem in Songs of Innocence? What allows the speaker to see things differently?

24. What is the "trembling cry"?
25. How do you understand the poem's references to natural things - sun, rain, fields, thorns, etc.?

### "Chimney Sweeper"

26. Compare the poem to its Innocence precursor. Again, what enables the child to interpret his situation so differently?
27. Is it significant that the child uses the present tense in the last stanza - "because I am happy, & dance and sing..."? What is the nature of his dancing and singing?
28. What is the logic of the child's statement that his parents, their conception of God, and that God's Priest and King "make up a heaven of our misery"? How can they all "make up" a heaven from the existence of misery?

### "Nurse's Song"

29. Compare this poem with its Innocence predecessor, "The Ecchoing Green." Characterize the difference in perspective that distinguishes the Nurse from the elders in the earlier poem.

### "The Sick Rose"

30. What does the worm or caterpillar symbolize?
31. Characterize the unhealthy "sexual economy" (as in "political economy") figured by this poem.
32. Compare this poem with its Innocence predecessor, "The Blossom" if you happen to have a full copy of Songs of Innocence - you can get it from David Erdman's Complete Works of Blake from an offsite hyperlink.

### "The Fly"

33. Is the speaker's identification with the fly a healthy one?

34. Refer to King Lear 4.1, where Gloucester says "As flies to wanton boys, are we to the gods. / They kill us for their sport." How similar is the thought about the fly in Blake's poem?

35. What power does the speaker attribute to "thought"? Is the attribution or perspective convincing?

## "The Tyger"

36. What emotional progression does the poem imply in the speaker's contemplation of the Tyger?

37. What is the answer to the question in line 20, "Did he who made the lamb make thee?" Why does the speaker need to ask the question? Who is "he," i.e. the lamb's creator?

38. What is the significance of the poem's references to "fire," "burning," and the "furnace"? What does fire often symbolize?

39. Examine the plate on page 55 - describe the Tiger's attributes. What sort of "tiger" is this that Blake has engraved? What effect does the odd spelling "tiger" create?

## "My Pretty Rose Tree" / "Ah Sun-flower"

40. What two states of love do these poems invoke?

## "The Garden of Love"

41. Explain the speaker's perspective on morality as a system of oppression.

42. To what extent is the speaker complicit in what is happening?

## "London"

43. What effects do the poem's insistent particularity and totality have - i.e. "charter'd," "mark," every"?

44. Why is the reference to prostitution the most significant one to the speaker, as we see from the last stanza?

**"The Human Abstract"**

45. This poem is the companion of "The Divine Image" in Songs of Innocence. Why is it significant that Blake uses the word "abstract" in the title of this poem? What exactly does that word mean in context, and how is abstraction perhaps the key to the erroneous thinking about mercy and pity that the poem laments?
46. What progression of mental states does the poem trace? What are the material consequences of those successive states?

**"Infant Sorrow"**

47. Refer to Songs of Innocence's "Infant Joy." Why is the child sad following upon the trial of birth?
48. What relationship to the father and mother does the infant-speaker assert?

**"A Poison Tree"**

49. What is the "apple," and why does it kill the foe? Why does the foe try to steal the apple?
50. As with "The Human Abstract," what progression of mental states does the poem trace? What are the material consequences of those successive states?

**"To Tirzah"**

51. Tirzah is Blake's figure for material nature, in addition to what the *Norton* editors say. Blake seems to have added this poem to Songs of Experience only in later copies. Does that mean we should take the speaker's attitude towards nature and the human body as definitive?
52. Look up the editorial reference to the Gospel of John 2:4 and its surrounding context. How does it affect your understanding of Blake's poem? (Time permitting, you might also look up Song of Solomon 4:6 and I Corinthians 15:44.

## "A Divine Image"

53. Refer to "The Divine Image" in Songs of Innocence. What was Blake saying about the relation between the human and the divine in that poem? How has it changed in "A Divine Image" in Songs of Experience?
54. The *Norton* editors say that "The Human Abstract" is subtler than this poem. How so? Which poem do you consider a more effective contrary to "The Divine Image" in Songs of Innocence?
55. What are Blake's favourite images of innocence, and how does he use them?
56. Discuss Blake's use of simple sentence structure and diction in these poems. What is the overall effect of this stylistic decision? What keeps the poems themselves from being simple?
57. How does Blake portray nature? How does the conception of nature differ in the Songs of Innocence and the Songs of Experience?
58. How does Blake use repetition in the Songs of Innocence and Experience?
59 How does Blake portray childhood?
60. What can you discern from these poems about Blake's views on religion?
61. What were (and are) the effects of Blake's mode of publishing his poems with handcrafted coloured engravings?

# Bibliography


Baulch, David M. "The Sublime of the Bible," on William Blake's Milton and how Blake's notion of the sublime differed from conventional ideas. In Romanticism on the Net, Issue 3 (August 1996).

Bentley, G.E. A review of Stranger from Paradise: a Biography of William Blake (Yale University Press, 2001)Reviewed in Criticism, Summer, 2002 by Kathryn Freeman.

Bidney, Martin. A song of innocence and of experience: rewriting Blake in Brodkey's "Piping Down the Valleys Wild." on William Blake, Harold Brodkey, in Studies in Short Fiction, Spring, 1994.

Connolly, Tristanne J. A review of William Blake and the Body (Palgrave Macmillan, 2002) Reviewed in College Literature, Spring 2004 by Longacre, Jeffrey.

Eaves, Morris, et al. "Once Only Imagined." An Interview with Morris Eaves, Robert N. Essick, and Joseph Viscomi on the future of Blake studies. In Romantic Circles Praxis Series, January 2003.

Eliot, T.S. Poet T.S. Eliot on William Blake from Eliot's The Sacred Wood: Essays on Poetry and Criticism (1922).

Essick, Robert and Joseph Viscomi "An Inquiry into Blake's Method of Color Printing." In Blake, an Illustrated Quarterly, Vol. 35, no. 3 (winter 2001/2002).

Goldberg, Brian. "Byron, Blake, and Heaven," in Romanticism on the Net, Issue 27 (August 2002).

Hobson, Christopher Z. A review of Blake and Homosexuality (Palgrave, 2000), reviewed in Criticism, Spring, 2002 by Harriet Kramer Linkin.

Höltgen, Karl Josef. "William Blake and the Emblem Tradition" in EESE 2/2002.

Hutchings, Kevin. "Gender, Environment, and Imperialism in William Blake's Visions of the Daughters of Albion" in Romantic Circles Praxis Series, Romanticism and Ecology, November 2001.

Paananen, Victor N. A review of William Blake (Twayne Publishers, 1996). Reviewed by David M. Baulch in Romanticism on the Net, No. 8 (November 1997).

Peterfreund, Stuart. A review of William Blake in a Newtonian World: Essays on Literature as Art and Sciene (University of Oklahoma Press, 1998). Reviewed in Criticism, Wntr, 1999 by Grant Scott.

Pfau, Thomas. "Bringing About the Past: Prophetic Memory in Kant, Godwin, and Blake." In Romantic Circles Praxis Series, Romanticism and Conspiracy, July 2004.

Phillips, Michael. A review of William Blake: the Creation of the Songs: from Manuscript to Illuminated Printing (The British Library and Princeton University Press, 2000).

Plotnitsky, Arkady. "Chaosmic Orders: Nonclassical Physics, Allegory, and the Epistemology of Blake's Minute Particulars." In Romantic Circles Praxis Series, Romanticism and Complexity, March 2001.

Punter, David. A substantial introduction to William Blake from the Literary Encyclopedia 17 July 2001. On Songs of Innocence (1789); On Songs of Experience (1794).

Punter, David (ed.) A review of William Blake, New Casebooks (Macmillan, 1996). Part of a round-up review, reviewer Michael O'Neill, Romanticism on the Net Issue 7 (August 1997).

Raine, Kathleen. A review of Raine's Blake and Tradition (Princeton Univ. Press, 1968). First page of article only. Reviewed by Jean H. Hagstrum in Modern Philology, Vol. 68, No. 1 (Aug., 1970).

Reilly, Susan P. "Blake's Poetics of Sound in The Marriage of Heaven and Hell." Contends that by combining many genres and choosing genres which originate in sound or speech, The Marriage of Heaven and Hell merges William Blake's Higher Criticism with an emphasis on oral culture. In Romanticism on the Net Issue 16 (November 1999).

Simpson, Michael. "Who didn't kill Blake's fly: moral law and the rule of grammar in 'Songs of Experience.' - William Blake - Rhetoric and Poetics, in Style, Summer, 1996.

Wright, Julia M. Review of Blake, Nationalism, and the Politics of Alienation (Ohio University Press, 2004) Reviewed by David Baulch. Romanticism on the Net, Issues 36-37 (November 2004-February 2005).

Yoder, R. Paul. Unlocking Language: Self-Similarity in Blake's Jerusalem. In Romantic Circles Praxis Series, Romanticism and Complexity, March 2001.

